The Vogue Of The Prophecy, The Plague Of The Nation

Volume 1

Moses O. Kingsley,
Keith Swearing,
Ivor Chevannes

WESTBOW·
PRESS
A DIVISION OF THOMAS NELSON
& ZONDERVAN

WestBow Press books may be ordered through booksellers or by contacting:

WestBow Press
A Division of Thomas Nelson & Zondervan
1663 Liberty Drive
Bloomington, IN 47403
www.westbowpress.com
1 (866) 928-1240

ISBN: 978-1-4908-7441-8 (sc)
ISBN: 978-1-4908-7442-5 (hc)
ISBN: 978-1-4908-7440-1 (e)

Library of Congress Control Number: 2015904605

Print information available on the last page.

WestBow Press rev. date: 03/31/2015

Contents

Preface

This book provides an in-depth analysis of the prophecy written in chapter 11 of the book of Daniel.

Few writers or organizations have ever attempted such a feat, and I believe this work highlights the profundity of the prophecy as well as its application to modern-day society.

Daniel 11 (KJV) symbolically explained the existence of certain nations governed and manipulated with greed as they strived for world power. Then there comes a defeat, bringing them to their end.

To understand this prophecy, people would have to devote themselves to relentless pursuit of knowledge. And so I encouraged all those who are desirous of new ideas or truth, to read this book.

I speak not as one who has the authority but as one who seeks knowledge and the Divine, whose name is Yahweh, and in the process of my research I have come to realize that no one can understand prophetical Scripture in isolation. One must refer to other biblical and historical references in order to arrive at a coherent conclusion.

The keen reader will observe that Daniel 11 is a complete narration from the reign of Nebuchadnezzar, king of Babylon, to imperial and papal Rome and the adjoining ruling powers of the northern and southern nations. I have painstakingly cross-referenced and linked each of these historic periods with the present in order to discern the revelations for the future.

Some prophecies are inevitable, and for time immemorial they have existed as a plague on mankind. I say, "Plague" because the events foretold have a sense of inevitability and have already been laid out at the hands of the Almighty. Without the revelations of prophecies and the conclusions of their interpretations for our own era, men will perish. And so this book of Daniel is no less timely than its forebear,[1] written and put together almost 2,200 years ago.

Although some scholars thought the book had been written between 167 and 164 BC during the reign of Antiochus IV Epiphanes, I personally believe that some historical manuscript must have been left by Daniel as some sort of evidence in providing information.

---

[1] The book came within its proper time, declaring the revelation of the ancestors who lived before the book was written and those who existed after its creation.

Introduction

During the early history of the Jews, Yahweh gave visions to His people. He forewarned them that all nations would be fighting for power in the last days, leading up to the appearance of the "Son of Man",[2] the judge of the whole world.

Let us review the second and seventh chapter of Daniel.

- Daniel 2 (KJV). This gives details about the "image's head was of fine gold, breast and arms of silver, belly and thighs of brass, legs of iron and feet part iron and part clay."
- Daniel 7 (KJV). This speaks of the four beasts coming up from the sea: "like a lion, like a bear, like a leopard, and a beast more dreadful and terrible" than the rest.

Now let us compare and contrast Daniel 2 and 7.

Daniel Chapter 2 **Images**	Daniel Chapter 7 **Beast**
1. Head of Gold (Babylon)	Lion
2. Breast and Arms of Silver (Medo-Persian)	Bear

---

[2] Daniel 7:9–10, 13, and 22 indicates that the Son of Man received power to judge the world. Mathew 5:22, 23 and 27 also give confirmation of Christ manifesting Himself as the "Son of Man".

3. Belly and Thigh of Brass (Greece)	Leopard
4. Legs of Iron with Feet Partly of Iron and Clay (Rome)	Dreadful Beast

In regard to the first beast, Babylon, Daniel 2 reveals the head of gold as the Babylonian Empire ruled by King Nebuchadnezzar, while Daniel 7 speaks of the Babylonian Empire as a lion.

As for the second beast, Medes and Persia, Daniel 2:32 and 39 symbolized the Medo-Persian Empire as a breastplate with arms of silver, while Daniel 8 (KJV) gives its symbolical view as the ram (male sheep). The verse goes on to say that the ram shall sprout two horns. These two horns represent the combined rule of the kingdoms of Medes and Persia.

Daniel 7 illustrates the Medo-Persian Empire as the bear. It goes on to say that the bear had "three ribs in its mouth." These three ribs are three kings that shall rule and expand the empire successfully via wars.

To my understanding these three kings are Cyrus, Cambyses (Ahasuerus), and Darius I.

The beast that had the "three ribs in its mouth" represents the king that stands on the shoulders[3] of the preceding three kings. This beast is the fourth king, and it is called Xerxes.

On the matter of the third beast, Greece, represented by the "he goat" (male goat) and also "the leopard," Daniel 7:6 (KJV) presents Greece as a leopard, saying, "After this I beheld, and lo another, like a leopard[4], which had upon the back of it four wings[5] of a fowl;

---

[3] Shoulder here means strength.
[4] This beast represents Greece.
[5] This represents the swift and vast uprising of the empire.

the beast had also four heads[6]; and dominion was given to it." In Daniel 8 by contrast, Greece is illustrated as a he-goat (male goat) becoming stronger after defeating the ram (male sheep). Afterward its great horn was broken, and from it four little horns spread toward the corners of the earth. Thus, its concluded that after the he-goat[7] conquers the *ram* (Medes and Persia), the *he-goat* (Greece) would have been established and subsequently broken up again into four major empires spreading toward the ends of the earth. Each of these kingdoms was ruled individually by the four last commanders of Alexander's forces.

In regard to the fourth beast, Rome, "the little horn", and "red scarlet dragon," Daniel 2, 7, and 8, as I gathered, all agree, saying that this beast would be great and exceedingly strong, subduing the previous ones. Chapter 2 speaks of its "feet of iron," symbolizing the strength of its dominion. The ten toes partly of iron and partly of clay illustrated the convergence of Rome with ten other kingdoms. While iron represents the strong link between Rome and some kingdoms, clay represents weak alliances with the others.

Daniel[8] continues by saying that after the establishment of these ten kingdoms, the Elohim (God)[9] of the heavens would set up a kingdom that could not be destroyed. Rather, it would destroy all preceding empires.

On this note, the reader should therefore recognize that these ten kingdoms, appearing as working partners with the fourth *beast* (Rome), was not a referral manifestation before the first advent of

---

[6] This symbolized the main dominance and existing ruler ship of the whole empire.

[7] The he-goat here represents the early stage of the Greek Empire.

[8] Daniel 2:44 (KJV) says, "And in the days of these kings shall the Elohim (God) of heaven set up a kingdom, which shall never be destroyed, and the kingdom shall not be left to other people, but it shall break in pieces and consumed all these kingdoms, and it shall stand forever."

[9] The word God, though not a translation of the Hebrew word Elohim, was introduced by the King James Version in the sixteenth century.

Christ, but it suggests such an event will take place just before the Second Advent.

My conclusion of the time of their appearance together was highlighted by these chapters:

1. Daniel 8:9–12, 23–24 (KJV): These verses indicated that this horn[10] becomes so mighty that he "magnifies himself above the Prince of the heavenly host[11] and takes away the daily sacrifice." In such doing, he destroys the sanctuary of Christ and casts the truth to the ground, which results in the destruction or dismantling of the church of Christ formed in the early first century. After the breakdown of the early church, the horn[12] begins his teaching, and it practiced and prospered.

2. Daniel 2:44 (KJV) gives the view that during the reign of these kings the God (Yahweh) of heaven will set up a kingdom. Certainly before this a few things happened.

   a) By AD 476, Northern and Eastern Europe merged into Western Europe, forming the Roman Empire.
   b) During AD 508, most European nations pledged to spread Roman Christianity by force.
   c) The nineteenth and twentieth centuries showed a change in European nations. They developed a greed for power and began to fight against one another. Consider the Napoleon War, which ended the Roman Empire, and the Triple Alliance against the Triple Entente in World War I.

---

[10] This symbolized imperial Rome ruled by Julius Caesar to Emperor Diocletian's vast persecution of the church in AD 303–313.

[11] This normally represents a large body of people, but on account of the word *heavenly*, it definitely speaks to an angelic crowd or celestial beings.

[12] This indicates papal Rome established by Constantine in AD 312, instilling Roman Christianity.

d) After World War II, the Allies[13] controlled Germany by sharing western and eastern Germany amongst themselves in 1949. Starting in the early 1950s, West Germany's federal parliamentary republic sustained their economic growth. West Germany and the United States then developed closed political ties, and both were economically interdependent. Germany then became a member of NATO in 1955, and by 1957 Germany played the leading role as one of the founding members of the European Economy Community (EEC), where ten nations came together and formed a league. In 1993, the EEC was renamed as the European Union (EU) with Germany still playing the leading role.

If Scripture said, "In the days of these kings He would set up a kingdom that shall never be destroyed," obviously He was speaking of a rebuilding of the one that was destroyed, and this rebuilding will take place during or at the time of the existence of these ten nations sometime during the twentieth century.

Daniel also said that this kingdom that would be rebuilt "will not be left in the hands of others."[14] Evidently the manuscript provided by Daniel is saying that the church will be grounded in the firm doctrine and teaching of Christ, His imperial majesty, and His holy highness, not being deceptive of the pagan doctrine set out by Rome.

The question to consider now is this: Why didn't Daniel come out and directly identify the fourth beast as Rome? Well, he certainly described it as dreadful, terrible, devouring and conquering.

---

[13] France along with the United Kingdom and the United States emerged on May 23 and controlled West Germany and formed the Federal Republic of Germany, while the Soviet Union was controlled East Germany, forming the German Democratic Republic on October 7.

[14] The word "others" used here indicates the Roman Empire and also the hypocritical (apostate) scribes and Pharisees and Sadducees.

My obvious answer to the question is this: It says in Daniel 2 that after he received the interpretation of the vision from the angel, his countenance changed within him and that he kept the matter in his heart. Again in chapter 8 (KJV), it says that he chose to keep the vision in himself. Therefore, I believe that this knowledge was to be kept a secret until the end of days, when it would be revealed to the people of Yahweh.

What can I say then? Am I one of Yahweh's people, for it has revealed to me that this beast is Rome? There is no other kingdom as dominant as Rome after Greece, as pointed out by the prophet Daniel.[15] Rome made its appearance immediately in 168 BC, after it conquered Greece, and it became the master of the existing world at the time.

---

[15] Daniel 2:40 (KJV), 7:7 (KJV), and 8:24and 25 (KJV) all indicated the political strength of Rome. According to Daniel 11, Rome continues its stride against the south, with the strength of a northern (European) religious union.

Chapter 1

Babylon—Chaldeans Monarchy

To begin this chapter, I will start by explaining the first symbolic feature of Daniel 11, which is Babylon described as *the lion*.

This is the empire once ruled by Nebuchadnezzar. He was identified as a great king of Babylon and was referred to as king of kings (not Christ).

In 588 BC, 112 years after Israel fell into the hands of the Assyrians, Jerusalem was taken captive by the king of Babylon.

Nebuchadnezzar kept the children of Israel in bondage, and it was during his reign that the curse[16] spoken of by Jeremiah, the prophet, concerning the seventy years of desolation came upon the Jews.

Nebuchadnezzar ruled with an iron fist until his death. During his rule, Daniel and other Hebrews were placed in difficult positions because they did not worship the gods of the Chaldeans.

When Nebuchadnezzar died, his grandson Belshazzar[17] succeeded the throne. Belshazzar, in his arrogant state of mind believed that he should be seen as a god. He also thought that the Chaldeans and the Jews should see him as a divine one and give reverence.

---

[16] The spoken words of the prophet that says Israel shall be in captivity by the hand of the king of the Chaldeans for seventy years (Jeremiah 25:8–12 KJV). (Compare this with Chronicles 36:14–21).

[17] Belshazzar was son of Nebonidus, son of Nebuchadnezzar.

Belshazzar, who compared himself with Yahweh, demanded to drink one night from the vessel[18] of Yahweh's tabernacle.[19] On that very night in 539 BC, Belshazzar was killed during the invasion of Cyrus the Medes.

---

[18] Daniel 5:1–4, 30 (KJV) indicated that these vessels were actually the golden and silver vessels that were taken from the Tabernacle of Yahweh, by King Nebuchadnezzar.

[19] This house *(tabernacle)* of Yahweh was destroyed by Nebuchadnezzar, during the invasion of Jerusalem in 586 BC.

Chapter 2

Medes and Persian Empire

In 538 BC, Cyrus of the Mede took over Babylon, including all the empires and provinces that had been conquered by the Babylonians.

Daniel 7:5 (KJV) speaks of the "bear[20] with three ribs in its mouth." The rib signifies the bear's offspring just as the metaphor in Genesis speaks of the creation of Eve, where Adam's ribs were taken to produce another of his kind.[21]

The three *ribs* are three heirs to the throne, but the beast itself would be the fourth heir with dominion over Medes and Persia.

Daniel 11:2 (KJV) explains that "there shall stand up yet three kings of and Persia; and the fourth would be far richer than they all." This same verse continues to indicate that this fourth king will spawn aggression against the Greeks.

Let us see how the prophecy unfolds concerning these four kings of Medes and Persia.

The First King (538–529 BC)

The first king, Cyrus II of Persia, began his reign when the Babylonian Empire was captured in 538 BC. During his reign the seventy years of desolation, which was foretold by the prophet

---

[20] This symbolically represents the Medes and Persian Empire.
[21] Eve.

Jeremiah,[22] came to an end, culminating in the rebuilding of Jerusalem.

Cyrus conquered Babylon by diverting the River Euphrates away from the fourth city wall, and then he entered through the unprotected riverbed. It has been said that the Babylonians were no match for the expert Persian archers, which lead to a victory for the Persians. When it reached hand-to-hand combat, there were not much Babylonian soldiers left to fight.

Cyrus also fought against Croesus, king of Lydia and overlord of the Greek states of Ionia at that time. Croesus lost the battle and his empire, including Ionia. Cyrus punished the Ionians, using them as slaves. Athens, also a Greek state, was furious at the treatment given to the Ionians. Athenians and some Ionians subsequently retaliated by burning the Persian city of Sardis.

Cyrus was the wisest, but he was not cruel or powerful as other Medo-Persian emperors. He allowed subjugated people to practice their own religious customs while they still paid taxes and tributes to the Persian king.

The Second King (529–522 BC)

The second king of Medes and Persia was the son of Cyrus named Cambyses, also known as King Ahasuerus. During Cambyses' reign his soldiers journeyed through Arabia and conquered Memphis in Egypt. As a result of this conquest, the Egyptians benefited from reorganized trade, and among others, there were repair of temples and monuments that had been destroyed.

The provinces of Persia were called satrapies, and they were ruled by governors called satraps. Persians kings always made sure their satrapies were well maintained. Roads were built, and they stretched from Egypt through Babylon to India in a bid to improve

---

[22] Jeremiah 25:8–12; Chronicles 36:21–23; Ezra 1:1–7.

communication and trade with dependencies. As the Persians gained control of more of the civilized world, they grew more cosmopolitan in their outlook, adapting to the culture and customs of the people in the lands they conquered. Cambyses, otherwise called King Ahasuerus I, ruled over 120 provinces, but the reign of King Ahasuerus II brought the provinces to 127 provinces. Read Esther 1:1.

The Third King (522–486 BC)

The third king of Medes and Persia was Darius I of the Medes, who killed the usurper that invaded the throne at that time. After he seized the throne, Darius then sat as king. It was during his reign that Daniel received the prophecy[23] concerning the seventy weeks (representing the 490 years) it would take the children of Israel to complete the rebuilding of Jerusalem.

In the quest of building his empire Darius brought skilled workers and tradesmen from Babylon, Egypt, Assyria, and Greece. In order to build the Persepolis,[24] the Persians pirated the architectural treasures of conquered lands and other nations. Egypt's calendar and astronomy was also studied by Persians scholars.

Darius I thought of himself as the ruler of the known world at that time. He levied taxes on land and water. Those who agreed to pay retained their land and became allies of Medes and Persians.

Darius I sent messengers to Athens, advising them of his new protocol. But instead of agreeing to his proposal, the Athenians threw some of the messengers down a pit while the others were pushed down a well.

In 490 BC, the Persian king decided to go to war against Athens. He landed at Marathon, a Greek city south of Eretria, with the help

---

[23] Daniel 9:1–3, 20–27 ((KJV).)

[24] A city built by the Persians.

of an exile named Hippias, who had been banished by the Athenians in 510 BC because of his continuous ambitions to remain a tyrant.[25]

Miltiades, an Athenian general, defeated Darius with the help of men from nearby Plataea. More than six thousand Persian archers were killed by Athenian swordsmen in an ambush organized by the Athenians. The Athenians claimed victory, and the Persians were forced to return home defeated.

The Fourth King (486–465 BC)

The fourth king of the combined Medo-Persian Empire was Xerxes, son of Darius I.

Xerxes was cruel and arrogant. He pulled his army from every nation within the empire, including Ethiopia and Libya. He also used slaves to carry weapons and luggage.

Xerxes saw himself as a god, claiming that no country could overcome his superb power. His army was said to consist of three hundred thousand men with also an additional one thousand personal bodyguards[26] to the king.

King Xerxes held a grudge against Greece since they had defeated his father in the battle of Marathon in 490 BC. His action ten years later (480 BC) in the preemptive strikes against Greece fulfilled the prophecy of Daniel.[27]

---

[25] Tyrant ((king)) was a dictator that governed Athens in 560–527 BC. An Athenian name Cleisthenes, who was also a tyrant, realized the misused of that kind of ruler ship and introduced reforms in 508 BC. By 507, democracy was introduced by the Athenians. By that time the tyrant Hippias was already being exiled.

[26] These bodyguards were known as the Immortals.

[27] Daniel 11:2 says, "And now I will tell you the truth, there shall stand up three kings in Persia; the fourth shall be … () and by his riches he shall stir up all against the king of Greece."

In 480 BC, during the annual Olympic Games of Athens and Sparta's yearly religious festival, Xerxes marched northward through Thrace, following the coastline.

The Olympic Games was such an important event that nothing was allowed to stop it. Similarly the religious festive in Sparta was so sacred that fighting and wearing armor was not allowed during the period. Xerxes uses the Greek's devoted season to his advantage and planned out his attack.

Leonidas, the Spartan king, learned of Xerxes's advance, and in spite of the festival at Sparta, he marched northward with a band of three hundred soldiers and slaves.[28] On the way a handful of soldiers from other places (Tegea, Mantinea, Arcadia, Phlius, Mycenae, and other parts of Greece) joined the advancing army.

The few thousand Greeks set out to meet the Persian king with his three hundred thousand men and one thousand guards.

Leonidas picked the narrow coastal mountain path at Thermopylae, a crucial point of entry into Greece. His intention was to ambush and hold the Persians at this location until the Olympic Games were over, giving other armies time to come to their aid.

Upon learning of Leonidas's plan through an informer, Xerxes decided to set up camp for six days.

On the sixth day Xerxes sent one of his armies to force their way through the pass. Leonidas held them off, attacking line by line until they were destroyed. The Persians dead bodies were used to block the path.

The next day Xerxes sent his Immortals. Nevertheless, even the Immortals were killed at the mountain pass.

Acknowledging that his men were failing, Xerxes once again enlisted the help of a Greek traitor[29] to gain access to the path from the south.

---

[28] These slaves were called helots.

[29] One wonders if this traitor was the same person who had informed Xerxes earlier of the blocked path to Thermopylae. On the other hand, this traitor could

On becoming aware of the stealth attack, Leonidas ordered three hundred to stay and defend the pass, while others escaped safely and carried a warning to Athens.

The Persian then entered Thermopylae from both ends and killed King Leonidas and the three hundred.

Having conquered the Spartans, the Persian king continued onward to Athens. There he burned the city to the ground after he realized it was deserted. He then continued onward to Salamis.

While Athens was burning, Themistocles, leader of the Athenians who took most of the people to Salamis and Aegina, traveled five miles onward to Piraeus to prepare a fleet for the Persian invasion.

In August 480 BC, the Persian army arrived on the shores of Salamis with huge fleet of ships. Seeing this, the Spartans and Athenians who took refuge at Salamis began to panic, but Themistocles's experience and courage emboldened his countrymen.

Themistocles placed his small navy between the channels of Athens and Salamis and waited until it was surrounded by Persian fleets. In this way the Persian king was deceived into believing that he had captured the enemy vessels. At this time Themistocles ordered his ships to take the battering rams of their ships and destroyed the Persians fleet. Xerxes, realizing defeat, then took his remaining army and fled along the icy roads.

Xerxes and his armies were driven from Greek soil for good after a few more attacks in the spring 479 BC.

The strength of the Greeks and Athenians were in their unity, and on realizing this, Xerxes gave up his campaign against Greece.

---

have been held as a prisoner or slave and forced to give information.

Chapter 3

Greek's Empire

The third kingdom of *the beast* is Greece, propelled to power by three main states, namely Athens, Sparta, and Macedonia.

Athens

Athens[30] existed as a kingdom until King Codrus died 1068 BC. Athens was then ruled by an aristocratic[31] oligarchy.[32] The chief magistrate was an archon that was initially elected for life but then later in the future for a period of ten years.

The rule of tyrannies[33] then developed in 560 BC and lasted for thirty-three years, after which Athens then began to reform, becoming democratized in 507 BC.

Athens's power and influence grew after the first Persian invasion in 490 BC. Unfortunately there was a setback after the second invasion in 480 BC.

Rebuilding had commenced, and to protect itself from any more invasions, Athens formed an alliance with the Ionian city-states of Asia Minor. The Delian League, as the alliance was called, was also

---

[30] Athens is on the plain of Attica in south east central Greece. It became the capital of Greece in 1834 BC. Its ancient name was Athenae.

[31] A person described as having high financial status.

[32] This means being semi-democratized.

[33] Tyranny (plural as tyrannies) is governance by dictators known as tyrants (kings).

collaborated to protect the coastline of Greece in 478 BC. By virtue of this league, Athens rose to pre-eminence amongst Greek city-states and ushered in a golden age. This advance continued under the rule of Pericles (460–43 BC).

Interest grew in developing their scientific knowledge and educational system. Athens then became a center of learning for mathematics, astronomy, philosophy, and medicine under teachers called Sophists.[34]

To institutionalize Athens as a city of learning, the citizens built a temple in honor of Athena, goddess of wisdom, on the high mountain called the acropolis. It became known as the Parthenon and housed a golden statue that stood forty feet high.

Since the society was also underpinned by a democratic[35] philosophy, gathering took place on every street corner to debate issues that affected the entire community.

Sparta

Sparta is situated to the west of Athens in the land called Peloponnesus. Spartans never encouraged tyranny rule. Instead they had a type of democracy and oligarchy with a model of kingship restricted and empowered in some ways to create a balance.

The kingship was shared by two kings equally empowered. They were restricted to hold any judicial power, and they vowed to stand by their oath of allegiance to the states. The kings were commanders of the army and were not allowed to gain too much power in the states. In the fifth century BC, two kings ruled Sparta concomitantly.

---

[34] Sophists include men teaching young men to think and solve problems in mathematics, astronomy, philosophy, and medicine.

[35] Athens had been a democratic society since 507 BC. Democracy was first introduced by the Athenians in 508 BC. Democracy is a government with representatives who are elected and removed by the people.

A typical example is King Leotychidas[36] and King Leonidas.[37] Both ruled together for thirteen years.

Sparta was a military state in which the king was both general and commander of the army. Day-to-day administrations were undertaken by councilors, and economic prosperity depended on the labor of slaves.

Athens's main strength was its navy, so Sparta sought to compensate on land by training boys to be soldiers from a tender age. Spartan males were indoctrinated to live and die as soldiers.

When a Spartan baby boy was born, the parents would take it to the elders to see if the child was healthy or weak. Weak babies were left out on the mountainside to die. Healthy babies were placed in barracks at the age of seven along with the other young men. There they began their military training. At thirty years of age they were honored by receiving a military placement.

When a young man was brave enough to fight for the country, he was given a suit of bronze armor, a red tunic, and a helmet decorated with dyed horsehair.

The best and strongest of the graduates joined a team of soldiers called the Three Hundred. Wives were chosen for the Three Hundred so that they could perpetuate the lineage by bearing strong babies.

Spartans Rivaled Athenians

Let us now review the circumstances that led to the fall of the first two Greek states and gave rise to the third.

After the Persian war of August 480 BC and spring 479 BC, Athens decided to form a league with other city-states as explained earlier. The alliance was completed between 478 and 477 BC with

---

[36] Leotychidas ruled from 491to 476 BC. His son, Archidamus II, reigned from 476 to 427 BC.
[37] Leonidas ruler-ship lasted from 489 to 480 BC. His son, Peleistarchus, reigned from 480 to 458 BC.

the understanding that all states in Asia Minor should provide money and ships for a joint fleet. The alliance was called the Delian League because the treasury was held on the island of Delos.

Later the Athenians moved the common wealth to Athens. This sparked criticism that Athens was benefiting more than other allies, using the money to build the Parthenon. Athens was also accused of forcing other city-states to obey Athenian law. Sparta in particular became afraid that Athens was trying to extend its influence over all of Greece. In response the Athenians issued threats against Sparta and its Peloponnesian allies, including Syracuse in Sicily, Kroton, Megara, Corinth, and Olympia. This led to the Peloponnesian War.

The Peloponnesian War (431–404 BC) lasted twenty-seven years. Both sides were cruel and merciless. The Athenians murdered men and took women as slaves, while the Spartans captured and enslaved the Athenians in quarries.

Sparta was strengthened by the financial aid received from Persia. This created a standoff that lead to the lack of food among the Athenians, which resulted in their surrendering between 405 and 404 BC. The Athenians were kept in subjugation for thirty-six years, sparking protests against the treatment in captivity under Sparta.

The Spartans lost the discipline formerly instilled by their warrior culture. They became fat and greedy, preying upon poorer classes and weaker states rather than aiding their economic development. Inequitable distribution of wealth and decaying cities incited a Greek rebellion by 362 BC. Poor Spartans united with enslaved Athenians and neighboring city-states, especially Thebes, resulting in the downfall of Sparta. Athens was then reinstated as the political and cultural center of Greece (read *Man, Civilization, and Conquest, by Margaret Sharman*, Chapter Ten, page 58-59).

As time went by, a new type of society developed in Athens and other parts of Greece. Individual wealth became such a priority that men would go to fight for other countries, even Persia, for financial gain. In this respect, Athens could no longer recruit a special army loyal enough to protect its borders.

Macedonian, on the other hand, was now strategizing ways to extend its own strength and dominion. After they defeated Thrace, the Macedonians built an army with the aim of appropriating Greek wealth.

After they defeated Thessaly, the Macedonians marched farther south. During this time the Athenians and Thebans worried about the thriving ambition of the Macedonians. Athenians and Thebans who decided to defend themselves against the Macedonians fought together at Boeotica just north of Attica, but they were defeated, placing the Macedonians in full command of most of Greece.

Macedonia

Macedonia was the greatest state of Greece during the fourth century BC and was situated at the northern end of the Aegean Sea. The Macedonians were mixed race, partly Greek and also descended from the tribesmen of Yugoslavia (Serbia).

During the Persian wars between 480 and 490 BC, the Macedonians fought against Greece, probably seeking well-being in the arms of the Persians. The Macedonians, who had no dominance at the time, showed Greece their desire for Greek power, proving their untrustworthiness. The Greeks even called the Macedonians barbarians.[38]

Phillip II (382–336 BC), who was very ambitious, ascended the throne in 359 BC and was determined to develop Macedonia in a powerful state.

The Macedonian force consisted of well-trained men, mainly foot soldiers armed with long spears called spikes. These soldiers

---

[38] Barbarians are a primitive, brutish, and uncultured set of people.

marched in a closed formation called a phalanx, their spikes pointing forward and their shields shoulder to shoulder protecting the next man's right arms

No time was wasted. Two of King Phillip early sieges already included Thrace and Thessaly (354–353 BC).

Demosthenes, an Athenian leader who was fearful of the king's ambition, encouraged the people of Athens to go at war against King Phillip. Isocrates, on the other hand, called for peace with the Macedonians and asked that Phillip II unite Greece against the Persians.

Athens then became divided in that some wanted peace and others wanted war with the Macedonian king. The king of Macedonia marched down to Boeotica and defeated the forces of Demosthenes. This resulted in a Greece united under Macedonian leadership, one that was now strongly opposed to the Persian threat.

Unfortunately before Phillip could consolidate his new empire, he was murdered by one of his own officials in 336 BC. Suspicion arose that his son Alexander had plotted the murder.

When he heard of the king's death, Demosthenes rejoiced, thinking that the Macedonians would retreat to their homeland. He believed Phillip's son Alexander was too young at the age of twenty to be a capable leader. He was soon proven wrong.

Phillip's son Alexander III, who was later known as Alexander the Great (356–323 BC), was half Greek. He was mentored by Aristotle, a remarkable Greek philosopher. After he was made king and he learned about Greek culture and their gods, Alexander supposedly started to see himself as a son of the gods. He thought that he had been sent by the heroes of old.

At the beginning of his rule he checked the rebellious Thebans, slaughtering six thousand and selling eight thousand as slaves. The demonstration and effect of this act quelled insurrection by other city-states.

As Alexander III began his conquest for power and wealth, he commenced the fulfillment of the following Scripture passages concerning the third *beast*: Daniel 7:5 (leopard), Daniel 8:5–8 (ram), and Daniel 11:3–4 (Greece broken).

Alexander, still not as wealthy as Darius III of Persia, was impelled to cross the Hellespont in the spring of 334 BC to get a hold on Darius's wealth and provinces.

At this time the Persian king was lord of Assyria, Babylon, and Egypt. His army consisted of men drawn from all parts of the empire as well as hired Greek soldiers. This resulted in mixed loyalties and a tendency to abandon the king during times of life-threatening situations during battle. Alexander, knowing this, used it to his advantage at times (read *Man, Conquest, and Civilization,* Chapter Eleven).

His superiority became apparent in 334 BC when he crossed over to Asia on the bank of the Granicus River on the western tip of Asia Minor (modern Turkey) and defeated an army of the Persians before he marched south to cut off the ports and coast of Syria.

In 333 BC, marching south of Asia Minor, the king of the *leopard* (Greece) met with the king of the *bear* (Medes and Persia). Darius III and Alexander III fought at Issus, where Darius was soon defeated. He was forced to flee farther east into Asia, while Alexander traveled south into Syria and besieged the city of Tyre. After seven months the Phoenicians of Tyre also gave in their lot. This was followed by another two-month siege at Gaza in southern Palestine, therefore extending the Syrian campaign into 332 BC.

Alexander then went to North Africa, where he was welcomed by the Egyptians as their Pharaoh. He stayed in the Nile Delta until 331 BC. During this time he founded the town of Alexandria and offered sacrifices to the native gods.

Having added Asia Minor, Syria, Gaza, and Egypt to his empire, the Macedonian king retraced his steps through Syria to Damascus and crossed over to Mesopotamia (modern-day Iraq) in order to reach the Persian Empire.

After his defeat at Issus, the king of Persia escaped to Babylon and rebuilt a new army. He subsequently moved north to Arbela (Erbil) and took command of the nearby province of Gaugamela.

At Gaugamela, Alexander met Darius's largest army yet. They were equipped with state-of-the-art chariots with sharp blades and wheels. However, Alexander's tactic was to divide his troops during the charges of the Persian's chariots, allow them to pass, and command his troops to turn around swiftly and slay both horses and the men steering the chariots. When Darius saw his defeat once again, he fled to Susa.

Alexander continued his campaign up the Tigris River to Babylon, where the governor surrendered without a fight, and, the treasure held at Susa that Darius used as army wages was taken. By 330 BC, Persepolis, the Persian capital, had been burned, and Ecbatana, the storehouse of great wealth, had being captured.

As the Macedonian Empire expanded, it became more difficult to administer. New and inherited territories could not be left unguarded while Darius was still on the loose. This then produced more work for Alexander's army.

Alexander's exhausted army was soon eager to return home. This idea drove the men to plot ways to frustrate the king so that they might be sent back home.

The king of Greece main priority at this stage was to confront Darius directly so that he could cut his campaign short. However, fate intervened, and Darius's jealous cousin, Bessus,[39] who also had his eye on the Persian throne, stabbed Darius to death. At this juncture Alexander declared himself ruler of all Medes and Persia.

In 330 BC, Alexander marched east, conquering other natives, tribes, and states. The Grecian conqueror built sixteen new cities

---

[39] Bessus was later hunted down and killed by Alexander and his men about 327 BC.

named Alexandria after himself. The ruler of the *leopard* (Greece) introduced Greek ideas to the newly conquered provinces and erected temples to the Greek gods of his homeland.

Problems emerged once more when the Greek soldiers became exhausted because of the continuous marches from state to state. Low resistance against diseases and infections in the bushy jungles and forests led to the frequent illnesses of dysentery and malaria, resulting in high fatalities. Many soldiers then became fearful of not returning home.

However, on the flipside, Alexander's development of commerce from the Mediterranean to the Orient resulted in the empire—and Greece in particular Greece—becoming very wealthy.

Alexander also employed clever tactics to subdue conquered people. For example, he insisted that Persia should be ruled by native leaders, often placing them in positions of authority above their kinsmen and other Greek soldiers. This strategy reduced tension between Persians and Greeks but created resentment on the part of the latter toward their own king.

King Alexander also encouraged his men to wear Persian clothing and marry native women. He led by example, marrying two Persian women.

Alexander's men were also troubled by the fact that he adopted other Persian customs, such as commanding his subjects to lie prostrate in his presence until permitted to rise. He then cleverly made an exception for the Greeks by allowing them to stand in his presence, while Persians continued to bow in his presence, acknowledging him as a god.

Despite logistical and cultural setbacks, the Macedonian king relentlessly continued his conquest eastward so that by 330–327 BC, all of eastern Persia had already been conquered. The Greeks then successfully captured the Afghan plains and subjugated the tribes[40]

---

[40] These tribes were located geographically in what is now known as Russian Turkestan.

near the Caspian Sea. The campaign finally crossed the Indus River to the Hydaspes (Jhelum) in northwest India in 326 BC.

In 326 BC, Alexander won his last and fiercest battle against King Porus of India despite the unequal matchup of large elephants against horses.

Alexander planned to continue eastward so that he would end up at his starting point because of the inspired knowledge[41] of his accompanied geographers. On the way he was strongly opposed by Greek soldiers who believed that monsters lived in that part of the world. The Macedonian king became furious and decided to continue alone until a consultation[42] with the oracle changed his mind.

He then built a ship commanded by Nearchus to carry some of his army down the Indus River to the Arabian Sea. The rest returned on foot.

When he arrived in Babylon, Alexander, realizing the bad governance and instability that had developed during the ten years of his absence, immediately set about making new laws to dispel quarrels and rifts that had arisen. He also put Greek and Persian men to work restoring buildings, rebuilding temples, draining marshlands, and reversing the decline that the neglectful overseers had permitted to occur.

Alexander continued to encourage Greek and Persians to live together in harmony and friendship, integrate, and intermarry.

In spite of all the Macedonian leader had accomplished, he was also planning an expedition against Arabia, Carthage, and Italian states when he was struck ill with malaria.

Alexander, king of Greece, by reason of his illness, died in 323 BC before he reached the age of thirty-three.

---

[41] At that time of Alexander's conquest, some philosophers thought that the earth was flat and that travelling from one point straight onward you will end up where you started.

[42] Alexander sought guidance and direction from his spiritual devices. The replied given was a negative response to the request of his continued journey. On account of this he changed his mind from going onward.

Chapter 4

Alexander's Kingdom Broken and Ruled Not to His Posterity

The king of Macedonia, the so-called king of Greece, died, leaving his empire well established. But before we go any further in this chapter, let us make comparisons of the following Bible verses: Daniel 7:6, Daniel 8:8, and Daniel 11:4.

> *Daniel 7:6 (KJV) says, "Behold I Daniel saw a leopard, and on his back four wings of a fowl and four heads, where as dominion was given unto it."*

We have already established that this leopard symbolized Greece. The four wings and four heads are four kingdoms established out of the Greek king's empire and borders in four different directions[43] accordingly.[44]

> *Daniel 8:8 (KJV) says "The he-goat waxed very great, and when he was strong, the great horn was broken, and for it came up four notable little horns toward the four winds of heaven."*

---

[43] These were placed geographically in the east, west, north, and south.
[44] These four subkingdoms shall be placed in four quarters of the earth with individual borders.

I previously postulated that the he-goat also symbolized Greece. By reading verse 21 of this same chapter, I understand that the first horn of the he-goat was the first king of united Greece that spread its empire from the north to the east, west, and south. My theory with history concluded that Alexander was this king and that after his kingdom was established, his dominion was broken, creating four subkingdoms ruling four different quarters of the earth. This is explained in further text.

> *Daniel 11:4 (KJV) says, "And when he shall stand up, his kingdom shall be broken, and shall be divided toward the four winds of heaven, not to his posterity, nor according to his dominion which he ruled, for his kingdom shall be plucked up with others."*

Here the prophecy declared that the Greek king's empire would be broken, resulting in the lands[45] divided in four and ruled by men not of his linage or seed. Ultimately it would result in the kingdoms being invaded and conquered by other forces.

The revelation of the prophecy was revealed after Alexander's death in 323 BC. His empire was fragmented, creating four notable subkingdoms. These kingdoms were then ruled by the four generals of Alexander.

These subkingdoms included Macedonia and Greece (northwest region), which was ruled by Cassander; Antioch of Syria and Mesopotamia (Mideast region), which was ruled by Seleucus Nicator; Egypt and Palestine (south region), which was ruled by Ptolemy Lagus; and Thrace and Asia Minor (northwest and east regions), which was ruled by Lysimachus.

---

[45] The lands within the regions of the empire were divided into four.

None of these generals were of Alexander's lineage or posterity,[46] yet they ruled, each having his own empire, although the capitals were named after Alexander.

The kingdoms of greatest importance were Syria in the east and Egypt in the south. Syria was ruled by the family of Seleucids, descendants of General Seleucus. The Ptolemy family, on the other hand, ruled Egypt for more than 270 years[47] as the Pharaohs[48] of Egypt.

There were ongoing wars between these generals for many years after. And of course, each individual dynasty continued the quarrel.

---

[46] This means family or kin.

[47] Other writer gives information that the Ptolemy family ruled Egypt as Pharaohs for nearly three hundred years. (Read the book titled, *Man, Civilization and Conquest.*)

[48] Pharaoh is the title given to the "head" of the government or "king" of Egypt.

Chapter 5

The Ptolemy Kingdom in the South

And the king of the south shall be strong, and one of his princes, and he shall be strong above him, and have dominion; his dominion shall be a great dominion.

—Daniel 11:4–5

This prophetic declaration manifested when the Ptolemy family took over the empire of the south in the fourth century BC. The kingdom of Egypt and Palestine, which was ruled by Ptolemy and his descendants, was dominant[49] from 330 to 304 BC.

The ruling oligarchy became progressively wealthy on the back of a nationalized state. Landowners were compelled to produce crops and livestock for the state at fixed prices. In broad term the citizens of Egypt were literally enslaved in their own country, surviving by lesser means while the ruling authorities exercised a claimed franchise off the labor of the poor.

Alexandria, the Egyptian capital, was second only to Rome in stature, commerce, and culture during its first few centuries after it was founded by the Macedonian king, and its time was known as

---

[49] Their rule was looked upon with great respect. The order of dominance was due to their remarkable effort of logistical rule with continuous control over that region, resulting with Egypt also on the rise geographically and economically. Some claimed that this rule began immediately as King Alexander died in 323 BC, while some record it as happening between 304 and 301 BC.

the Alexandria Age. This period began its decline when Cleopatra VII (Thea Philopator)[50] and Mark Antony were defeated in 30 BC, resulting in the end of the Ptolemy reign as king and Pharaoh.

During the reign of Ptolemy I (Soter)[51], he established[52] one of the most noted university libraries, which his son Ptolemy II (Philadelpus)[53] then built on.

Many other interesting improvements had been done up to the time of Claudius Ptolemy (AD 90–168), who was one of the first geographical scientists to write books explaining the distance between the earth and the sun, eclipses, the movement of the planets, and the formation of the Milky Way. Ptolemy thought that the earth was the center of the universe and that the other planets orbited around it.

The Arabs and the Christians communities in the second century AD were influenced[54] by the geographic and scientific teachings of Claudius Ptolemy.

---

[50] Cleopatra VII was daughter to King Ptolemy XII (died 51 BC).

[51] Ptolemy I was born 367 BC, ruled from 323 BC, and died 283 BC.

[52] The library was initially organized by Demitrius, a student of Aristotle during the reign of Ptolemy Soter 306 BC.

[53] Ptolemy II was born 309. Ruled from 283 BC, and died 246BC. He continues the construction of the university libraries of Egypt that his father had started.

[54] It is widely known that some of the work of Claudius Ptolemy, which is celebrated and called the almagest by the Arabs, was a collection of works and ideas cited by Hiparchus in the second century BC. The almagest was interpreted as the bible of astronomy for some thirteen centuries.

Chapter 6

The Extended Rule of the South, by One of His Princes

And the king of the south shall be strong; and one of his princes[55], and he shall be strong above him, and have dominion; his dominion shall be a great dominion.

—Daniel 11:5

Many theologians and historians made reference to this part of the verse[56] as the war between Alexander's generals. I stand to be corrected, but this (my) view is an alternative one, showing Carthage as "one of his princes" of the south. This city was an extension of the south with an uprising that waged war against the Romans, who also sought to become the stronghold of the north.

---

[55] Many descriptive forms have been given concerning the *prince* of the south. Seleucus I (Nicator) of the Seleucid dynasty was also symbolically spoken of as the *prince* of the south (*The Jerusalem Bible—Readers Edition*). Some other editions refer to the prince as the southern king official. Prophecy is interpretive, and other views have factors that one should take into consideration. My inference is that it is more likely the prophet was pointing to another country in the south as with its initial ruling power as a prince but not to one of the king's son, kinsmen, or officials. Prince here would symbolically speak about a lesser authority and rule. Therefore, this prince kingdom would not be as powerful as the Ptolemies, rulers of the south at that time.

[56] "And one of his princes" (Daniel 11: 5)

While the Ptolemy dynasty was ascending on the southeast side by conquering the region dominantly controlled by the Seleucid dynasty, Carthage, south of the toe of Italy across the Mediterranean Sea, was also rising to prominence. Their ambition also would materialize, organize, and control the region.

They were not originally from this part of the south, but to sustain and gain prominence, their habitat reaches this part of the African continent.

Their Origin

The Carthaginians were from a Semitic[57] civilization of the Afro-Asiatic tree known as the Phoenicians (Byblos, Sidon, Tyre, etc.) in the Eastern Mediterranean. The Punic, as they were referred to, spoke Canaanite language. Located in the Western Mediterranean, the city of Carthage was founded at Tunisia[58] and for centuries had been one of the most important trading ports.

Rivals in previous eras against the Greek colonies and Italy resulted in the Carthaginians' dominance at sea by 500 BC. The Carthaginians' two main rivals were the Greeks and Italians (especially the Romans).

Rivaled with the Greek

In the middle of the sixth century BC, the Phoenicians and the Etruscan-Punic allies joined together against the Greeks. This

---

[57] The Phoenicians should not be looked upon as a clear blood line of the seed of Shem but a fused seed of Esau and Ishmael with the seeds of Ham (*especially Canaan, Noah's grandson*), since their origin begins some times after the flood.

[58] Carthage, present day Tunisia, was founded 814 BC by a queen of Tyre name Elissa, otherwise called Dido. Her aunt was Jezebel, wife to King Ahab (878–853 BC) of Israel.

resulted in the loss of Corsica to the Etruscans[59] and Sardinia to the Carthaginian.

In 480 BC while the Greeks were at war with the Persians, they were also involved in the Battle of Himera against the Carthaginian army, which was trying to invade Syracuse[60], but the Carthaginians failed.

In 405–367 BC, Hanno I the Great of Carthage and Dionysius I of Syracuse fought a long naval battle. The Syracuse king lost the battle, trying to take Punic Lilybaeum in western Sicily.

In 311 BC near Syracuse, Punic armies defeated the Greek leader Agathocles. Agathocles failed to admit defeat and retaliated by landing a vessel at Cape Bon near Carthage. They fought at Cape Bon and the Greek leader was defeated once more in 307 BC.

When he accepted defeat, the Greek gave up fighting Carthage for Sicily, placing the attention to the invading Persian forces from the east. Rome, willing to claim victory, became the new rival against the Carthaginians.

Rivaled with Rome

Rome[61], under the sovereign of the Etruscan king[62], decided to end the Sixth century with a change of governance. This was a result, because of the Etruscan king's contributions to the Punic allies and their various attacks on the Italians and Greek colonies. After, which they became a republic and entered three treaties with the Punic allies.

---

[59] This was a name given to a set of people of ancient Italy. Ancient Romans called them Etrusci. The Etruscan joined forces with the Carthagians during the sixth century BC.

[60] Eastern Sicily.

[61] This was ancient Rome then governed by Etruscan kings during the sixth century.

[62] King Tarquin the Proud was the last of these seven kings of Rome, before its Republic. Tarquin the proud was deposed 509 BC.

The first two Romano-Punic treaties happened in 509 and 348 BC. These were designed to define the trading boundaries and individual zone areas. Then in 280 BC, another was enacted to make a compromising effort between the Carthaginian and the Greek leader Pyrrhus.

Opposing interest developed between Rome and the city of Carthage, which resulted in disagreement, suspicion, and conflict. The contentions between them created a series of wars called the Punic Wars.

The First Punic War (264–241 BC)

The war broke out in 264 BC between Rome and Carthage when the former encroached on the trading port at Sicily.

In 262 BC during the initial stages of this war, Rome gained its first experience of naval battle, and by 261 BC, they had built their first fleet. The war continued for twenty years until the Romans eventually captured Corsica, Sardinia, and Sicily in 241 BC.

Because of the loss of these territories to Rome, the Carthaginians forces led by Hamilcar Barca began a series of campaigns to expand their control over the peninsula. Their control extended to Ebro Valley (in Spain), where they founded the city "New Carthage" (in Spain) in 228 BC.

Their development[63] and expansion in Spain led to their decision to besiege the Roman protected town of Saguntum (in Spain) about 219 BC. This attempt ignited the conflict with Rome, leading to the Second Punic War.

In the meantime, the Ptolemy dynasty was facing confrontation with the Seleucid dynasty. Between 221 and 204 BC, Ptolemy IV Philopator kept launching counterattacks against Antiochus III of Syria.

---

[63] The Carthaginians dominated the Spanish mainland, built an empire, and constructed towns and trading ports all along the south coast during 228 and 206 BC.

Antiochus III Megas of the Seleucid dynasty made campaigns in Phoenicia and Palestine. He also went up against Ptolemy IV at the fortress of Gaza during the Battle of Raphia in 217 BC.

It is interesting to note that Hannibal Barca (during his reign) had closed ties with Antiochus III in the battle against Rome. In 195 BC while in exile in Tyre, Hannibal acted as a tactical advisor for Antiochus III in various battles against Rome.

Carthage as the prince city of the south did not ponder at the attacks of the Romans but, as the "prince[64] of the south", continues to develop their trading port at the cost of the Second Punic War.

The Second Punic War (218–201 BC)

In spring 218 BC, this ambitious Carthaginian leader named Hannibal Barca (son[65] of Hamilcar Barca) arose and decided to attack Rome once more.

Hannibal's decision for this attack was triggered by few reasons. The army of his father (Hamilcar Barca) that fought during the First Punic War sought revenge. He wanted to recapture Sardinia and other lost island. The Punic allies had a new power and base in Hispania that had been created by the Barcid[66] family.

Hannibal's army consisted of a mixture of Carthaginians, Iberians, Celts from Spain, and trained African troops, including Numidian horsemen.

Approaching from Spain, Hannibal had to use incredible charm to encourage his army to continue. This was so because of the immense misfortune they encountered along the way. Even before

---

[64] The word prince used here represents some one next to power. In this case, Carthage was the next city in that part of the south to be equally recognized next to Egypt.

[65] Hamilcar Barca had three sons who participated in the commanding leadership of the empire. They were Hannibal Barca, Hasdrubal Barca, and Mego Barca.

[66] Barcid was a family household name given to the Barca's bloodline.

they reached the Alps, many fell ill. Others were either killed or wounded by hostile tribesmen.

In the narrow mountain passes of the Alps, horses carrying food supplies fell over the cliffs, resulting in food shortages and starvation, leading to the cannibalism of dead soldiers.

On descending the path from the Alps, before reaching North Italy, Hannibal's men were impeded by winter and had to camp in the narrow snow-clad valley.

Rome dispatched Consul Scipio[67] on hearing of Hannibal's arrival, but by the time Scipio could confront the "Prince of the South", Hannibal was already across the Pyrenees.

After a brief and bloody battle at Trasimento (Lake Trasimene) in 217 BC, during which the Numidian (present day Algeria) horsemen attacked from left field, Scipio was force to retreat.

Hannibal, encouraged by his victory, attacked Rome by night at the Battle of Ager Falernus in 217 BC. The Roman dictator Fabius Maximus fought a losing battle. The Carthaginian emerged victoriously as Rome co-opted and offered him status as a foreign exile under scrutiny.

The king of Carthage stayed in Italy for fourteen years. However, during this time the Carthaginian soldiers were frequent victims of guerilla attacks.

In 216 BC, a resumption of war led to the army of Hannibal marching into Campania and capturing Capua, the second largest city of Italy. Capua was also used as headquarters for the king of Carthage and his army. During this same year the Carthaginians were also victorious at the Battle of Cannae, which decimated more than eighty thousand men in one day.

Apart from the established empire of the Ptolemies, who were noted as the "king of the south" during the third centuries BC, Hannibal was revealed as the "strongest[68] prince of the south" and

---

[67] Scipio had just come from Spain.

[68] Strongest here denotes that apart from the Ptolemies, Hannibal was above all

was the only subject to stand against the Roman Empire, winning the first part of the Second Punic War.

Even after the decimation of their army, Roman pride prevented them from making peace with Hannibal.

However, after Hasdrubal's head was cut off and sent back to his brother Hannibal in 207 BC, the latter realized the futility of trying to take Rome itself.

In 206 BC, the patience of Rome benefitted when Scipio Africanus,[69] a Roman general strengthened by the death of Hasdrubal, led an army across the Western Mediterranean Sea to the peninsula (Spain). There he defeated the forces of the Punic allies at that fort, capturing all Carthaginian towns except Cadiz.

In 204 BC, the military genius, who was still filled with raged, went south and landed in Utica near Hannibal's home capital, Carthage. The strategic effort of Scipio Africanus compelled Hannibal to immediately quit his attention in Italy and return home to defend his homeland.

Hannibal was finally defeated in 202 BC by Scipio. The eastern Numidian,[70] strengthened by Rome victory, dethroned the king of Massyli,[71] ending the long Second Punic War. Carthage lost all trading cities, and its leading influence over the Western

---

other rulers in that part of the south. One must realized that Ptolemy was not mentioned as a prince but a king of the south.

[69] Publius Cornelius Scipio (Scipio Africanus) was the son of Consul Scipio who fought Hannibal at Lake Trasimene in 217 BC.

[70] These Numidians were from the eastern tribe of the Massylians. They were ruled by King Gala who died in 206 BC, and his son Masinissa became king. King Masinissa, being an ally of the Carthagians, switched side during the Second Punic War and joined forces with Rome. King Masinissa, being encouraged by Rome victories, went against the western Numedians and defeats them.

[71] This was a Northern African tribe of western Numidia, who supported Rome against Carthage during the Second Punic War. In the latter part of the Punic War (in 208 BC) they switched allegiance, and "rejoined" Carthage again. The king of Masaesyli (western Numidia) at that time was King Syphax.

Mediterranean was repudiated, leaving Carthage to reduce and restrictive surroundings.

Reformed methods done by Hannibal revived Carthage once more. In 191 BC, Hannibal offered to pay off the indemnity owed but was opposed by anti-Punic factors in Rome.

Corrupted oligarchies in Carthage joined Rome in its opposing actions against Hannibal, forcing him to flee to Asia as a refugee. Scipio, who was in favor of Hannibal's reform methods, encouraged his returned with an agreement of peace with the nearby allies of the Western Mediterranean. Despite the agreement of peace, war still broke out between Hannibal and the king of the Numidian Berbers.

The Third Punic War (149–146 BC)

War broke out as a result of the Numidian king Masinissa constantly provoking the Carthaginians. The retaliation of the Carthaginians provided a reason to determine the end of the peace treaty.

Rome challenged Carthage, and the defeat was imminent. The Carthaginians were presented with an ultimatum either to vacate the city or be destroyed with it. Hannibal decided to go to war.

By 146 BC, Carthage was decimated after three years of siege. The naval fleet was destroyed, and foreign territories captured by Hannibal ceded to Rome. Carthage became the new province of Africa.

So strong was Roman hatred for the Carthaginians that they ploughed salt into the agricultural lands, making it infertile for a long time.

Under Julius Caesar, emperor of Rome, the city of Carthage was rebuilt in 46 BC and became the leading city and capital of that African province.

Chapter 7

The Fourth Beast—Rome

As Rome became dominant, the significance of Daniel's prophecies became evident. Let us examine the following Scripture passages: (A) Daniel 2:40–43 (KJV), (B) Daniel 7:7 (KJV), and (C) Daniel 8:8–9 (KJV).

A. Daniel 2:40–43, as I understand, indicates that the beast should be strong as iron with the power to subdue and crush all other kingdoms. This verse could be interpreted as Rome being the beast that shall manipulate and maneuver the other kingdoms. The iron and clay represented inequality and confusion amongst the kingdoms, weakening Rome in its cause.[72] During the existence of the Holy Roman Empire, these kingdoms or subkingdoms[73] were France, Germany, Spain, Portugal, Britain, Italy, Switzerland, Hungary, Yugoslavia, and Poland. In the beginning of the sixth century AD, three of these ten subkingdoms were plucked out from the union. These three subkingdoms were Hungary, Yugoslavia, and

---

[72] Rome's cause and determination was to rule the world both religiously and politically.

[73] Subkingdoms are kingdoms that are a part of a whole empire. These ten subkingdoms warred amongst themselves. In the end it resulted in the fall of the Holy Roman Empire in 1806 as well as World War I and II, and by 1957, the EEC was formed.

Poland. The Holy Roman Empire disintegrated in the early nineteenth century after Napoleon defeated the European powers that opposes him at the battle of Austerlitz in 1805. Later a new Germany confederacy was formed in 1814, of which Austria became the leading power. Another shift in the leading powers of the hemisphere was appointed again after World War II when the European Economic Community (EEC) was founded in 1957 and then reorganized as the European Union (EU) in 1993, the members of the powerful countries forming the G8.

B. In Daniel 7:7,[74] the prophet again declares that the "fourth beast is dreadful and terrible, and strong exceedingly." The iron teeth[75] symbolized the beast's devouring action with strength to subdue all other nations[76] before him. The verse states that the beast would be different from all other beast before him. The beast's diversity could be explained as a characteristic of strength, especially with its iron teeth, how it approached and stamped the residue with its feet, and the magnificent outset of the many horns it had. This chapter also explained that this beast had ten horns. These ten horns represent the ten nations he would affiliate with to establish his kingdom.

C. Daniel 8:8–9 explained that shortly after Alexander the Great's kingdom had been divided to the four corners of the earth, out of one of these corners came forth a horn strong and great that waxed exceedingly to the south, the east, and

---

[74] This prophecy refers to the same beast in Daniel 2:40–43.

[75] An animal uses its teeth to consume its prey. The beast's teeth represent the same. However, its strategies will be of vast consummation, which represent its iron teeth.

[76] These nations include the Babylonian Empire, the Medes and Persia Empire, and the Greek Empire, which were conquered by Rome.

the pleasant lands. Note that the Scripture passage did not mention the north in regard to the horn's direction of flight, so in my view the horn would be coming from the north and proceeding to the south, the east, and the pleasant lands (western lands).

Geographical Position

Italy is situated just below the Gaulic and Germanic tribesmen countries of the northern lands.

Rome is the capital of Italy, which many, including myself, acknowledge to be the ideal set of people who represented the horn. This horn extended out of one of the four preceding horns of the he-goat.

History[77] reveals Rome as a conqueror, conquering many nations and empires, such as the Babylonians, Medes, Greeks, and Carthaginians.

So if history proved this city, to be unconquerable in the north, spreading to the south, east and west of its empire, then who can say otherwise?

Rome Assured Manifestation as the Beast

As Rome, represented by this fourth beast, made its approached to stamp the residue and made its mark in world dominions, one must take careful observation of Revelation 13.

Revelation 13 speaks of the beast in his full appearance. He was clothed as a leopard, his feet as the feet as a bear and mouth as the mouth of a lion.

These features[78] are symbolic to the characteristics of Rome, and I will speak with conviction and authorization.

---

[77] References can be drawn from the book 'Man, Civilization and Conquest.

[78] The beast's features are comprised of the skin of a leopard, a bear's feet, and a

A. Leopards are known to leap as part of their species' special development. Likewise, Rome leaped from the least to the greatest, showing their greatness and versatility in comparison to other empires.

B. When a bear faces his opponent or prey, he always stands upright on his two hind legs as a man. So Rome always stood up to its enemies until victory or defeat. That is why Rome was always involved in long and devastating battles.

C. A lion mouth serves like a trumpet and produces a sound so loud that its enemies are warned by it. His roaring proclaimed the demand for the clearance of his surrounding or domain. Rome speaks with that authority, demanding that its enemies surrender or accepted defeat.

I should further establish that though the beast in Revelation 13 was clothed with all the features[79] of the three beasts before him, this simply represents the addition of the possession of the empires they had. Seeing that the fourth kingdom (Rome) conquered and devoured the third kingdom (Greece), it can be interpreted that all of these kingdoms conquered by Greece were ceded to Rome.

The Fourth Beast Cited as a Man

I have observed Scripture and its prophetical views concerning the fourth beast, and I was able to relate to the following passages in the King James Version: Daniel 7:20 and 25, Daniel 8:23–25, and Revelation 13:8, 17, 18.

Daniel 7:20 and 25 gave indication of a "horn that had eyes, and mouth that speak very great things…" The verse goes on to say "he shall speak great words against the Most High, and wearing out the

---

lion's mouth.

[79] The three beasts that came before the fourth beast were the *lion* (Babylon), the *bear* (Medes and Persia), and the *leopard* (Greece).

saints." According to these verses, isn't it clear that at some time in the future, this "horn" must reveal itself as a kingdom or a man?

Daniel 8:23–25 says that in the "latter time of the kingdom…, a king of fierce countenance, and understanding dark sentences, shall stand up… he shall also stand up against the Prince[80] of princes," and by so doing, destroying His[81] holy people. A kingdom is never without a king, and this *king* will manifest as man *standing* against Christ and his people.

Revelation 13:8, 17 (KJV) gives prophetic explanation that this kingdom will exist with power over churches and states. Verse eight says "all that dwell on the earth shall worship him, whose names are not written in the book of life of the Lamb[82] slain…" Since the words "worship him" were used, obviously, this kingdom in its latter stage would be a religious government. Verse seventeen suggested "buy or sell", indicating the power of this man with the economy. So evidently this is a man and a kingdom empowered by the church and states.

Verse seventeen continues to indicate that the *signature* of the beast would manifest in three ways. These are, "a mark," "a name" and "the number" of his name. These indications show that all three *signatures* represent the title of the *beast*.

Verse eighteen specifically emphasized on the title of the "beast", "man" and the "number", by saying "let him that hath understanding count the number of the beast, for it is the number of a man: and his number is six hundred and threescore and six (666)."

Irenaeus, in his book title *Against Heresies*, linked the word "Lateinos"[83] with the number six hundred three score and six (666),

---

[80] The Prince here represents Christ.

[81] Prince of all princes who is Christ the Saviour

[82] The Lamb symbolizes Christ.

[83] Latin is the name of the language used by the people of the fourth prophetical kingdom known as Rome.

by suggesting that it might be the name of the fourth kingdom in Daniel's vision.

Others believed that the vision was pointing to Nero (Neron)[84] Caesar. By adding the numeric equivalent of the letters of his name, the total was six hundred threescore and six (666).

Another interesting thing to look into is the Latin word *Vicarius Filii Dei*, which adds up to six hundred three score and six (666) when adding the numeric equivalent of the words.

There are many disputes surrounding the words *Vicarius Filii Dei* (Vicar of the Son of God), where persons are saying that it is a title used by the Pope. Many hold the view that anyone bearing this title, other than the Messiah, is an Antichrist. However, it has been said that the Catholic Popes never used the title *Vicarius Filii Dei* but the title "Vicarius Christi" (Vicar of Christ) instead. Nevertheless, when adding the numeric equivalent of this title (Vivarius Christi) it also adds up to six hundred three score and six (666).

Viewing all indications, the number six hundred threescore and six (666) has always being shown to be associated with Rome (*the fourth beast*).

As for me, this *number* is the title of a man that ruled a kingdom, which is the fourth kingdom in Daniel's vision. The kingdom would initially[85] govern by church and states under the leadership and advice of this *man*[86], then some time in the future the power of states would be taken away.

Rome will no longer be imperialistic[87] but a country under a religious leadership, fighting against the commandment of the Prince of

---

[84] *Neron* Caesar without the "n" (Nero Caesar) would only add up to 616. The "n" was added to give the total of six hundred three score and six (666).

[85] *Initially*, because it starts out as a governed body united with the Church and States. Sometime after that the power of the States was removed by Napoleon Bonaparte.

[86] This man is the religious leader of Rome.

[87] This is imperial Rome ruled by emperors.

Princes and breaking the staff[88] of any opposing kingdom, relinquishing their power and subduing[89] their kingdom to His domain.

One will argue about the existence of this man, making disagreeable suggestion about certain conclusions, but assuredly this man will reside in Rome, maybe not holding a political post but having the power of a religious voice.

If this man is the head of Roman's religious trend, you should look and make your assumptions of this man and decide who he is for yourself.

---

[88] The staff represents one concept or belief.

[89] At this time one will agree and accept his religion, and be a part of his kingdom. Any opposition would be destroyed.

Chapter 8

The Birth of Rome

In his conquest Alexander the Macedonian lived to achieve the unification of the Greeks. Being united, they were able to build a better empire under the rule of the Macedonian king named Alexander the Great.

The Greek Empire grew, colonizing all islands around the toe of Italy.

After Alexander's death (323 BC) the most advanced people in Italy at that time were the Etruscans. The Etruscans were the largest tribesmen living in Italy, but they were originally from Lydia of Asia.

Amongst other tribes was a small community of people called Latin living near the Tiber River. Their chief town was called Rome, and they were then known as the Romans.

A legendary story says that a prince of Troy named Aeneas was ordered by the gods to lead his people westward to find a new nation. The prince of Troy landed in Italy and joined forces with the Latin-speaking countrymen who were living there. He then ruled a town called Alba Longa for generations.

It is said that two sons were born from Aeneas. One was called Remus, and the other was Romulus. When they reached manhood, an argument developed amongst them. They argued about who is to be king. After a long quarrel, war broke out between them and their followers. Remus was defeated, and Romulus ruled the city and called it Rome. That was about

750 BC, and at the time the Greek Homer was taking notes and recording all these legendary stories.

In 640–500 BC, the Etruscan kings conquered and ruled Rome. Under Etruscan rule, the Romans were treated with civility. The treatment was better than that of the upcoming era of Grecians colonization with King Philip II and Alexander the Great of Macedonia.

Years after the period of Etruscan colonization and civilization, Rome decided that they did not want any more of these Etruscan kings to rule over them.

At the time of this dispute an Etruscan king named Tarquin the Brud was in power. During his rule the state of Rome had been developed. New buildings, towns, and provinces had been erected. While this Etruscan king was away on some particular business, the people of Rome dethroned him, claiming that they never again wanted to be ruled by any more kings.

They decided then to have two chief magistrates who would hold offices for only one year. Hence, Rome formed their first republican government.

Rome then started to push the frontier of the Roman Republic farther north and then southward, westward, and eastward by striking their enemies at every turn. Shortly thereafter, Rome became the leading power in Italy, subduing all, including the Etruscan and Greek cities of southern Italy.

The reformation and reconstruction of the infrastructure was now the order of the day, stimulating the building of roads, providing proper access throughout the country, and encouraging all to obey Roman laws.

Consuls or chief magistrates were selected every two years from amongst the praetors.[90] An individual who had been elected many

---

[90] Individuals who preceded their professions and became judges were known as praetors.

times to be a consul attained the top rank of the ladder, which was a proconsul.[91]

As Rome began to claim other provinces outside of Italy, the people saw the need to appoint leaders of these provinces. Some of these new provinces were Sicily, Sardinia, Corsica, Port of Spain, and North Africa, which was conquered during the Punic Wars. Syria, Palestine, Macedonia, and most of the Greek Empire was conquered by 167 BC. Rome then made them into Roman provinces as well. Elected proconsuls were made governors of these provinces.

After a while, Rome's expansive society and republican form of government did not elevate all of the lifestyle of the citizens equally. The richer class of individuals in Rome controlled all the lands and took advantage of the poorer set of people, treating them as slaves and paying cheap wages.

Another thing that was also disturbing was that the soldiers that fought for Italy during the wars had nothing to show for their heroic performances. Various reformers tried to give back lands to these heroic soldiers, but the rich individuals, especially those in the senate, opposed such action.

The empire was then on the verge of a civil war but as a result of positive changes in the economy and improvement in the life of some people, the civil war intended was placed on hold. Later this reform did not make any difference in that there remained an upper class of individuals called optimares and an ordinary set called populares. Those who were poor kept undergoing economic pressures, which resulted in hostility between the senate and the people.

Apart from the rivals between the senate and the people, there were also rivals within the senate as well. The senators took sides for and against the present consuls.

During the year 88 BC, there was a consul (chief magistrate) name Suela who was very cruel and merciless and made himself a

---

[91] This is the governor of a province.

dictator for the two years he was in office. During his government he killed six thousand men who were supporters of a senator that opposed him.

The Roman republic deteriorated drastically, but before it could end, it brought about a long civil war and much Roman bloodshed.

Chapter 9

Julius Caesar and Rome

Julius Caesar, born around 108 BC, ruled Rome until his death in 44 BC. Caesar is one of the most popular kings of the Roman Empire. He began his career as a quaestor.[92] During this appointment he made himself a good fortune and was known as a rich man in Rome. Caesar's ambition encouraged him to think that without wealth he would never achieve the level of power he desired.

By the virtue of the wealth he had acquired, he bribed his way to the top. One of his methods included paying for expensive shows, some of which included gladiator in combats and chariot races. This was done in the effort to win the love and favoritism of the people.

In 64 BC, he was given the highest priestly rank of the land known as Pontifex Maximus, the chief priest. This position was an elected position for life.

In 59 BC, Julius Caesar became a praetor,[93] and then he became a consul. Two consuls were elected each year by a judge (praetor). These consuls were then the chief magistrates of Rome.

After he used his wealth to achieve the position of a consul, Caesar was now in financial difficulties, so he decided to seek financial support.

At this time there were two important men in the senate. Pompey, who had led Rome to war against the Syrians and made Palestine

---

[92] A quaestor is a junior official.

[93] A praetor is a Judge in rank.

a province of Rome, and the other, Crassus, a wealthy landowner. With these two, Julius joined forces and formed the triumvirate.[94] With the power of three they excelled over the other senators.

In 58 BC, Julius Caesar became proconsul, as he ensured that he was elected more than once as consul. Being proconsul, he was now supposed to be a governor of a Roman province. He was then elected as the governor of Cisalpine Gaul and Illyricum (North Italy and the modern coast of Yugoslavia).

War then broke out in Gaul, and so Julius had to subdue the German tribesmen from the north in their attempt to attack the Helvetii, a tribe from western Switzerland. During his next visit to Gaul (north Italy), he made an agreement with the locals to fight with him against the German living east of the Rhine River, preventing the German tribesmen from invading their countries.

Between 58 and 49 BC, the governor and his legion carried out a purification conquest in Gaul. They destroyed all who disobeyed his principles of peace, and took possession of their cultivation and land. The tribesmen of Gaul, desperate for their irrigated lands, tried to resist Julius, but to no avail. Vercingetorix, the Gaulic king, was forced to surrender because of the threat of starvation. At the end Caesar claimed the entire city of Gaul for Rome. The senate, showing their appreciation to Caesar, declared a public holiday that lasted for twenty days.

While Caesar was engaged in the purification at Gaul, Crassus[95] was engaged in a battle in Asia, where he was killed. His passing left Julius and Pompey fighting each other over the remaining wealth.

In Caesar's absence from Rome, Pompey gets the opportunity to become a powerful individual amongst the upper class (optimares) that controlled the senate. Luckily for Caesar, he was already the beloved idol of the ordinary (populares) class of people.

---

[94] A triumvirate is a three-man government.

[95] Crassus was one of the members of Caesar's "three men government."

In 49 BC, when Caesar was returning from his Gaulic journey with an intention to beset all who opposed him in Rome, he was ordered not to enter or approached Italy with his army. Instead of complying, Julius marched southward across the Rubicon River with his army. At this moment the Romans realized that Julius was determined to take Rome to fulfill his thirst for power.

Pompey, understanding Caesar's thirst for power, accepted that he could not defeat Caesar. He saw that the triumvirate they once had was now broken, so he escaped with his legion to Greece.

Now that Julius Caesar had no one to oppose him, he became the new conqueror of Rome. The invasion of Rome and the senate brought stipulations. The citizen believed that Caesar would be just as evil to them as he was to the other natives. Anyway, Caesar disappointed them. He did not use his bloodthirsty method as he did in Gaul and other places, as that would have encouraged a civil war resulting in unrest amongst the citizens. Instead he treated the people generously and won his enemies over to his side. Although he had won over the hearts of the people, he still thought of Pompey as a threat to the society of Rome that he had started to develop, so he went in search of him. Caesar and his army, which was accompanied by Mark Antony as his chief lieutenant, followed Pompey and defeated him at Pharsalus in Thessaly. Pompey escaped into Egypt, leaving behind his followers.

Chapter 10

Caesar and Egypt

After King Alexander's death Egypt was separated from the combined empire of Alexander and placed under subjection and the rules of Ptolemy's generation. The Ptolemy generation ruled Egypt, and was the pharaoh of Egypt for many years. They were one of the most triumphant countries in the south at that time

Ptolemy XIII (Theos Philopator I)[96] was the pharaoh of Egypt when Pompey fled[97] from Caesar for refuge. Ptolemy, in need of Caesar's friendship, have Pompey murdered rather than receiving him in Egypt as a friend.

When Caesar entered[98] Egypt in search of Pompey, he was welcome by Ptolemy with Pompey's embalmed head while showing off how he had killed his (Caesar) enemy.

With this action Ptolemy believed that he had found a friend and that with this gift Caesar would soon leave Egypt, knowing that the man he had sought was now dead. But Ptolemy did not know that he had brought troubled on himself.

When Ptolemy XIII tried to take full control of Egypt, Cleopatra VII insists on her leadership of the kingdom. She was then

---

[96] Ptolemy XIII Ruled Egypt from 51 BC until his death 47 BC.
[97] Pompey tried to escape from Caesar after his defeat in August 48 BC.
[98] Julius Caesar reached Egypt, a few days after Pompey, in 48 BC.

strengthened[99] by the hand of Caesar, which result was the death of her husband (Ptolemy XIII)

With Caesar's help, Ptolemy XIV (Ptolemy Philophator II) took his sister's hand in marriage, indicating the will of the old ways to safeguard the throne and ensure it would stay in his family.

Nevertheless Cleopatra became Caesar's Mistress in 47 BC.

Caesar and Cleopatra in Marriage

> *"And in the end of years they shall join themselves together, for the king's daughter of the south shall come to the king of the north to make an agreement" (Daniel 11:6 KJV).*

Some historians believed that this verse[100] refers to the marriage between Bernice[101] and King Seleucus (Antiochus II Theos) of Syria.

Looking into the history of the shared broken kingdom of Alexander, this marriage[102] between Bernice and Antiochus II is of no significant to verse six of Daniel eleven. It is so because the Seleucid kingdom had controlled the "Middle East"[103] not the northern region. The northern kingdom of Alexander was shared between Lysimachus[104] and Cassander.[105]

One should note that there were other marriages between the Ptolemy females and kings of other dynasties. An example of such

---

[99] Caesar and Cleopatra were victorious against Ptolemy XIII, with the aid of Romans reinforcement at the Battle of the Nile 47 BC,

[100] Daniel 11:6

[101] Bernice (Berenice) Phernopherus was the daughter of Ptolemy II Philadelphus.

[102] The marriage took place around 250 BC, which does not correspond to the time of Daniel prophecy that referred to a marriage that should take place in the latter part of the Ptolemy dynasty.

[103] The Seleucid's share of the Macedonian kingdom was Antiochus of Syria and Mesopotamia.

[104] Lysimachus received N. West and East region.

[105] Cassander received part of N. West region.

marriage is between Arsinoe II[106] and King Lysimachus of the northern region, which placed her marriage as a better revelation of the prophecy[107] of Daniel than Bernice's marriage. However, seeing that Julius Caesar of the northern kingdom was more a remarkable figure and a powerful king compared to King Lysimachus, Arsinoe II's story was not that outstanding as that of Cleopatra. Also, most of these marriages took place during the earlier part of the Ptolemy dynasty, which makes these marriages of no link to Daniel 11:6 (KJV).

One important detail of verse six is that the prophecy should occur during the *latter* part of the dynasty. Daniel 11:6 (KJV) says, "And in the end[108] of years they shall join themselves together ..." There is no other marriage that occurred during the reign of the Ptolemy that adjoined such prophecy as the marriage between Cleopatra and Julius Caesar of Rome.

Daniel 11:6 (KJV) says "the king's daughter of the south shall come to the king of the north to make an agreement."

Lucius Mestrius Plutarchus (Plutarch), in his book titled *Life of Julius Caesar,* explained how Cleopatra smuggled herself secretly into the palace with the help of her loyal friend[109] to see Caesar.

This Cleopatra, who was the queen of Egypt, fell in love with Caesar, the king of the north, and "made an *agreement*"[110] that both would gain the kingdoms and rule Egypt together.

Caesar thereafter took sides with her against Ptolemy, her brother, the pharaoh of Egypt, and they defeated him in battle. It was reported that Ptolemy drowned when his ship was capsized in the River Nile.

---

[106] She was sister to Ptolemy II Philabelphus.

[107] The prophecy of Daniel 11:6.

[108] The word *end* refers to either of two things, which is the end of the Ptolemy reign or in the latter part of the dynasty.

[109] This friend's name was Appollodorus.

[110] Cleopatra's agreements were basically of two reasons. Firstly, she was in exile and wanted to regain her rightly place, which is on the Egyptian throne. Secondly, Egypt was in debt (financially) to Rome, which one of her way of payment was to marry the Roman Emperor.

After Ptolemy XIII died, Cleopatra was forced to adhere to the old ways[111] of Egypt, so she married her younger brother, who became Ptolemy XIV.

Caesar and Cleopatra got married after a while in Egypt. They had a pronounced Egyptian ceremony, and together they had a son named Caesarion. It had been said that because of the marriage of Caesar and Cleopatra, the Egyptians feared that the Greek dynasty[112] was ending and the Roman dynasty had begun.

Caesar stayed in Egypt for one year. When he returned home, he was so powerful[113] that he made himself a dictator for ten years. After that, he left in search of Pompey's remaining followers, conquering Libya and Spain before the civil war was over.

Caesar Back in Rome

After Caesar returned, he acquired full control of Rome. To celebrate this, he held the greatest feast and offered the best entertainment ever in a Roman arena at that time. Many chief kings were led through Rome in chains, including Vercingetorix, the great Gaulic king, who was then murdered at the feast. Luckily, because of the love he had for Queen Cleopatra, he releases her sister, Arsenal.

Caesar, wanted to be seen as a god, ordered his statue to be placed with the statues of the gods of Rome in public places with inscriptions stating, "To the unconquerable god." Appearing to fit the cause, he always dressed in purple and sat on his golden throne in the

---

[111] The old custom was that any individual bearing the title Queen or Pharaoh of Egypt could not marry anyone outside of the family, but to keeping the dynasty in the bloodline by marrying to someone in the family.

[112] The Egyptians were referring to the ending reign of the pharaohs by the Ptolemy family and the beginning of the reign of the Caesars.

[113] Caesar was now king of Egypt and a proconsul of Rome.

senate house. Though never crowned king, some of Caesar's senators decided that they should call him the king of Rome. Therefore, Caesar was then the so-called king of Rome.

Caesar's Assassination

> *Daniel 11:6 (KJV) says, "She shall not retained the power*
> *of the arm, neither shall he stand nor his arm."*

Caesar and Cleopatra planned to gain power and rule Egypt and Rome together, but unfortunately the prophecy of Daniel revealed itself in conjunction with the treacherous work of two of his senators.

Cassius and Brutus, two of the senators who feared Caesar's power in Rome, thought of refusing and opposing Caesar's declaration as king of Rome. On the other hand, they thought that their decision would not stand, seeing that the other senators would not vote against Caesar. After all, they were his chosen senators.

The court chamber of the senators was finally called to discuss the matter of making Caesar the king of Rome officially. This meeting was planned for the March 15, 44 BC.

As Caesar, the soon-to-be king of Rome, sat at the meeting and listened to the petition of the senators, Brutus and his confederates passed through the gathering of the senators with a hidden dagger and stabbed Caesar to death. Caesar had the chance before he died to look to Brutus and say, "Et tu Brute," meaning "You too, Brutus." At his death Octavius[114] ascended to the throne and preceded the ambition as Rome's first king and emperor.

---

[114] Octavius was Caesar's nephew.

Mark Antony Emulated Caesar's Footsteps

Daniel 11:6 (KJV) says, "She shall be given up, and they that brought her … and him that strengthen her in these times."

Mark Antony III, born in 83 BC, ascribed himself as a brilliant military leader and orator. He accompanied Caesar in many distinguish campaigns in Greece, Egypt, and Palestine. Antony was Caesar's chief lieutenant when he fought against Pompey and his army, and he destroyed them at Pharsalus. He was very ambitious, and like many others, he sought the opportunity to gain power.

Antony was consul when Caesar was assassinated. Being a relative of Caesar by his mother, Antony became so upset with the conspirators that at the funeral he gave a speech, during which he threatened them. On account of this threat they fled the city.

Not long after, Antony, Lepidus, and Octavius[115] formed another three-man government.

They then went in searched of Caesar's two main conspirators. The two, Brutus and Cassius, were caught and killed by the triumvirate at the Battle of Philippi in 42 BC.

After this battle they divided the Roman Empire amongst themselves, Lepidus receiving the governorship of Africa (although he was disposed of in 36 BC). Mark Antony III received Alexandria and the east, and Octavian ruled Rome and the west.

Mark Antony decided to continue the task of Caesar, which is to create a bond[116] with the Egyptian queen to strengthen ties with Egypt. So while he was pursuing the agreement[117] of the bond, he fell in love with Cleopatra.

---

[115] Octavius, after ascending the throne was called Octavianus (Octavian).

[116] Antony's action proved that he agreed with Caesar that whosoever ruled Egypt must also rule Rome.

[117] Anthony wanted Cleopatra's promise to support his intention to war against the Parthians.

Cleopatra responded to the request of Antony and met with him at Tarsus to answer question of loyalty. On arrival, her charm moved Antony from off his feet that he chose to spend the winter of 41 BC with her at Alexander.

On 25 December 40 BC, Cleopatra gave birth to twins, which Antony accepted as his children. Four years later, while on his war journey to the Parthia, he renewed his relationship with the queen of Egypt. From there on, Alexander (capital of Egypt) became his home.

Antony's decision to marry Cleopatra angered Octavian because Antony was also his sister's husband. So the governor of Rome falsely accused Antony, saying he was squandering Rome's wealth on the Egyptian queen and had turned his back on his wife (read *New Standard Encyclopedia Volume A,* page 293, subheading *Antony, Mark).* This action Octavian took against Antony was definitely a sign of a superstition, believing that Mark Antony planned to use the power of Egypt and acquire Rome's wealth and throne.

Octavian succeeded in his strategy against Mark Antony. As a result, Antony's powers and positions[118] in Rome and Alexandria were stripped from him. The Egyptians responded against Octavian and his decision, which resulted in a civil unrest. This was an illustration from the Egyptians, showing that Antony was well beloved and seated as their pharaoh and king in marriage with their queen, Cleopatra.

According to the outcome of Cleopatra and Mark Antony, we should take keen note of the Scripture as follows:

> *"She shall be given up and they that brought her, and he that begat her, even he that strengthen her in these times"* *(Daniel 11:6).*

---

[118] Antony served as governor of Egypt and the east.

It was obvious that her husband, Antony, had "strengthened her" and he showed it practically; Antony, on behalf of Egypt, made conquest against Armenia, Media, Parthia and Libya. He extended the empire by adding more provinces to its claim, while Cleopatra was honored (by Antonius)[119] with her knew title, "Queen of Kings."

As Antony began to strengthen[120] Cleopatra ruled within the south, Octavian, ruler of the north, (Rome) became jealous and envious of Antony's progress.

The expansion of the empire of Egypt threatened Rome's dominance in the north, which left Octavian Caesar believing that Cleopatra was planning a war against Rome to establish herself as empress of the world of the north (Rome).

In 31 BC, Antony and Octavian fought at the Battle of Actium.[121] The forces of Octavian defeated the army of Antony in the naval battle. Antony then fled to Egypt in search of Cleopatra. On arrival at a certain destination, he heard that Cleopatra was dead. The defeated ruler of Egypt, not knowing that the report was false, fell on his sword and died immediately. When Cleopatra received the news that her husband was dead, she committed suicide as well on August 12, 30 BC.

Caesar's son, Caesarion,[122] was also killed on August 23, 30 BC to make sure that Caesar's offspring had no chance to inherit the Roman throne. It is said that Octavian (Octavianus or Octavius), Julius Caesar's nephew, who succeeded the throne after his death, gave the order to kill Caesarion (Caesar's son).

---

[119] Her husband

[120] Antony attacked the provinces of the Roman Empire and placed them under Egyptian rule.

[121] Actium was an ancient name of a promontory on the west coast of Greece.

[122] Caesarion was born June 27, 47 BC. He became Pharaoh and reigned with his mother from September 2, 47 to August 23, 30 BC. After the death of his mother he remained the sole pharaoh, and he was the last pharaoh of the Ptolemy dynasty to rule Egypt.

After this victory at the Battle of Actium, Octavian became master of the Roman world.

The outcome of the deaths of Cleopatra and both of her husbands[123] marked a real revelation[124] at that time, fulfilling the prophecy about the Egyptian queen ruling Egypt and Rome with either of her husbands. It was of course Cleopatra's main aim to bind Rome with Egypt when she gave her hand in marriage to both of these high-profile Roman celebrities.

---

[123] Her husbands were Julius Caesar and Mark Antony.
[124] Daniel 11:6 (KJV) gives full details on the prophecy.

Chapter 11

Rome Imperial Successors

After Caesar was assassinated in 44 BC, his will and testament made Octavius[125] his adopted son and heir to the throne. After he ascended to the throne, Octavius changed his name to Gaius Julius Caesar Octavianius (Octavian).

Octavius (Octavian) had a quarrel[126] with his brother-in-law, Mark Antony III, in 43 BC. They fought at the Battle of Mutina (Modena), where Octavian was victorious with the help of some of the soldiers who were loyal to his adopted father and the senate. After this battle, the first quarrel between him and Antony, he was made consul (read *Standard Encyclopedia Volume A,* page 482, subheading *Augustus*).

During the year 43 BC, his ambition led him becoming a proconsul, which was usually appointed as a governor of a province. At the end of 43 BC, Octavius rejoined forces with Mark Antony and General Marcus Lepidus to form the second triumvirate.

In 42 BC, after the triumvirate defeated the army of the conspirators that had assassinated Caesar, they divided the Roman Empire amongst themselves.

One of Octavian's first acts was to build a temple to his predecessor, Julius Caesar, indicating to the people under Roman sovereignty that

---

[125] Octavius was Caesar's nephew who was also known as Octavian.

[126] This quarrel or battle did not refer to the battle between them at Actium in 31 BC.

they should think of Caesar as a martyr and a god and by extension all Roman emperors as their gods.

To enhance the power of the emperors so that people would see them as Romans gods, all ancient statues and monuments bearing the images of Roman gods, including the flags going to battle, were removed and replaced with statues of the emperors of Rome. The only ancient statue allowed to stay was the statue of Jupiter.

Although conquered natives under Roman subjects were allowed to worship according to their own beliefs, they were still commanded to bow to Roman emperors as gods. Any individuals who refused to bow were punished or killed.

Regardless of Octavian intentions, he did not dress ornately. Octavian wore simple clothing and did not live imprisoned in the palace. In fact, he ate simple meals and wore leather sandals. His administration was very encouraging, inviting the Italian citizens to become Roman citizens.

In order to have absolute power, Octavian decided to limit the power of the senate. This limitation of power allowed him to wield absolute power of all Roman provinces.

During Octavian early ascension to the imperial throne, had he took on the entire proceedings as a king and tried to rule as a dictator, he would have been assassinated like Caesar. As a dictator, if he had demanded the proceeding act of the senators as if they were impotent in their jurisdiction, he would have made the senate to feel as if they were being pushed around. That would have led to bad blood between Octavian and the senate and perhaps strengthened a plot to assassinate him. Foreseeing this, Octavian combined his ruler ship with the leadership of the senators by keeping them occupied with the imperial business. He gave them a chance and a say in all Roman issues irrespective of the limitation of their powers.

In 29 BC, during the reign of Octavian Caesar, the Temple of Janus was closed for the first time in two hundred years. This was established as a way of restoring peace in the Roman Empire.

Octavian succeeded in becoming the first Roman emperor in 27 BC, which brought the beginning of imperial Rome. Although honored by the people in this powerful fashion, he did not gravitate or administer maturely to the title. Nevertheless, he called himself Augustus Caesar, meaning the *Supreme*. Augustus's reign was known as the Augustus Age, and he was known to the later generation as the best emperor that had ever ruled Rome.

The gates of Janus were closed for the second time in 25 AD, and Augustus Caesar (Octavian) closed them again for a third time in 13 BC, marking another act of peace in Roman Empire. These administrative[127] acts by Augustus Caesar had cleared the way for more than two hundred years of Roman peace (Pax Romana)[128] lasting from 27 BC to AD 180.

The emperors of Rome desired to extend Rome's culture and power in every direction, and Augustus played an integral part in that effort. During his reign Rome grew in wealth and was stopped only once in AD 9, when Arminius defeated the Romans at Teutoberg Forest (Germany).

Nevertheless, Rome's population grew rapidly, and because of that, the Roman emperor had to take census of the people. Augustus Caesar decided that "the world[129] by Rome should be taxed," which "brought Joseph in Judea with Mary his espouse wife to be taxed also" (Luke 2:1–5 KJV).

In his honor the Roman month Sextiles was named August. At his death in AD 14, his adopted son, Tiberius, succeeded the throne and became Rome's second emperor until his death in AD 37.

---

[127] The quote, "closing the gates of Janus," was a Roman ceremony held to mark world peace.

[128] *Pax Romana* was started by Augustus Caesar in 27 BC, and the peace ended in AD 180, when Marcus Aurelius died. During the time of the *Pax Romana* (sometime between 3 and 4 BC), the Messiah was born.

[129] *World* here represents the existing countries and people in and around Rome, living by its sovereign laws.

Emperors during the Pax Romana

During these times not all Roman emperors ruled with good intent like Augustus Caesar (Octavian) did, but in spite of that, Rome strived in wealth and development. The conquered cities around Rome's borders were upgraded so that the people would feel at ease. Laws were also established to encourage the auxiliary soldiers to become Roman citizens.

The Roman leaders with the help of their laws kept the Pax Romana despite the troubled moments.

After the death of Tiberius Caesar in AD 37, Caligula succeeded the throne and ruled from AD 37 to 41. Emperor Caligula, who had given his horse a marble stall, a purple blanket, and the seat of a consul, was symbolically giving a statement to his senators. His statement was that anyone who desired to strive to the seat of a consul would be nothing but a horse, likely to be chained and given a bridle, and the person would be treated as such and be placed in a stall. The emperor made clear that he alone should attain such position as an emperor. He believed that anyone with the ambition to reach the level of a consul would also be elevated as proconsul. His fear of the proconsul is the intention to plot against him and remove him from office.

He also forced rich men to leave their wealth to the state, which would agitate a depreciation of wealthy men who were not able to excel. This forceful action of Caligula caused uproar against him.

Under his (Caligula) rule, wealth was bestowed upon King Herod Agrippa I,[130] who was made king of Judea from AD 39 to 44. During the reign of Caligula, King Herod Agrippa I was authorized to put the Jews under much suffering and persecutions. After the death of Caligula, Claudius succeeded the throne in AD 41.

---

[130] Herod Agrippa I was the grandson of King Herod the Great.

Emperor Claudius was also another firm ruler of Rome from AD 41 to 54. He also persecuted the Christian Society. It was in his hands to satisfy the request of the hypocritical Jews regarding the destruction of the Christians. Between AD 46 and 48, Claudius encouraged what is known as the devastating decline and deaths of the Christian Jews, fulfilling the prophecy of Agibus (Acts 11:27–30). Paul also inherited his share of this demise when he was placed before the judgment seat of Claudius Caesar and was judged concerning the doctrine of the Christ (Acts 26 KJV).

This emperor of Rome also extended the kingdom of King Herod Agrippa I so that it was as large[131] as his grandfather King Herod the Great.

Between late AD 43 and early 44, this same Herod also used a sword[132] and slashed off the head of James, the brother of John, both disciples of the Messiah.

Peter himself also tasted some of the terrible deeds of Herod Agrippa I when he was placed in prison[133] (Acts 12:1–4 KJV).

All these atrocities were encouraged and authorized by Claudius Caesar, the emperor of Rome. At his death in 54 AD, Nero succeeded the throne.

By then Herod Agrippa I had already died and his son[134] succeeded the throne.

---

[131] Herod the Great sought to destroy the Messiah at birth but died the same year in 2 BC. That is probably why his offspring took the mantle (deeds) up so drastically.

[132] "Now about that time, Herod the king stretched forth his hands to vex certain of the church, and he killed James the brother of John with a sword" (Acts 12:1–2 KJV).

[133] Peter was placed in prison during Easter, which is a season of Roman celebration, but for the Jews that season of celebration was called the time of unleavened bread or Passover, which was held in the month of April. It is said that Peter miraculously escaped. (Read Acts 12:7–11 KJV.)

[134] This son's name was Herod Agrippa II.

Herod Agrippa II ruled from AD 44 to AD 100. Although he was a Jew, he was devoted to the Roman cause. It also made him happy to persecute and destroy the early Christian Society, furthering the bad examples set out by his father. Nevertheless, when the demise[135] was set out against Paul by the high priest Ananias and the elders of the Jewish church, it was in Agrippa's interest to free Paul; however, Paul requested that he be brought before Caesar (Nero). Paul was imprisoned in AD 61 but was set free in AD 63 by Emperor Nero. By the end of Nero's rule, the hands of the *enemy* slew Paul.

Nero ruled Rome from AD 54 to AD 68, during which time he killed his mother and half brother. There was also a mysterious fire that broke out in the city of Rome during the night of 18th July AD 64. Many accused Nero of starting it. Nero in his defense sought for an answer, which he found in the Christians.

With wicked intentions toward the early Christians, Nero blamed them falsely for lighting the fire and gave orders that they should be placed in the arena with the lions. This was a regular procedure the emperors of Rome endorsed. The Christians were placed in the arena to confront brutal animals, just as gladiators were placed in the arena as a means of entertainment.

Nero, who had a mental disorder as was cited by the praetors and others in the senate, was dismissed from the throne and was replaced by Galba as emperor of Rome in April of AD 68. Nero committed suicide in June of the same year.

After the death of Nero, a peculiar chain of events took place from AD 68 to 69, when four emperors ruled Rome one after the other.

The first of these emperors were Galba. Then Otho was made emperor by the power of the praetorians in January AD 69. Vitellius was later made emperor by the hands of the Germans in the same year. Vespasian became emperor the same year and ruled until AD 79.

---

[135] Ananias (the high priest), about five days later, descended with the elders with an orator named Turtullus, and informed the governor against Paul (Acts 24:1 KJV).

Emperor Vespasian was recognized for his contributions in putting an end to the civil unrest of Rome at that time.

During the Pax Romana, many individuals were allowed to become Roman citizens. Some could even become emperors.

Trojan, who ruled from AD 98 to AD 119, was the first non-Italian emperor. He built a forum in AD 100. Trojan and Hadrian were Spaniards. As said by Roman citizens, they both were also excellent emperors.

The death of Marcus Aurelius in AD 180 heralded the end of the Pax Romana.

Commodus, emperor of Rome from AD 180 to AD 192, decided to increase taxation in the provinces to cover expenses that the country had incurred. His decisions led to civil war. The unrest resulted in Commodus being murdered by one of his own guard in AD 192.

Septimus Severus, a soldier from North Africa who ascended the ranks, became an emperor of Rome from AD 193 to 211. He was born in Leptus Magna in April AD 145, and died in North England at York in AD 211. For the next hundred years the army took control of the provinces and elected their own emperors. As this new form of governance took its toll, disagreements[136] amongst the generals became common, resulting in quarrels and revolts.

During these internal problems the empire became vulnerable to its enemies and invaders. Some of these enemies were the barbarian tribes of Germany (Frank, Goths, Visigoths, Saxon, Huns, Vandals, etc.). In spite of all these atrocities, Rome still made its strides as the master of the world.

As Rome exercised its world dominance, the disturbances within its empire continued nonetheless. One of the problems[137] it faced was created by Christianity.

---

[136] The disagreements were about the next emperor of Rome, which is to be selected from amongst them.

[137] There were many problems Rome faced by the Christians. Worst of all, the

Instead of concentrating on Rome political problems, Rome put more of its effort into eliminating the strong hold that Christianity had on the people.

---

citizens were encouraged by Christianity to disobey the laws of Rome and not worship Caesar as their supreme god.

Chapter 12

Persecutions of the Early Church during and after the Pax Romana

One of the main reasons for these persecutions was that they did not adhere to Caesar and other Roman gods. The Christians believed in only one Supreme Being[138] and His Son (Yeshua).

In the first century AD, Annas,[139] Caiaphas[140] and some members of the Jewish religion[141] rejected Christ's teaching of the New Covenant. The reason was that they respected Moses' law and would continue in them.

Christ Himself also had many encounters with the scribes, Sadducees and Pharisees. He was blamed for not encouraging His disciples to do according to the traditions of the elders. The Pharisees and scribes accused Him by saying that His disciples "eat bread with unwashed hands" (Mark 5:6 KJV). In His defense "He said unto them, full well ye rejected the commandment of God, that he may keep your own tradition" (Mark 7:9 KJV).

---

[138] The Supreme Being was called Yahweh by the prophet Moses, but before the time of the Christian era he was openly evoked as the Elohim.

[139] Annas was former high priest and father in law to Caiaphas. He accused the Messiah, and with trial proceedings tried to attain a confession from the Messiah.

[140] Caiaphas was the chief priest.

[141] Some of the religions were that of the Pharisees and Sadducees.

Again He was accused[142] by the Jews when He spake of Himself as God, and as they were about to stone[143] Him, He sought to defend his words by saying "Say ye of him, whom the father hath sanctified and sent into the world, Thou blasphemest: because I said, I am the Son of God" (John 10:36 KJV). At that point, the elders, Sadducees and Pharisees along with some of the Jewish community sought ways to get rid of him.

The high priest, with the elders, then accused the Messiah of declaring himself as the King of the Jews, which they presented before Pontius Pilate as one of the reasons[144] for him to be held and placed in prison.

The crucifixion was then set, and as it seems, it was encouraged by the elders of the synagogue. The chief priest, the high priest and the elders were so committed to dishonoring the glory of the Christ, in that they perpetrated[145] false report about his resurrection. After the resurrection, they worked mischievously against the Christians, acting as perpetrators and deceivers.

However, many still accepted the Christian faith and the church grew rapidly. During its growth, the church was plagued by the Roman emperor and members of the senate.

The Christians were hated for their religious belief and were always searched out. If caught, they were persecuted or put to death. After the crucifixion most persecutions were carried out by public

---

[142] The Jews were annoyed when Christ declared Himself as the Son of God, so they accused Him and say that they stoned Him "for blasphemy: and…, being a man, makest thyself God" (John 10:33KJV).

[143] The Jews were so angry with the Messiah, in that they were ready to pick up stones to throw at Him. John 10:31 says "then the Jews took up stones again to stone Him."

[144] They could not find a more suitable cause to get Pilot's attention, but to say that he was "perverting the nation, and forbidding to give tribute to Caesar, saying that He Himself is Christ a King" (Luke 22:2).

[145] When the knowledge of the empty tomb was made known, the chief priest "gave large money unto the soldiers, Saying, Say yes, His disciples came by night, and stole Him away while we slept" (Mathew 28:12,13KJV).

officials or government bodies. These persecutions were linked to a particular individuals or persons who played leading roles. However, for the first two centuries of the Christian era, according to the history of the Great Persecution, no emperor had ever issued a general law against the Christian assembly.

In AD 64, when Emperor Nero allegedly accused the Christians of setting a fire in the city of Rome, it was his local officials that commanded the persecution, but it did not spread beyond the city of Rome. At Birthynia in AD 111, it was Imperial Governor Pling that committed the persecution. At Smyrna in AD 156, it was the proconsul. At Lyon in AD 177, it was the provincial governor, and at Sicily near Carthage, it was the proconsul again that persecuted the Christians.

So according to historical facts, we can draw the conclusion that earlier Roman emperors did not officiated publically any Christian persecutions that spread throughout the entire Roman province.

In spite of these actions by the fanatical leadership of Caesar and his senate, the Christian faith made a superb growth at the end of the second century. The growth was enhanced because the citizens of Rome, rich and poor, were impressed with the faith the Christians had in Yahweh, even when they were thrown in the arena to face the hungry lions. During such demonstration the Christians had said that they would never bow to Caesar or any other Roman gods. This angered the emperors, and they knew they needed to stop the growth of the church at the beginning of the third century.

We already mentioned that the full effect of the Pax Romana ended around AD 180, so many emperors after that began to show signs of hostilities toward the Christians in order to ultimately hinder the growth of Christianity.

The Historia Augusta, a fourth-century history, declared the anger[146] of Emperor Septimus Severus (AD 193–211) in AD 202

---

[146] Septimus Severus enacted the law under heavy penalty

when he forbade conversion to Judaism and Christianity. The words of the *Historia Augustia* indicated this act to be carried out "under heavy penalty." Emperor Severus thought of this as a method to eliminate the population of the Christian families.

Maximini (AD 235–238), in his attempt, tried to eradicate the church leaders (bishops) by persecutions.[147]

Religious life for the Christian society became difficult because of these actions set out by the council of Rome. The Christians became exhausted due to imperial pressures, and because of weaknesses of the spirit (not flesh) some elders apostatized.

The growth of apostasy took a hike when Emperor Decius, (AD 249–251) acting in fury, commanded church leaders to enforce the offering of sacrifices to the gods of Rome. Some bishops, in fear of their lives, agreed to conformity[148] and persuaded their followers to submit.

In AD 253, Valerian became emperor of Rome. By AD 257, he began expressing his anger for the Christians who refused to accept the sacrificial law of Rome.

The forceful hands against Christianity gave way to the absence of Christians' traditional values and practices by church leaders. The locations of churches that held firm traditionally were revealed to the emperor by the apostate church leaders (hypocritical bishops).[149]

At the death of Emperor Valerian in AD 260, his son, Gallienus (AD 260–268), ascended to the throne and established a little peace with the church. Although at times it was disturbed with occasional and isolated persecutions, this timely peace continued until the reign of Diocletian (AD 284–305).

---

[147] The Fabian bishop of Rome and the Babylon bishop of Antioch were two church leaders that were persecuted to death at that time.

[148] This is to accept Roman tradition and ways of worship.

[149] Apostate church leaders had similar behavior to the hypocritical scribes, Sadducees, and Pharisees (Matthew 15:7–9; 16:11–12; 23:1 KJV). The Euctemon bishop of Smyrna was an apostate church leader in the third century during the reign of Emperor Decius.

Diocletianic Persecution

The Diocletianic Persecution is known as the Great Persecution and was said to be the most severe[150] persecution the Roman Empire ever enacted against Christianity.

In AD 284, Diocletian took the throne and became emperor of Rome. He was a religious conservative and faithful to the traditional Roman cult. Diocletian idealized himself as a restorer, forming the tetrarchy rule (ruled by four emperors) and returning Rome to the Golden Age before his death in AD 311.

Before the reign of Diocletian, the church enjoyed the peace during the reigns of Gallienus and Aurelian (AD 270–275). The benefits of the peace was evident in some areas, especially in the East, North Africa, and Egypt, where the Christians grew rapidly and influentially in the society, which resulted in the traditional deities of Rome losing credibility.

Around AD 290, Porphyry, a philosopher of Tyre, expressed shock at the rapid growth of the Christians in the fifteen-volume work titled *Against the Christians*. Porphyry, who disregarded Christ's action concerning the disposition of the demons in the pigs, suggested that Christians were committing blasphemy by worshipping a human being rather than the "supreme god"[151] and behaving treasonably by disregarding traditional Roman practices and beliefs. He also

---

[150] Severe is suggested here because after the Diocletianic Persecution, Constantine sanction freedom of religion and the Edict of Milan 313 was enforced. There are no known persecutions against Christianity of this nature or magnitude since the fourth century.

[151] Here I presumed that Porphyry must have been comparing *his god* as in any other form (as he was a pagan) but surely not as *Yahweh* or *Yeshua the Christ*. He denies the claim that Christ is God and should not be worship as such.

suggested that they be punished, saying that these Christians were fugitives[152] from their fathers' traditional customs.[153]

When the tetrarch government was formed, a senior emperor (Augusti) and junior emperor (Caesar) were appointed. During Diocletian's tetrarchy rule, Diocletian and Maximian were senior emperors, while Constantius and Galerius were junior emperors. Amongst the tetrarch, Diocletian was always encouraged by Galerius, who was his subordinate, to walk a thin line between life and death concerning the Christians.

The tetrarchy government was established so that they could have proper control of all Roman provinces with proper guidelines to beset the overspreading and growth of the Christian church. In AD 295, the tetrarchy established laws that were enhanced by an edict issued by either Diocletian or Galerius, forbidding incestuous marriages and affirming the supremacy of Roman laws over local laws. This edict insisted that all Roman emperors should abide by the sacred precepts of the Roman law and in extension should logically enforce compliance[154] in religion. Galerius took great courage in performing such exercise.

It is said that his mother,[155] who was a priestess in Dacia, was bitterly anti-Christian. She saw that their presence and growth weakened her aspects of divinations, and this could be one of the main reasons he contributed to such terrorism among early Christians.

In AD 299 at Antioch, Lactantius (a Christian rhetor)[156] recorded that Emperor Diocletian and his subordinate Galerius were present at a sacrifice to summon the oracle for the prediction of the future, but

---

[152] He used the word *fugitive*, to say the Jews were running away from the ancient customs of their fathers.

[153] The Jews worshipped an unknown *Supreme Being* without any specific form or shape, but in representation it's "mostly" in the form of a man.

[154] This meant that all religions were expected to accept Roman culture and religion.

[155] Her name was Romula.

[156] Rhetor refers to one who records daily happenings.

at the time the diviners were unable to read the sacrifice. Christians were blamed for this inability because one among them was seen making the sign of the cross at the divination. For this Christians were purged from the army with or without rank. It was said that Galerius did most of the purging.

At Antioch in the autumn of AD 302 during a religious ceremonial sacrifice, a deacon name Romanus entered the court and denounced the ceremonial act. Diocletian imperial consulates (including Galerius) suggested the punishment of setting Romanus aflame, but Diocletian instead ordered that his tongue be cut out.

In Nicomedia in AD 302, Diocletian and Galerius had continuous arguments on what should be the imperial punishment for Christians. Emperor Diocletian suggested that they should be forbidden from entering the military and getting any public position, while Emperor Galerius agreed on extermination.

Both emperors set to resolve this dispute. They then referred the issue via a messenger to the oracle of the temple of Apollo at Didyma. The reply from the messenger said that the "just on earth" hindered Apollo's ability to speak. The *just* were referred to as the Christians within the empire. Diocletian then accepted to universal persecution. The Great Persecution was set, and the call for the first edict was proclaimed.

First Edict

February 23, was the day of the feast Terminalia, which was done in honor of the god "Terminus."[157] It was the day Rome would terminate Christians. On this day of February 23, AD 303, Diocletian ordered the destruction of the newly built Christian

---

[157] The word "terminus" is a Latin word meaning boundary or limit. The name Terminus was a Latin word for a "boundary stone" and Rome centered there worship around this boundary stone as the god "Terminus." In Roman religion a ritual was performed annually to *sanctify* this stone with the blood of a sacrificial victim.

church at Nicomedia and the burning of its scriptures. And on February 24, the edict was further enforced.

Second Edict

In the summer of AD 303, following the rebellion of Melitene (Turkey) and Syria, a second edict was published, one giving an additional order that all bishops, priests, and deacons be imprisoned. Historian Eusebius[158] declared in the letters of his manuscript that the prisons overflowed because of the recent imprisoned Christians, which made way for the release of the imprisoned Romans.

Third Edict

On November 20, AD 303, there came the twentieth anniversary of the Diocletianic reign. To celebrate this, Diocletian ordered the third edict demanding that all clergymen and elders of the church be freed if they agreed to make sacrifices to the gods of Rome. Many clergymen apostatized and became entwined with the ceremonial cult of Rome, mixing Jewish religious customs and traditional ways with that of the Romans.

On account of this edict, factions in the churches developed. This resulted in the splitting of the Christian church in many ways. There were Christians who subdued themselves to the ways and customs of the Romans to secure their own safety, while there was the rigorist who opposed the oppression and remained uncompromised.

The Donatist was once a rigorist group that fought in the streets of Rome against Christians, proving themselves as traitors, accepting compromised position.

---

[158] Eusebus was a contemporary ecclesiastical historian.

Fourth Edict

In January AD 304, the fourth edict was published. It proclaimed that all persons in the empire should stand collectively in any public place and make a sacrifice. However, most of this edict was not strongly enforced by Maximian and Constantius I in the west of the empire.

After the Fourth Edict

On May 1, 305, Diocletian and Maximian resigned. Constantius I and Galerius became Augusti (senior emperors), and Flaverus Severus and Maximinus became Caesar (junior emperors). With the second tetrarchy, only Galerius and Maximinus continued the persecution.

Constantine succeeded his father Constantius I, on July 25, 306, ruling the western end of the empire, and Maxentius[159] went against Emperor Severus and seized Rome on October 28, 306. They both encouraged tolerance of religion within the empire.

During such time Emperor Galerius was an opposing force, still persecuting the Christians. He made many attempts (accompanied by Severus) to dethrone Emperor Maxentius but was unsuccessful.

When Galerius sent Severus to suppress the revolt in Rome 307 BC, Severus and Maxentius were engaged in battle where he was defeated by Maxentius and held captive. Galerius retaliated by invading Italy, while Maxentius in rage, ordered the death[160] of Severus.

On Emperor Galerius's deathbed he encouraged the end of the persecution, but after his death in AD 311, Maximinus, who was a junior emperor at the time, took his place, ascended the throne as

---

[159] He was the son of Emperor Maximian who governor of some western Roman provinces and resigned on May 1, 305.
[160] Severus died in April 16, 307 BC. His death was either by execution or suicidal.

a senior emperor, and continued persecuting the Christians at the eastern end of the empire.

Time passed, and tensions increased between Constantine and Maxentius. It seemed that Constantine was determined to rule Rome and its provinces all by himself.

As the war pursued, Emperor Constantine decided to build a strong army of people that would be dedicated, eager to war and would gain richly[161] at the end.

Constantine political militancy gain the trust of the nonvoters and those who are reluctant to take part in government matters, and also those who were once a militant part of the army but were thrown out for particular reasons. Most of these individuals were characterized as Christians

Maxentius, who was not that popular with the Christians, tried his best to gain favor by restoring lands that were taken from the Christians during the edicts set out by Diocletian. This did not work to his advantage because most of the lands were already on the path of restoration by the active tolerance set out by Constantine.

Favor was given to Constantine on account of his father's inapplicable response to Christian harsh persecution and the great technical and psychological relationship that Constantine had with the Christian society.

Therefore, the army of Constantine was cloaked with Christian soldiers, which gave strength to his arms and resulted in a defeat for Maxentius at the Battle of Melvian Bridge outside of Rome on October 28, 312. At the death of Maxentius, Emperor Constantine became emperor of western Rome.

When Maximinus learned that Constantine had defeated Maxentius and started fearing for his life, he issued a letter restoring

---

[161] "Richly" does not necessarily mean wealth but benefits such as freedom of religion and the right to work in any capacity available.

Christian properties with the intent to persuade his fellow emperors[162] to show pity.

In the early spring of AD 313, Emperor Licinius, who had replaced Emperor Severus and ruled only a part of his provinces, advanced toward the eastern provinces of Emperor Maximinus.

Maximinus failed to gain support from the people of the provinces under his control, became angry, and retaliated by killing and torturing his own citizens and the Christians that opposed him.

Maximinus tried again sometime later to win the hearts of his competitors and gain public support by issuing one more edict of tolerance, but this was to no avail. Licinius continued to advance, defeating Maximinus at the Battle of Adrianople on April 30, 313. Maximinus committed suicide at Tarsus in the summer of AD 313.

With Constantine as emperor of western Rome and Licinius emperor of the eastern Rome, the Edicts of Milan were published in Nicomedia in June AD 313, proclaiming tolerance and freedom of religion and peace between both emperors.

Emperor Constantine, still hungry for power, continued his quest to be master of the entire Roman world. In AD 324, Constantine waged war by land and sea and defeated Licinius. Constantine, now emperor of the Roman Empire, proclaimed Christianity Rome's religion and encouraged Roman citizens to convert. With that proclamation, he managed to remain popular in Roman provinces. He contained revolts and preserved his imperial power throughout his reign.

Although there was an outburst of conversion in the fourth century AD by virtue of Constantine's declaration,[163] the new converts were not exposed completely to the ways and concepts of the first-century Christians. After all, most of the true and original disciples who were followers of the divine cause of the Messiah had

---

[162] This included Emperor Constantine and Emperor Licinius.
[163] Constantine declared Christianity as roman's religion.

already been killed in the arena of Rome, or they were persecuted by the end of the third century AD.

On account of the new converts' truth, the true doctrine was overshadowed by the deceptions taught by some hypocritical[164] bishops.

Deception

Let me first say that Christianity is not a deception, but some of those who aligned themselves with it are deceivers. I for one love the divine cause, connecting daily with the Savior.

Because of deception, many of us seem not to grow spiritually. Growth is evident when we first accept the weakness of our spiritual and moral endeavors. At that moment the missing link to our spiritual growth is made evident.

The way might be difficult for some; however, the principles of the early church are pure, and we must stick to them.

Paul, who was enlightened by the Jewish religion and foreknew the intrusion[165] of deceit, stated in 2 Corinthians 11:13–15 KJV that there would be "false apostles and deceitful workers transforming themselves into the apostles of Christ." Paul declared the pattern of Satan transforming his ministers of darkness[166] to appear as ministers of righteousness, whose end shall be according to their works. Furthermore, Galatians 1:6–9 lays out the intrusion of another gospel seeking to pervert the gospel of Christ, teaching and preaching a doctrine not aligned with that of the Messiah.

---

[164] Matthew 23 shows how Christ denounced the Pharisees and Sadducees, calling them hypocrites, and it also shows how they stopped people from entering the Holy Land and how they themselves would not enter.

[165] Paul was saying that because invitations were not given out to the angels of deceit, they became imposters, entering in the fold of Yahweh, appearing to be committed to the cause of righteousness.

[166] Darkness illustrates individuals who are not inspired to do Yahweh's will and are under the influence of deceitfulness.

This gives real reason why John had to admonish the churches in the book of Revelation. In his letters[167] he wrote concerning these individuals who "said they were apostles" of the true church but instead "were of the synagogues of Satan" (Revelation 2:2, 9, 14, 20; Revelation 3:9 KJV).

On account of the intrusion by these *angels*[168] of deceit and the gospel laid out by them, which was contrary to the teaching of the Devine Word, many sacred and religious rites were defiled[169].

On the other hand, as of the teaching of perversion, the emperor was not interested in the doctrine pursued, but just the mere fact to give Rome a chance to be governed more easily.

By the beginning of the fourth century AD, Christianity became a namesake[170] in Rome, which began the process[171] of forming the Christianity we have today.

The apostate bishops (Scribes, Sadducees, and Pharisees) played an integral part in building a new essence[172] surrounding Christianity.

It is common sense to note, that in the event the emperor moved to encourage Christianity, the bishopric would in this wise be given to the elders[173] of the temple (synagogue) who were then called bishops.

---

[167] The Book of Revelation is actually a manuscript of prophetical details, but chapters 2 and 3 are directive letters to the churches.

[168] False apostles

[169] Daniel 8:12 (KJV) says "it cast down the truth to the ground; and it practised, and prospered."

[170] At that time and age, the suppression of Christianity ended, and thereafter it became an essence of Roman culture and religion.

[171] Roman's Christianity is a result of Roman culture being instilled into Jewish customs, which is now affixed to Christianity.

[172] This in essence provides the thought concerning the doctrine of immortality only after death and the binding of the culture of Rome with Jewish customs (e.g., Roman Easter with Jewish Passover) to encourage that Romans accept Christianity.

[173] Some high priests, Scribes, Pharisees, and Sadducees were known as hypocrites (Matthew 23 KJV).

Chapter 13

Constantine—The God of Roman Christianity

Constantine, born at York in North England (modern-day Serbia) on February 27, AD 280, to a British mother,[174] was the last emperor to rule from Rome.

Constantine, emperor of Rome (AD 306–337) maneuvered and governed Rome through the instillation of Western Roman Christianity. This emperor became so deeply involved in the cause of keeping Rome united in peace, with its new Christian culture, that he was automatically drawn into it by means of his personal[175] interest.

On this ground the Roman throne that had always being worshipped as the seat of the Roman gods and sovereigns became twisted when it became Christianized[176] in Jesus' name. Yet, at no time when Constantine was advertising the divine Word, which was written in Latin on his triumphal arch in Rome, had he declared the divine to be the Messiah.

One day on the way to Rome when he was returning from the battle[177] at Melvian Bridge in AD 312, Constantine saw a vision, a

---

[174] Her name was Helena, a prostitute and barmaid.

[175] Alexander uses Christianity as a source to enable many victories beginning at Melvin Bridge and his victory against Maxentius.

[176] This *Christianization* implies to Christianity mixed with paganism. This was the way *cut* to instill Roman culture into Christianity and maintained tolerance.

[177] It was the battle between Constantine and Maxentius.

message written across the sky concerning the sign of a cross with the words *Hoc Signo Vince*. These words translated into English mean "By This Sign Conquer." One does not know if Constantine really saw this vision, but he did make Christianity the official religion of Rome. Hence, it was declared Roman Christianity. For sure one can understand why Constantine legalized the Christian faith, seeing that more than half of the army was made up of Christian converts. He instigated that the sign of the cross to be used as the religious emblem[178] of Roman Christianity, and he also used it on flags when they went into battle.

Looking at other perspectives regarding Constantine, and Rome declaring and claiming Christianity, there are a few points to consider. These points show that the emperor used Christianity to his own advantages, and the points are as follows:

1. Constantine was already a solar henotheist.[179]
2. For Constantine, this god, Sol, was the visible manifestation of the invisible highest God[180] behind the universe.
3. This god (Sol) was the companion of all Roman emperors, including him.
4. He, Constantine, was a believer of such faith[181] because he, too, declared seeing Sol in a vision while he was taking his meditation walk in the Apollo grove in Gaul as recently as AD 310.

---

[178] Constantine replaced the eagle with the cross for the emblem of Rome. *(Ref. Eusebius, Life of Constantine)*

[179] A solar henotheist is someone that believes in the Roman sun god sol.

[180] Probably Constantine wants to denote some similarities with Yahweh and the highest God of the Romans, but as stated in #3, Yahweh could not had been a companion of no Emperors of Rome including Constantine.

[181] This faith was of the sun god, Sol.

5. Constantine vision of the sun god, (Sol),[182] and the vision of the cross[183] serves as a symbol of the emperor religious intent. This was manifested when he combined paganism with Christianity.

6. By my conclusion it is clear that the god, Sol, represents "paganism" and the cross represents "Christianity."

By these five declarations it seems unacceptable that Rome and its confederates, who had crucified the Adoni (Lord) and Savior, could declare the foundation of the re-established kingdom of our Christ.

Is it not widely accepted, especially among most theologian and individuals who have studied the prophecies, that the Bible declared the *beast* was Rome? If this *beast* is Rome, was it not mentioned in the books of the prophets that this same kingdom of the north (Rome) was cursed and its downfall would indicate the end of days?

This is the same *beast*[184] which was spoken of by Daniel the prophet saying that the "beast make war with the saints and prevailed against them" (Daniel 7:19–21 KJV).

Daniel also said that this "beast would speak against the Most High, His testimonies and laws" and by this pattern he shall "persecute and wear out the saints of the Most High" (Daniel 7:25 KJV).

The prophet indicated that the *beast*[185] would transgress the commandment of Yahweh and would deceive many who sought His ways. Being overcome, they would believe in his[186] way as the way of light, thus resulting in "the truth being cast to the ground" (Daniel 8:9–12 KJV).

---

[182] This is a name given to one of the "pagan" gods of Rome

[183] The cross represents the crucifix. Constantine used it as a sign for the Church.

[184] This is the seat of Caesar, but in the last days it will be "apostasy with state." The apostate church will take the seat of Caesar, thus ending Imperial Rome.

[185] Here the "beast" becomes strong and manipulate church and states. The end result would be Rome and the apostate religion against the true Church.

[186] The apostate religion

Furthermore, Daniel magnified his thought concerning this kingdom by saying that in the last days, "he shall cause craft to prosper" (Daniel 8:23–25 KJV).

John, on the Isle of Patmos, also declared that the *beast*[187] was glorified[188] by the *dragon,* "by the means of the miracle which he had power to do" in the sight of the people (Revelation 13:11–16 KJV). So here again we see religion in action working miracles, which in effect will blind those who have not the seal of Christ.

So if all these prophecies were pointing to this throne, then the throne of Caesar should never have been undertaken[189] by Christianity. Can Christ's kingdom be reestablished by the power of Rome and the throne? I say no. On this note I cannot see Emperor Constantine being glorified with this gift to reestablish Christ's kingdom, which had been trampled by the rulers of Rome and his confederacies.[190]

Irenaeus,[191] a great scholar and father of the principle of the Church, in his book titled, *Against Heresies* gave his idea regarding the manifestation of Rome and its apostasy. In his Fifth volume of *Against Heresies* he addresses the figure of the Antichrist by referring to him as the "recapitulation of apostasy and rebellion." Irenaeus linked the number six hundred sixty and six (666} with the apostate religion. In his book he stated that the ten horns were the combined Roman Empire.

---

[187] The apostate religion

[188] Imperial Rome handed its authority to the apostate religion.

[189] This undertaken commenced when Emperor Gratian decided to omit Pontifex Maximus from his title and referred it to the Church of Rome. The title was then used by the Roman Catholic Church; hence imperial Rome was later empowered by the Papacy introducing Papal Rome.

[190] The apostate church leaders are the ones who shifted the mantle of the Messiah, bringing paganism over to Christianity.

[191] He was born in the second century AD and died 202 AD.

Tertullian (Tertulianus)[192] held the view that the Roman Empire was the restraining force Paul mentioned of in II Thessalonians 2:7-8 (KJV). Tertullian interprets the Scripture by saying that the ten kingdoms mentioned in Revelation 13 will make way for the Antichrist.

Others may think, otherwise, but my love of Christ urges me to believe that the church was rejuvenated through the will of the Almighty, not man.

Fall of Imperial Rome

The Church expanded as with the population of Rome during the reign of Emperor Constantine.

Division amongst the senate became an issue because some senators were Christians while some were of the pagan cult of old Rome. The divided senate clamored for the return to republican government while some differed to the same monarchy rule. Religiously some favored the bishop of Rome (pope). In the end imperial Rome died with the ascension of the bishop of Rome.

Despite the internal quarrels amongst the Romans, and the nearly defeat by the barbarian countries, Constantine remained emperor of Rome. Consequently he decided to move the capital of Rome to Byzantium, one of the cities of Alexander the Great, which he renamed Constantinople[193] in AD 330.

Constantine, realizing that he was losing his grasp on Rome, decided to flee to save lives in the midst of civil unrest. His destination was Constantinople the then capital of Rome, but the fight against the barbarian countries continued.

---

[192] Tertullian was born 160 AD and died 225 AD. He was a Christian author from Carthage. He was known as "the father of Latin Christianity" and founder of Western theology.

[193] Constantinople is now called Istanbul.

Nevertheless, without a ruling emperor residing within its borders, Rome continued to exist. All emperors continued to reside outside of Rome, leaving Constantine as the last emperor to live and rule from Rome. Constantine died AD 337, and Emperor Julius I (337–352) put on the purple robe.

As times passed, it also became difficult for Roman emperors to rule Rome from Constantinople, and there was probably mixed feelings amongst the elders who resided in Rome concerning the emperor's position.

The highest office in the pagan pantheon held by Roman Caesars was now held by Emperor Gratian (375–383). This title and office of the pagan pantheon was called Pontiff Maximus (meaning supreme pontiff). Unlike Emperor Constantine, Gratian, who adjusted to Christianity, believed that the title of the "Pontifex Maximus" was not something for a mere Christian or just any one to wear. He considered it holy and thought that it should be worn by the holy pontiff, the bishop of Rome. Precedence took its course as he handed it to Damasus (366–383), the bishop of Rome at the time.[194]

The bishop of Rome achieving that honor placed him as the highest priest in Rome, and in the end, the sovereign of Rome. This brought the end of imperial Rome and the beginning of papal Rome. Although there were other upcoming emperors after that period, it is said that they were mere puppets of the papal dynasty.

---

[194] This could be somewhere around AD 383, when the pagan senators requested the restoration of the Altar of Victory in the Senate House. Emperor Gratian had removed it since AD 382.

Chapter 14

Papal Rome

During the first century in the time of the early evangelistic period, Scripture was written on documents called manuscripts.[195] Selective documents[196] were then translated into Greek to accommodate and facilitated the teaching of the elders.

Being written in Greek, the documents were secured and placed in the synagogue. Access was given only to certain individuals. Whenever the Bible was displayed, it was time for the religious ceremony of the moment. At that moment its religious contents[197] were preached to give the detailed picture that the authorized organization had agreed upon.

In the fourth century Pope Damasus put an end to the controversies of certain text in the Bible at the time. He empowered a highly respective scholar[198] to do a revision of the Old Latin version of the Bible by comparing it with the Greek's version. From this the Latin Vulgate was produced.

---

[195] These manuscripts where then put together and called scrolls.

[196] Some of these documents included the four gospels (Matthew, Mark, Luke, and John).

[197] Since most of the original manuscript had been given up by the bishops and had been destroyed by the consulates of Rome, some of these Scripture passages may have been tampered with. Therefore, they may not give the proper detail of the true history of the gospel and the church.

[198] This scholar's name was Jerome, and he helped put together the Latin Vulgate.

It is certainly a necessity that Scripture went through some translations, clearing the way for a new set of people to hear and understand a new religion in their own tongue and language. Translation was surely one of the factors that encouraged the growth of the church, and it helped the church to grow and take control of the world. Nevertheless, these translations left us with many controversies and the denial of some expressions.

The Christianity of Constantine spread and developed and became more dominant during the reign of Emperor Gratian and Damasus, the bishop of Rome. Roman Christianity developed as a backbone, giving critical support to the monarchy of Rome. Synagogues were placed all over the empire, and the congregations of local churches were headed by local bishops.

These local bishops themselves held grudges against one another, striving for the power to become the next bishop of Rome. Often times the selecting of the papal successor disturbed the peace of the Church, which calls for the emperor and the prefects[199] of the community to intervene and promote peace. One occurrence was after the death of Liberius on September 24, AD 366, Damasus and Ursinus fought for the papal throne, and Damascus was later accused of Ursinus's death.

There were many schisms within the churches that bewailed separations. The Aryanism in Milan and the Meletian schism of Antioch were two main factors that threatened the Roman church. However, there were other issues surrounding the relation between the church at Alexandria, the church at Rome, and the church at Antioch in respect of the pope's position. As a result of these bewailed desires and sentiments against the bishop of Rome, the Bishop of Rome was not recognized[200] in general as the head of this new

---

[199] These are persons set over the provinces of Rome as senior administrators or military officials.

[200] Some persons might have referred to this recognition as in the sixth century when he was placed head of Christendom.

Roman Christian organization until the sixth century. The local bishops were then placed under the archbishops.

As the seat of Caesar was placed in the hands of the pope of Rome, where royalties were just confined to pay tributes to the papacy, it was then clear that the estate of Rome was now controlled by the Pope, giving him authority over the empire and Roman Christianity. Papal Rome then established an empire known as the Holy Roman Empire, and the Roman emperors then became instruments of the pope.

Jewish and Roman Festivals Intertwined

Rome, which was now under the full authority of the pope, went through some changes. The desires of the Roman Christians were addressed in that the Romans could now seek their immortality and still practice the customs and traditions of Rome. The old traditions and customs of Rome were then intertwined and modernized.[201] Old pagan festivities were changed bit by bit until they were called and looked upon as Christian fellowship and ceremonies.

Rome used to have a feast day called Saturnalia. This was a feast given to the god Saturn. On this day Roman citizens gave one another presents, and a mock[202] king was crowned as ruler of the feast during the celebration. Slaves would get the day off, and their masters would honor them by dining with them. Saturnalia was later celebrated as Christmas in Rome. I guessed that one could say that the demonstration of the mock king was placed presumptuously to represent the Christian Jews Adoni (Lord) and King.

The Roman Easter festive was celebrated in April as the returned of the corn. This tradition is now intertwined with the yearly Jewish feast, Passover or the Adoni Supper.

---

[201] The new Roman culture was now Western Roman Christian culture.
[202] The verb *mock* demonstrates ridicule, showing shame and imitation.

Barbarians Incursion on Papal Rome

As Rome was undergoing its changes because of the intertwining of Roman's paganism and Christianity, it still did not vanquish the incursion of the barbarian tribesmen.

As early as the end of the second century AD, Rome always faced continuous fights with the barbarians. After two hundred years of successive victories and defeats, the invaders of the barbarian countries (Goths, Visigoths, Franks, Saxons, and Vandals) crossed over the Rhine River and defeated the Roman frontier in AD 407.

People then realized that it was a good thing that Emperor Constantine had shifted the capital to Constantinople in Asia Minor. If the emperor had not moved Rome's wealth and its ruling kingdom to Constantinople, all would have been lost, and the kingdom of Rome would have been totally destroyed.

After the middle of the fifth century, Western Roman Empire was placed under much pressure again by the barbarian tribesmen of Germany invading its borders, and by AD 476, most of Western Europe and Italy was lost to the barbarians.

Soon after that, the fight was aborted, and the barbarians aligned themselves with the empire and its sovereignty, upholding the cause of the new religion of Rome.

The barbarians were involved in the life stream of the Romans, that the king of Franks called Clovis (barbarian) married the daughter of a Christian king. As a result of this marriage, Clovis was later converted to Christianity.

Burgundy Clovis ruled the Franks from AD 482 to AD 511. With the support of many other European nations during the year AD 508, he pledged that he would support and establish by force the Catholic faith. By AD 538, the pope was pronounced the head of Christendom, confirming him as master of the new Christian order, lord of religions, and the only channel for the remission of sin.

The result of this union between the king of Franks and the daughter of this Christian king led to the conversion of many rough and cruel warriors.

The Kings of Franks in Aid of Rome

During the seventh century AD, Muslim armies of the south started to cross from Arabia into Asia, invading and conquering new territories in the name of Allah.

As a result of this invasion, a continuous war between Roman Christians and the Muslim ensued. The Roman Empire then united to face off against these invaders.

In the years that followed, the Muslims carried their religion northward into Spain and France, which alarmed the pope in Italy. The pope, with the help of his neighboring Christian king of Franks, Charles Martel (the Hammer), who was an able commander, led his armies to meet the advancing Muslim invaders and defeated them at the battle of Poitiers in AD 732.

In AD 751, the pope of Rome was offered assistance again by the king of Franks, Pepsin the Short. In honor of his assistance he was given the title "Father of the Romans" by the ruling pope of Rome.

In AD 768, Pepsin the Short's son was crowned king of Franks and received an even higher honor than his father. This new king of Franks was named Charles the Great or Charlemagne. Charlemagne was not educated, but he was a very smart king who took lessons from monks. In spite of this drawback, he tried to improve the education and standard of living amongst his people.

Charlemagne defeated the pagan tribesmen of the east and the Muslim Arabs of the south who were attacking his borders. He was very successful in aiding the pope of Rome, and by the end of his reign the empire extended over most of Western Europe.

Pope Leo III (795–816) was so impressed by Charlemagne's loyalty to Rome that he disregarded the living emperor of Rome, a female[203] at the time, and pronounced Charlemagne as the Holy Roman Emperor of the western province on Christmas Day in AD 800. This king of Franks was honored as the worldly ruler and protectorate of the Holy Roman Empire, while the pope was the religious leader.

The growth of Christianity during Charlemagne's rule was rapid. His way of encouraging conversion to Christianity was not that of the way of the earlier and original Jewish Christians. This king's way was said to be cruel and forceful. This king of Franks had killed thousands of Saxons refusing to accept Roman Christianity.

During his campaign individuals were forced to accept the faith, anyone who refused to accept would be dragged to the river or watershed, and if the person refused to be baptized, he or she would have his or her head slashed off with a sword.

Charlemagne died in AD 814. Nevertheless, because of the gruesome act Roman Christianity had encouraged, a horrible war loomed between Roman Christianity and the Muslims.

---

[203] Empress Irene of Athens was ruling from Constantinople at the time.

Chapter 15

The Conquest of the South and Triumph against the North

Daniel 11:7 says, "Out of her roots one shall stand in his estate and shall come against the king of the north."

Daniel 11:8–9 continues the prophecy and says that the "king of the south "shall also carry captives into Egypt their gods, with their princes, and their precious vessels of silver and gold." Scripture goes on to say that he would claim the provinces of the conquered kingdom longer than the king of the north.

Some individuals explained that the Scripture passage was pointing to the birth of a woman, but here Scripture did not reference a *root* as in the "root of David" but rather *roots*.

In my opinion, when Scripture speaks of "her roots," it is simply explaining the similarity of her culture, which could also mean some one of her nativity. On the other hand, when Scripture speaks concerning "his estate," it is simply saying that another king of the kingdom or region shall ascend to power.

Africans and the Arabians Early Religious Ties

Africa, also embedded in the south, consisted of a set of people whose Christianity was called Coptic. These Christians had claimed their conversion had come from a man name John Mark, a follower of the Messiah. John Mark, also an apostle, had visited Egypt during his evangelical mission from AD 46 to 52. During this mission he brought the gospel of the Messiah to the Egyptians. Therefore, Coptic Christianity originated in Egypt long before Constantine instilled Roman Christianity.

These Christians did not accept the gospel of Roman Christianity. Nor did they validate Constantine or the pope of Rome as divine. On account of this the Roman emperors, Western Catholics, and Eastern Orthodox Christians persecuted Coptic Christians.

The Coptic culture and their way of life were said to be accompanied by the laws and ways of Moses and Father Abraham, which similarly the Muslims claimed to be a pattern. On this note, Coptic Christians and the Muslims were seen as being against the developed Roman Christianity in the north.

The kings of Saba, who ruled in the Sabean dynasty in the second century BC—a dynasty that was then followed by the Himyarites, who were from South Arabia—accepted the Jewish religion,[204] but they were soon overthrown by the Ethiopian Christians in the fourth century AD (read *New Standard Encyclopedia Volume A,* page 310, subheading "Arabia-history"). So the Jewish religion was a part of the Arabian culture and religion long before the original Christians who adopted Christ's teaching.

So the Arabians, the Egyptians, and the Ethiopians were earlier embedded in the life of Jewish Christianity, which Judaism was its initial religion, founded by the ancient prophets including Father Abraham. This similarity gave them the call of their roots.[205] This is why I believe the prophet denotes the similarity when speaking of "her roots" of the south, although after a while they instilled in their culture the familiarity of many pagan gods.

One must also remember that the Arabian Peninsula was occupied by the Semitic[206] race in ancient times.

---

[204] Judaism was then known as the Jewish religion before the advent of the Messiah.

[205] Roots indicate their culture.

[206] The Semitic tribe is a bloodline of Shem, the father of Abraham.

The Origin of the Muslim Faith

In AD 570, there was a boy born in Mecca, a busy town in Arabia. His name was Mohammad, and he belonged to the Quraysh tribe, which controlled the city of Mecca. Mohammad's family was influential in the society, and the people of Mecca looked up to them.

The community in which he grew believed in many gods. With other communities, they helped erect all types of different statues and idols in many places around Mecca.

It was said that Jews and Arabian Christians[207] often visited the marketplaces in Mecca where they discussed their religion. Listening to the discussions about their one true Theos[208] (God) captivated the mind of Mohammad. This was interesting to him. He realized that the old pagan ways of his people were a bit illusive.

The teaching and stories of these Christian Jews took hold on Mohammad. He spent most of his early childhood thinking of this one true Theos (God) until he reached manhood.

During his fortieth year he got a vision one night and saw the angel Gabriel, who came to him with a cloth of brocade. On it there was some writing. He was frightened by the sight of the angel, and then he heard a voice saying to him three times, "Read." Mohammad replied, "I cannot read it." The angel besieged to him over and over by saying to him, "Read in the name of the Lord[209] that created man from a clot of blood, read, your Lord is most beautiful who thought by means of a pen, thought man what he did not know."

Mohammad was disturbed and told his wife, Khadija, what he had dreamed. His wife immediately took him to her cousin Waraqa,

---

[207] The Jews and the Arabians were now Christianized by Roman's Christianity.
[208] During the early sixth century, instead of the Hebrew word *Elohim*, the Greek word *Theos* was already in use. Later the King James Version with the Roman Vulgate replaced this with the word *God*.
[209] The English word *lord* would not have been used in the language of the Arabians, but for the Christians at that time the Greek word *Kyrios* would have been used instead of the Hebrew word *Adonai* (Adoni).

who was a Jewish and Christian scholar. Waraqa told him that this angel was a messenger of God sent to embrace him and anoint him as a prophet. Mohammad then began his prophetical teaching about this one true God he accepted, the God he called Allah.

His first followers were his wife, his adopted son, Zaid, his cousin Alli, and some of his closest friends. Mohammad's teaching began to reach the ears of the people. Even the elders of his tribe were alarmed.

Mohammad then made a campaign to destroy all the Arabian pagan gods that were placed in the sacred temple Caba. His tribe, the Quraysh, thought of his religion as a downturn to the economy of Mecca, so they refused to do any business transactions with the followers of Mohammad.

During the year 615 AD, with finances running low, Mohammad encouraged his followers to migrate to the Coptic and Christian country of Ethiopia while he continued to stay with his family in Mecca.

One can imagine the close relation between the uprising Muslim and the Egyptian Coptic Christians. Over the years of exile in Egypt, Mohammad's followers and the Coptic Christians of Egypt consulted each other on religious thought. During such time they agreed on the immense opposition of the Roman religious customs and the vast devastation it implied.

Finally in AD 622, Mohammad decided to leave his countrymen and sought refuge in a city called Yathrib. In Yathrib, Mohammad had many friends who were intrigued by his teachings. Fortunately for Mohammad he had friends in Yathrib, as his tribesmen were plotting to kill him that very night he left his home town.

The Basis of Mohammad's Teaching

Mohammad declared that he had not found a new religion but that he was just following the teaching of the old prophet Abraham, who had given the Hebrews the thought of one God.

The Arabian prophet pointed out that the Jews had corrupted the ways of the Elohim[210] of Abraham, so Moses and Christ were sent to correct them, bringing back understanding, simplicities, and truth to its meaning.

He also believed that the Christians of Rome were in this dispensation, once again deceiving the people, and for that reason Mohammad was sent to correct the path once more.

Mohammad did not use the name Iesous (Jesus) and Theos (God) that the Roman Christians called upon. With new inspiration, he pronounced the name as Allah and by interpretation, he called his religion Al–Islam, meaning submission. Those who followed the ways of Islam were called Muslim, submitting only to Allah.

Muslim's Loyalty

Mohammad took refuge in Yathrib from his Quraysh tribesmen. The city Yathrib was later renamed Medina, meaning "the city of the prophet."

In Medina, loyalty was only given to Allah and fellow Muslims. These loyalties were so intense that if war would have broken out between Medina kinsmen and Mecca kinsmen, who were opposed to Islam, their loyalties would lay only with Muslims. Their loyalties would even result in the killing of mothers, fathers, relatives, and even the closest of friends living in Mecca.

The old ways of tribal recognition were made void. Tribesmen would fight amongst one another in Medina. Instead, no matter what tribe you were from, as long as you were a Muslim, all the backing and allegiance would be accorded.

---

[210] Here, as the author, I use *Elohim*. It is appropriate for me to use the originally transcribed title, as *Theos* or *God* was never a translation but was used in place of words. Some theologians might see this as unnecessary; however, I view names as sacred, and a title being divine must be consistent when invoked.

Another thing was certain. No Muslim was allowed to kill another Muslim, but as a Muslim soldier, you were to fight against any individuals who placed a stumbling block against the spreading of Islam.

Later more Arab tribes joined the cause, and soon they were fighting on the frontiers of the Persians and the Byzantine Empire and other parts of the Roman Empire.

I see this collaboration of the Arabian forces as the fulfillment of the following verse:

> *"Which shall come with an army, and shall enter into the fortress of the king of the north, and deal against them and prevailed"* (Daniel 11:7 KJV).

The Besiege Africans

During the early seventh century AD, the Arabs did most of the colonization of the continent of Africa. As they were encouraged by religious inspirations, these fierce Muslim warriors swept across northern Africa along the Red Sea to reach the Atlantic Ocean.

All the captured people who were Roman converts and otherwise were forced to accept Islam, except the Egyptians who retained their Coptic belief and the Ethiopians who preserved their Ethiopian Christianity (read *New Standard Encyclopedia Volume A*, Page 69, subheading "Africa").

The religious differences between the Muslims and both the Egyptian Coptic and the Ethiopian Christians were tolerated.[211] Though they were different in certain spheres, they held certain beliefs in the teaching of Abraham and the older prophets, and of course, they, too, were not affiliated with Roman's doctrine.

---

[211] Tolerance continues until the death of King Armah (615–630 AD), a king of the Kingdom of Askum (northern Ethiopia), who granted asylum to the family of the Prophet Mohammad.

Mohammad's tolerance was strengthened by the close relationship that the migrated followers of Mohammad had when they were in exile in Egypt and Ethiopia.

It is possible that during the early conquest of the Muslims, Egypt and Ethiopia were also used as some sort of fortress or postwar base. Seeing that Muslims were in control of some of these areas, it is likely that goods and prisoners were brought there.

This postwar base was an area usually used to celebrate and store goods that were brought from conquered lands.

Let us review the following Scripture passage:

> *"And shall carry captives into Egypt their gods, with their princes, and with their precious vessels of silver and gold"* *(Daniel 11:8 KJV).*

Many prisoners were brought from the conquered cities to Egypt and were forced to accept Islam. These prisoners were used as slaves while some were held in confinement camps.

It is possible that Mohammad brought the princes and priests as captives to demonstrate the superiority of Islam over other religions.

Mohammad religious rule lasted longer in these countries and continents than the past ruling Roman Empire had reigned.

With that in mind, it is a small thing to accept that these countries in the south, so rooted in their culture, would continue to oppose Roman Christianity, especially that within their borders.

Mohammad Returns to His Homeland

> *Daniel 11:9 (KJV) says, "So the king of the South shall come into his kingdom, and shall return into his own land."*

This prophetic revelation took place a few years later after the Muslims multiplied in Yathrib and other places, and became strong in numbers as they decided on a clear-cut intention to march into Mecca, the birth place Islam.

The prophet and his followers marched into Mecca without any resistance or opposition.

As the founding father of Islam encamped in the city, he went to the temple Ka'ba and threw out the statues and idols that the Arabians worshipped. Many then accepted the Muslim faith, while others who were defiant were killed. In a short time Arabia became a Muslim state.

When the Muslims conquered new territories, they asked the captives to choose the Muslim religion and served Allah as the one and only true God. If they accepted, living was much easier for them.

Mohammad lived to unite almost all of the Arabian lands, and he brought order out of chaos. He later died in AD 632.

Chapter 16

The Successors of Mohammad, King of the South

But his sons shall be stirred up, and shall assemble a multitude of great forces.

—Daniel 11:10 (KJV)

I considered that when Daniel spoke of the "sons of the king of the south," he was not referring to biological sons but successors as the spiritual leaders.

After Mohammad's death, Aba Baki, who was one of the first Islam converts, became his successor. The successors were called caliphs.

Aba Baki and the two caliphs that followed continued the war. It was such a victorious campaign for Muslims that within a few years they conquered much of the Persian's and the Byzantine Empire.

The Jihad or Holy War

During the course of the spreading of Islam, things began to get out of hand. The forceful teaching of Islam was overbearing and paralleled the pattern of the kings of Franks and his religious mission.

Muslims adopted the model of how the Romans spread Christianity. They began to compel others to accept Islam, and all opposition was met with brute force.

This escalated into a holy war, and thousands of people were killed on both sides. The Muslims speak of this ongoing battle as a jihad or holy war.

The caliph, now the leader of a huge empire, appointed governors to rule each state. All governors vowed allegiance and loyalties to him, the caliph.

The rulers or governors left their sons as their successors. Each dynasty bore the bloodline of the initial governor at his death. Hence, there was the Umayyad dynasty (661–750) and the Abbasids dynasty (750–1258).

Pursuits by the Caliphates

As the prophecy takes its toll, one must take into consideration the prophetical declaration of Daniel, pointing out that the south shall pass through the domain controlled by the north and shall conquer and claimed victory over various strongholds of the northern empire (read *New Standard Encyclopedia* subheading "Arabia-history").

These are the words of the prophet,

> *"And one shall certainly come and overflow and pass through." (Daniel 11:10 KJV)*

While the Arabs were exploring and conquering as they went, the already conquered territories were being invaded by their neighboring inhabitants. This encouraged the Muslim warriors to advance their conquest beyond the borders of these already conquered lands and to protect the Muslim fortresses and domain.

In AD 639, the Muslim warriors then decided to go westward to the Nile in conquest of Libya and Egypt. In this conquest the Coptic Christians in Egypt were left to continue their religious practices. By AD 641, Alexandria (Egypt) was then taken over by Caliph Omar, the Muslim leader at the time.

The Ommiad dynasty[212] of the Arabian Empire then went and conquered parts of India in AD 709, part of central Asia, the Berbers of North Africa, and all of Spain in AD 712.

In AD 732, they pushed northward as far as France. This alarmed the pope in Italy and his Christian defender, the king of Franks. Luckily for this Christian kingdom, King of Franks Charles Martel was an able commander who led his forces to meet the advancing Muslim army. Charles defeated the Muslim army at the Battle of Poitiers the same year. These are the words of the prophet, "Then shall he return and be stirred up, even to his fortresses" (Daniel 11:10 KJV).

When one sees the prospect of the manifestation of the prophecy, one can only conclude and admit to the divine order of the prophet and his connection with Yahweh.

However, the pope would not hold his breath in spite of his victory. The Pope of Rome and king of Frank had realized that the king of the south would continue to push at the fortress of the north. His main aim was to conquer all of the Roman territories and enforce the Muslim religion.

This defeat at Poitiers angered the Arabian caliph, which led to a change in his strategy of attack, which resulted in many defeats for the Roman Christian Empire.

Thereafter, the king of the north organized many mighty armies to defend his borders, but the multitude was given into the hand of the caliph. The following verse gives details of the prophecy.

> *"And the king of the south shall be moved with choler, and shall come forth and fight with him, even with the king of the north, and he shall set forth a great multitude, but the multitude shall be given into his hand." (Daniel 11:11 KJV)*

---

[212] The Ommiad dynasty was the family of Caliph Omar that was left in power after his death.

As the Arabian Muslims continued their conquest, the heart of the caliph was lifted up. He was encouraged by the many triumphs that he had over the Christian kingdom. These victories and invasions of Roman Christian territories resulted in the expansion of the Muslim Empire.

As the Umayyad (Ommiad) dynasty came to an end in AD 750, the Abbasids dynasty continued carrying out the Islamic religious conquest. The Abbasids ruled from Mesopotamia (Iraq), where the Sumerians, the Persians, and the Greeks had once ruled. The Muslim faith ruled and did so with power and "cast down many thousands" who opposed Islam.

In AD 751, the Arabian king of the Abbasids dynasty *pushed* at the king of the north, but luckily the pope of Rome was aided again by this king of Franks, Pepin the Short.

During the extensive rule of the Muslim faith, especially under Caliph Harun Ar Rashid, ruler of Mesopotamia, the Arabian conquest grew and developed.

The Muslims continued to push at the legions of Rome but were stopped on many occasions, as Charlemagne was now king of Franks and the new defender of the north as of AD 768.

During the rule of the Abbassides dynasty, the empire included all of Arabia property, all of Asia Minor going up to the Caucus Mountain, including part of the Byzantine Empire, and all of North Africa.

Eventually the grip of the south began to decline steadily, but they managed to hold on to Sardinia, Sicily, and Crete from AD 801 to AD 900, and they maintained a hold on some of Asia Minor and part of the Byzantine Empire until AD 1097.

The Turkish Muslims' Repudiation

Although the Muslims were "casting down many thousands they were not strengthened by it," the base[213] of the Arabian Empire weakened under the Abbasids Dynasty.

> *"And when he had taken away the multitude, his heart shall be lifted up: and he shall cast down many ten thousands: but he shall not be strengthened by it" (Daniel 11:12 KJV).*

During the period of the Abbasids dynasty there arose an eastern set of people in Asia Minor called the Turks who claimed to accept Islam. The Turks, who were conquered in the conquest of the Arabians Muslim, converted and developed a craving for power. This process of crave continued with the ambition to claim the Arabian Muslim territories. The decision was to overthrow the Caliphates of the Arabian dynasty and take over Arabia.

Eventually tribal war broke out amongst the Arabians Muslims and the Turkish Muslims, which further weakened the Muslim Empire.

The conflict between both Islamic countries continued from the tenth to the eleventh century. Muslims from the east (Turks) rivaled the Arabian Muslims and captured some of the Muslim cities[214] of Asia Minor and Europe.

They also approached the holy places of Palestine and proclaimed war on the Byzantine Empire, threatening the Christian stronghold of Constantinople in Asia Minor. This alarmed the pope of Rome once more. By then the schism of AD 1064 within the Roman

---

[213] This means that the core principles of Islam were defiled. The same Turks from Asia Minor who accepted Islam eroded the principles of the *Muslim law of loyalty.* Hence, the Turks Muslims rivaled Arabian Muslims.

[214] These were cities conquered during the Arabian conquest, including part of the Byzantine Empire.

Christian community had already taken place, separating the church into Western Roman Christianity (Catholic) and Eastern Roman Christianity (Orthodox).

However, the Byzantine Empire appealed to the pope of Rome for help in AD 1095. The pope thought it also a good opportunity to help the Eastern Roman Empire in Asia Minor, using it to unite the western[215] and eastern[216] body of Roman Christianity in strength to recapture Jerusalem once again.

---

[215] The western body was named Roman Catholic.
[216] The eastern body was named Eastern Orthodox.

Chapter 17

The Return of the King of the North

For the king of the north shall return, and shall set forth a
multitude greater than the former, and shall certainly come
after certain years with a great army and with many riches.
—Daniel 11:13 (KJV)

The Eleventh-Century Crusades

Papal Rome continued to be the main city of the north, both
spiritually and politically. To maintain this standing, the pope decided
to beset the *evil*[217] approaching after he realized the disaster it would
bring on the Christian Empire if he was to allow Constantinople to
fall into the hand of the Turks. The Turkish Muslim who overthrew
the Arabians, the founders of Islam, now made himself the central
power of the south and its religion called Islam.

Irrespective of the pope's approach, the cunning Muslim Turks
continued their quest and captured Palestine, which the pope of
Rome admitted was detrimental. It remained in the pope's best
interest to recapture Jerusalem from these powers from the east.
Some of these individual were also known as the Saracens.[218]

---

[217] To the pope, this was a disaster of a great magnitude.
[218] The Saracens are a member of a one of the nomadic Arabic tribes (Muslims),
especially of the Syrian Desert, who harassed the borders of the Roman Empire.

The Pope's Religious Quest

On this note Pope Urban II *preached* a crusade (a holy war) against the Saracens (Seljuk Turks). It was said that thousands of soldiers and knights answered the call of this religious quest.

At that time the fight was not just against the Turkish Muslim but against the entire Muslim Empire. All European countries were encouraged to stand up against Islam.

The Prophet Daniel foresight the answer to the request against the south and says "And in those times there shall be many that stand up against the king of the south" (Daniel 11:14 KJV).

Rome united the European armies from the north, including three armies that set out from France and another from Italy, marching across Europe to meet with the Byzantine Empire in Constantinople and confront the Turks in Asia Minor.

The response to the quest was great so that it was said to be much more than the pope determined.

Pope Urban II tried to forbid women, the sick, and monks as well, but that had no effect. The turnout was enormous. Most of them were peasants (slaves and freemen), serfs, and knights.

Mostly, some of these individuals were looking for a way out to find new homes in the new lands after the crusade. Though some did not make it home, the order was given by Pope Urban II to make sure the crusaders were paid.

The European submission to the call of the crusade demonstrates the commitment from the local to the upper class to stop the disaster that is ahead.

Interestingly, there were even a particular set of European that were also keen about their allegiance regarding the Roman Empire. The prophet Daniel addressed them as *robbers*. I refer to them as *European Inmates.*

European Inmates

> *Daniel 11:14 (KJV) says, "Also the robbers of thy people shall exalt themselves to establish the vision: but they shall fall."*

To me the word *robbers* here mean someone acting against the laws of the land or someone committing an atrocity against one's abode. I am not sure if the word *thy* referred to ownership or the opponent of the south, but for sure they were prisoners.

Some of these soldiers in the European army were prisoners charged with murder or robbery.

These criminals in this crusade probably intended to rob and loot the wealth of the land they set out to conquer. Most of these prisoners were not paid with cash but an excused of the crime charged known, whereas the peasants' payment or subsidy would have been access to land conquered.

The main reason for this expedition was to recapture Jerusalem, as it was thought to be one of wealthiest and most prosperous lands in the east.

I supposed that during the crusades, many or perhaps most of these prisoners of Europe were placed at the fronts of these battles.

This exaltation led to many of them placing their lives on the line. These robbers were paid with their release if they returned home alive, and those who had death sentences had them commuted.

There was speculation as to whether the families of the deceased inmates were compensated, seeing that the trade-off was freedom from prison if they survived the battles.

On the contrary, the European crusaders were victorious at the end. Some of their goals were met, especially some important cities that they had lost to the Muslim crusaders.

Some Important Cities Taken

> *Daniel 11:15 (KJV) says, "And the king of the north shall
> come, and cast up a mount, and take the most fence cities:
> and the arms of the south shall not withstand."*

The Roman Empire did not quit, but set the crusaders to the task,
advancing against the Muslims Turks until the goals[219] were met.

Since AD 1095, the Muslims fought three years continuously
against the Romans, but to no avail.

During the three years of war, Asia Minor and part of the
Byzantine Empire were taken by the Roman Empire in AD 1097.
The Christian kingdom gained most of the territories controlled by
the Muslims and reclaimed them as Roman territories with a renewal
of Roman Christianity.

In the year AD 1099, the Romans finally took Jerusalem and
built new townhouses with the intent to settle in this new Christian
kingdom, Jerusalem.

Restructuring of Jerusalem

> *Daniel 11:16 (KJV) says, "And he shall stand in the
> glorious land, which by his hand shall be consumed."*

To ensure that Jerusalem stayed in their hands, the Romans
fortified the city with fences and large castles of great strength as a
protection from any Muslim invaders from the south.

Claiming to bring civilization within the walls of Jerusalem,
the crusaders destroyed historic sites and buildings, and with force
they changed the old cultural aspects of the Western Roman way
of life.

---

[219] The goal was to "retake" the Byzantine Empire and the holy land, Jerusalem.

Religious ways of worship were enforced by Rome, and the accepted traditions of Abraham, Moses, and the prophets were discredited.

The pope gained prominence and represented the Christ.

Enforcing traditional practices and Western customary culture in Jerusalem resulted in the destruction of the Holy Land and risked its honorary religious concepts. Thus, this fulfilled the Scripture, "He shall stand in the glorious land, which by his hand shall be consumed."

Chapter 18

Muslims Retake Jerusalem and Asia Minor

Jerusalem Recaptured

During the next 170 years, the fight between both religious groups became widespread in Europe.

The so-called Christians of Rome organized many more crusades against the Islamic faith, but apart from the crusades during AD 1095–1099, all other crusades were a failure.

Over these years the Muslims gained strength. By AD 1187, Saladin, the sultan of Egypt and a devoted Muslim, recaptured Jerusalem.

The crusaders of Europe were so threatened by the unrelenting attitude of the sultans of Egypt that even Baibars, who reigned from AD 1260 to AD 1277, continued to feel frustration as well.

Baibars, as the sultan of Egypt, regained most of the castles and towns in the east that had been captured by the crusaders of western Rome.

Asia Minor Taken by the Turks

The Holy War continued, and both the Roman Christians and the Muslims were against any opposition that came against them.

Apart from the Arabian Muslims, there were still the Turkish Muslims, who found themselves constantly at war with the Roman

Christian kingdom. Thousands of lives were lost on both sides during these wars.

One wonders about the doctrine of the Roman Christians. Should the doctrine be about love, which was in accordance with the teachings of the gospel of Christ two thousand years ago? Yet unlike the teaching of the original Christians, the pope of Rome, on the other hand, blessed the soldiers and mercenaries and sent them out to battle. Naturally the pope had to strengthen the will of his countrymen, persuading them of sure victory in Jesus' name, but one has to wonder what says the pope. Is it that the pope is saying that *killing* in Jesus name is legal? I could understand the sentiment of the pope being in rival with adversaries, but what about the *killing* of those Saxons who refused to be baptized? (Read *Man, Civilization, and Conquest, Margaret Sharman* Chapter 17 page 95).

The Turks, in similar fashion as any other Muslims, were so dormant and in need of victory that they went out and fought any opposition and killed in the name of Allah. Even Muslims began to slaughter other Muslims in the name of Allah.

Greedy to take over the Muslim states and empire, the Seljuk Turks and the Mongols fought together against the Arabian Caliphates and destroyed the Arabians dominance in AD 1258.

In AD 1453, the Turks accomplished one of their main tasks in capturing Constantinople, the main Christian state of Constantine, and they made Asia Minor the center of the Ottoman[220] Empire. The victorious invasion and the rule of the Ottoman Empire in Asia Minor lasted until World War I.

---

[220] Ottoman was the name given to the dynasty or empire of Osman (Othman), a Muslim leader from Asia Minor.

Chapter 19

Rome Strengthened by European Counterparts

He shall also set his face to enter with the strength of his whole kingdom, and upright ones with him: this shall he do.
—*Daniel 11:17*

Although there were continuous wars between the Christian crusaders and the Muslim warriors, many developments occurred in the Christian territories of the north. Some of these new developments produced some strong defenses for the Christian kingdoms of the north.

In earlier days the territory that is now Austria was a frontier colony of the Roman Empire. In AD 811, Charlemagne made Austria his Eastern March or frontier defense.

In AD 976 under Leopold of Babenberg, Austria's power began to rise, and the region became the Eastern Realm. During these times proclamations were made, and many mercenaries were sent to various countries, cities, and states to indoctrinate and spread on Roman Christianity. Those who refused to accept the religious concept would be severely punished, tortured, or even put to death.

Doubtless, although the kingdom of the north was making strides, they were still undergoing difficulties and striving to further their achievements, probably because of the strident attacks by and against the south.

While the Muslim faith was fighting against one another in the twelfth and thirteenth centuries, the Europeans were seeking ways to unite in strength.

Daniel pointed out that the kingdom of the north "shall enter with the strength of his whole kingdom..." (Daniel 11:17), and of course, this was the alliance of Rome with Europe (other kingdoms of the north) so that they could pursue their main objective much easier.

On this account, many marriages took place between kings, queens, princes, and princesses in creating a great Hapsburgs Empire.

One of these marriages allowed Austria to be acquired by the house of Hapsburg and to become the center of the Holy Roman Empire in AD 1282 (read *New Standard Encyclopedia* page 506 subheading "Austria").

Daniel referred to these marriages as follows:

> *"And he shall give the daughter of women, corrupting her"*
> *(Daniel 11:17 KJV).*

Many chapters[221] of the King James Version referred to woman as mountains and places. The prophet Ezekiel[222] represents cities as mother, daughters, and sisters.

My prophetic pronunciation of "daughter of women" symbolized the church or city-states. Therefore, this part of Daniel tells us that Europe shall give papal Rome the power over other territories and religions to forecast *his own devices.*[223]

The entirety of Europe then became a Catholic state because all royalties embraced Catholicism in the Holy Roman Empire, the pope being superior to all.

---

[221] Galatians 4:25–27.

[222] Ezekiel 16:45, 48, 53, 55.

[223] Daniel 8:12 (KJV) says "And an host was given him against the daily sacrifice by reason of transgression, and it cast down the truth to the ground: and it practiced, and prospered."

An example of the pope's superiority was given during the twelfth and thirteenth centuries when there was a religious sect other than the Roman Catholic faith, a sect that began to flourish in Europe. This sect, situated in the south of France, was called the Albigeneses.

One of their main beliefs was that there were two forces, good and evil, fighting constantly for the control of this world. They believed that matters of the soul were good, while matters of the flesh were evil.

The Albigenses got the attention of the Catholic faith when they denounced the resurrection and incarnation of Christ in their teaching (read *New Standard Encyclopedia Volume A,* page 153).

Catholics despised these teachings of the Albigenses, and the ruling pope (Pope Innocent III) ordered a holy war against them in the thirteenth century because he thought that their religious and social teaching would disrupt the growth of the Roman Catholic Church. He then sent mercenaries and adventurers on behalf of the Catholic Church to exterminate this sect.

As the middle Ages progressed, most Christian countries were ruled by kings, dukes, or princes. As a matter of fact, Christianity enforced this as a way of life in which all kings, dukes, and princes obeyed the pope's rule of law, which was not held up for questioning.

So the pope, the ruling monarch of the gospel of the north, had thus spread his wings and the gospel throughout Europe, where most if not all Europeans countries accepted the Catholic's supremacy.

Nevertheless, although Catholicism spread throughout Europe, religious opposition within the heart of the north became a key factor. So the union and strength of Catholicism became *infected,*[224] and the *virus*[225] spread to the throne of papal Rome, which led to the Renaissance, Protestant, and Reformatory periods.

---

[224] Weakened and breaking with disagreement.
[225] Disagreement and confusion about religious aspects spread in Rome.

Chapter 20

The Renaissance, Protestant, and Reformatory Periods

But she shall not stand on his side, neither be for him.
—Daniel 11:17 (KJV)

Consider the phrase "She shall not stand on his side" simply means to be in opposition or being against, which in the end will encourage rivalry (revolt). On this note my revelation was as follows.

There are three periods during the reign of the Holy Roman Empire that contributed to certain religious opposition and confrontations. This created uproar against the religious and spiritual ethics of the Church in the fifteenth, sixteenth, and seventeenth centuries.

These three are the Renaissance Period, the Protestant Period, and the Reformatory Period.

The Renaissance Period

During the fifteenth century, which was known as the middle Ages, things started to change slowly in the Roman Empire, beginning at Italy, the birthplace of the Roman Empire. At this time people had developed some eagerness to learn and discover more about the arts and culture.

Many people began to realize that someone they would often declare a witch for displaying evil traits was just displaying the presence of advanced age and concealed science.

The interest of this period spread rapidly over Western and Eastern Europe, and this brought trouble for the king of the north. Nevertheless, the benefit of this period was still evident and was called the Renaissance Period.

Due to the Renaissance Period, the intended European Union of the churches that the ("king of the north") Pope proposed was not going to plan. European *(city-states)* religious union became a path of a confused religious state. The aim of the Renaissance movement was to open up new ideas and stand against some aspects of the teaching of the Church, and seek to declare a new religious path. The outburst resulted in the great religious break away in the fifteenth, sixteenth, and seventeenth centuries. This then fulfilled the prophetic declaration of Daniel 11:17.

The Renaissance Intriguing Inspiration

Instead of remaining together in unity both spiritually and politically to fight the forces against Roman Christianity, the European body was falling apart, beginning at Italy.

Italy then was divided into many city-states (politically) ruled by dukes or princes, while the pope, who was the head of Christendom, ruled Rome.

The interest of each state to have its individual sovereignty and power instigated war in Europe. These states sometimes fought against other kings and dukes from other kingdoms and dukedoms in France, Spain, Germany, etc.

Italy then became a prize worth fighting for, which resulted in Italy under the rule of the French and then Spain.

This result triggered the people of Rome to commence evaluating the authority of the pope and his power.

If all these kings and dukes who had been set up by the pope and his councils could be so easily removed by opposition, greed, and internal European warfare, then the authority of the pope, bishops, and clergymen could be scrutinized and removed as well.

Seeing that the pope, bishops, and clergymen were mere showcases, the people then realized that they didn't need to rely on the nominal status and the so-called intellectuality of these leaders of the church anymore.

One could search the letters of the gospel by him or herself, and that was now encouraged; however, there were still obstacles to gain access to the Scripture, for only the scribes and bishops could access the written Word. This authorized access encouraged the elders of the churches to conspire, teaching deceptive doctrines that should not be opposed by any local individuals.

The church tried to pressure the people's self-learning attitude, but despite that, as early as AD 1388, John Wycliffe produced an English Version of the Bible. However, in AD 1530, the English Version, which was done by William Tyndale, was prohibited to be read in the Church. Obviously people reading Wycliffe's English Version was not applicable for the pope of Rome and his Roman Christian affiliates at the time.

John Guttenberg, who lived in Germany from 1398 to 1465, produced the first version of the printing press. Guttenberg had his printing press established in the height of the Renaissance Period in the fifteenth century. He also printed the *"common"* Bible of St. Jerome, known as the *Latin Vulgate*, but it could only be read by highly educated individuals. Therefore, the common people would have to depend on these educated people to give translations or interpretations. Probably this dependency[226] led to the controversies we have today.

---

[226] Due to this dependency, the Scripture was understood by the readers according to the given translations of the scribes, theologians and the fathers of the Church. On relentless studies, because of the newly self independency, people of all walks

During the Renaissance Period, the Bible was scarce and could only be seen in churches, and it was often chained to the pulpit; however, because the people eagerly wanted to read and understand the Book for themselves, the printers took up the demand and worked hard so that people all over Europe could own a Bible if they so desired. Those who were literate enough were then able to read and understand on their own terms. The vast distribution of this newly printed Bible translation allowed biblical education to become dominant, which resulted in opposition against the teachings of the pope and the Catholic faith. Those who opposed the teachings of the Catholic faith were then called heretics and were accused of the sin of heresy.

To stop this uprising, the pope sent investigators (inquisitors) to search the land for these heretics. If accused by these friars (inquisitors), you would be burned to death, or your properties or assets would be taken away. Sometimes you would suffer excommunication.

Read the following Scripture passage:

> *"After this shall he turned his face unto the isles and shall take many"* *(Daniel 11:18)*.

The pope made it his duty to take these drastic actions against the opposition all over Europe during the Renaissance Period.

Papal Rome was troubled by the uprising against the Catholic faith, and it feared the downfall it might bring. The pope of Rome realized this rebellion would not be so easy to deal with in comparison to the holy war against the Albigenses in the twelfth and thirteenth centuries. On this account the pope sent out loyal subjects to rid the land of religious opposition in Europe.

---

of life began to interpret the Bible according to their own intellectuality. Due to the many interpretations that came after, the end result gave way to other denominations all over Europe.

The main aim and command given to these loyal subjects was to force these religious sects to relinquish their faith and opinions, but if these people refused, they were to be excommunicated or burned to death.

Uprising against Tribute and Indulgence

For hundreds of years, Christian kings and princes from Germany, Spain, France, England, and all over Europe paid tribute and respect to the pope of Rome. During the Renaissance Period this was interrupted, as individuals opposed the pope's position and began seeking to understand the ways of the holy Son, Christ.

Enhancing the cause, Pope Leo X (1513–1521) thought of popularizing Catholicism as the only true religion and the way to God's throne, so they preached that forgiveness could be granted only through the Catholic Church.

Hence, the pope introduced indulgences. Indulgences were the payments of money to the papacy for any known sins committed. By the hand of the Catholic Church, these sins would be forgotten, and the sinner's conscience would be freed of guilt and the event would not await the person in judgment after death. With this redemption, one could even save loved ones who had already died with sin.

New criticism then spread inside and outside of Italy concerning the indulgences charged by Pope Leo X.

The people of Europe began to realize that these tributes and indulgences were not needed. They were just paying for Pope Leo X's luxurious and earthly glory.

The people thought that he was living more a life of a worldly prince than one of a religious leader. One must also understand that this worldly living was not an exclusive pattern of Pope Leo X. It was also the lifestyle of some popes before and after him.

This issue of payment for the forgiveness of sins stirred up an Augustinian monk name Martin Luther. As a result of the oppositions made by the Augustinian monk, the Protestant Period began.

The Protestant Period

The Protestant Period was strengthened by the Augustinian monk Martin Luther. He opposed some of the teachings of the Catholic Church with a strong voice.

By his own interest in the truth of the gospel, this *prince* of Saxony decided to take it upon himself—even if it could cost his life—to oppose and renounce the frivolous lifestyles of the popes, the cardinals, the laity, and the Holy Roman Empire as a whole.

When Pope Leo introduced indulgences, he automatically implanted a reproach upon the people and himself.

His kingdom was now in trouble and the turmoil begins.

> *"But a prince for his own behalf shall cause the reproach offered by him to cease; without his own reproach he shall cause it to turn upon him"* (Daniel 11:18 KJV).

Daniel did see the chaos as a prophet and said, "A prince for his own behalf shall cause the *reproach*[227] offered by him to cease" and turn the *judgment*[228] upon him.

The Triggered Moments of this Period

This *prince*[229], also a Catholic Christian, was known as Martin Luther (1483–1546). Luther lived in Saxony, part of the country governed by the holy Roman emperor, which included present-

---

[227] This *reproach* (reproof) is because of the people sinful act by turning from the purpose of Yeshua's (Jesus) death at Calvary and believing in forgiveness by way of purchasing indulgence.

[228] This *Judgement* is the result of his deeds and the *affirmative* (especially by protestant) that the pope was now accused of a sinful nature, whereby some persons (especially protestant) no longer admire Pope Leo X as they did before.

[229] *Prince* here does not means that he was a prince ascending to a throne but that he was a person with a deep religious connection to the Catholic faith.

day Germany, Austria, Belgium, and the Netherlands. Luther was a devoted Christian who also believed that there was something missing from the Catholic faith.

He desired to visit Rome, a place he likened to heaven itself. Luther one day got his heart's desire, and he gladly accompanied a friar to Rome.

On Luther's arrival, he was disappointed when he saw that Rome was not the holy and devoted place he thought it was. Luther was also terrified when he saw that the ruling pope (Pope Leo X) was dressed in luxurious apparel. He also gather information that popes were said to be in marriages and having many children. The rich and the privileged individuals would pay their way to be elected as cardinals, and the Christians lived worldly lives.

Although not all popes before were guilty of these acts, it was enough to cause gossip, and for sure Luther found Pope Leo X accumulating and hoarding money for wealth. The indulgence was also set up to enhance the hording of money collected by Pope Leo X.

Pope Leo X was taking advantage of the ignorant and poor, allowing them to believe that indulgences were the only way to receive forgiveness and telling them that Catholicism was the only true religion. People then thought that the papal position served as the mediator between the Elohim (Theos)[230] and man.

Luther—The First Protestant

On October, 31, 1517, Luther expressed displeasure with Pope Leo X after he sent the monk John Tetzel to Wittenberg. John Tetzel was surrounded by individuals seeking to purchase indulgence, with

---

[230] I supposed that the Latin Vulgate of Jerome was still in used, so the word Theos instead of the Elohim was in use. Nevertheless, a copy of the Old Testament translated from the original Hebrew version into English by Williams Tyndale in 1530 shows that the word God was also in use at that time in the sixteenth century.

the promise that they and their loved ones would receive forgiveness. Luther thought that "Those who say that a soul flies to heaven when coin tinkles in the collection-box are preaching an invention of man." (Read *Man, Civilization, and Conquest, Margaret Sharman.* Chapter 22, Page 122*).

31ˢᵗ Otober 1517, Luther then posted his *95 Theses*[231] publicizing his rejection of certain practices in the Catholic Church. His main argument was against indulgence, baptism and absolution.

Luther also stood firm in opposition when the imperial diet (convened by Emperor Maximilian) imposed the collection of tithes to provide money for war against the Turks. This was accompanied by a *papal bull*[232] on November 9, 1518, saying that all European Catholic Christians should believe in the pope's power and authority to forgive sins (i.e., grants indulgences).

In 1519, Emperor Maximilian's death ended his chapter, and Charles V of Spain was elected on June 28 of the same year. Emperor Charles V (1519–1558) ascended to the imperial throne.

Nevertheless, Luther continued his protest, and I supposed he argued publicly that this imposed proposal and demand for the collection of tithes and indulgence was a *reproach* on mankind and that it was impossible and ignorant and would encouraged a sinful nature. Wealthy persons would think that they could just purchase their freedom from sin in a convenient way.

The Protestant Movement moved throughout Europe, causing a widespread revolt, indicating to the people that Pope Leo X was as sinful as any human living in the world.

The pope and the cardinals could not believe that such a young man (Luther), the son of a poor miner would bring such a *"reproach"*

---

[231] A thesis is a documentation of arguments put forward for discussions. In Luther's situation it was a list of arguments opposing and proposing practices of the Catholic Church.

[232] *Papal bull* is a formal document written and sealed by the pope.

on them. Pope Leo X ordered that Luther's 95 Theses be condemned and that he should be excommunicated.

As a result of this, on May 21, 1521, King Henry VIII of England sent the pope a book on the *Seven Sacraments*[233] against Luther. The pope was encouraged by this book and conferred on the king the title "Defender of the Faith."

After this, the trial at the *Diet*[234] *of Worms*[235] on May 26 of the same year was held, over which Emperor Charles V presided. At this trial Luther was declared an outlaw.

At the trial the emperor in his statement remark said "A single monk who disagrees with what all Christianity has said for a thousand years must be wrong". Luther was then banned (excommunicated) from the empire and the Catholic faith. Despite this farce, Luther still continued his duties as a Protestant.

The Reformatory Period

The Reformatory Period began with Martin Luther, and his intensive Protestant Movement started the motion of reformation within the Catholic Church.

The threats, religious oppositions, and the reformatory issues that confronted Catholicism displeased the pope, and he turned his attention toward these matters, taking precedence in his own borders of the north.

---

[233] The *Seven Sacraments* (Latin word *sacrementum*) are the sacred values that are important to the Church. The Catholic Church lists them as Baptism, Eucharist, Reconciliation, Confirmation, Marriage, Holy Orders and Anointing the Sick.

[234] The term *diet* was mainly used historically for the *"Imperial Diet"*, an assembly for the *Imperial Estates* of the Holy Roman Empire.

[235] The *Diet of Worms* was like an *imperial court* held by the Holy Roman Empire. This court session was held at Worms in Germany.

Read the following Scripture passage:

"Then he shall turn his face toward the fort of his own land, but he shall stumble and fall and not be found." (Daniel 11:19 KJV)

Pope Leo X had to "turn his face (attention) towards the fort (borders) of his own land" to see if he could stem the growth of the Protestant Movement. Luther's ideas spread all over Europe, and this result in Germany becoming the Protestant country with the strength of Luther's ideas.

The Protestant monk had warned the Catholic Church to commence reformation, but the pope was too adamant to admit defeat. His rejection was clear, and it went as far as France, where the Protestants who were formerly known as the Huguenots[236] were prosecuted by French Catholics, forcing many to migrate to other parts of Europe and later to South Africa.

The Church neglected to reform, and its negative approach to the Protestant Movement highlighted the arrogance of the Catholic Church in the sight of the public. Seeing this, the common people were dismayed yet encouraged to follow Luther's example.

It became too late for the Catholic Church to commenced reformation because the monks were now also aligned with Luther against the teachings of the Catholic Church and its leaders.

Pope Leo X was no match against the growth of the Protestant Movement. The pope did more harm than good to the Catholic Church in persecuting the Protestant.

This rift between the Protestant and the Catholic Church created a challenge for the pope. The Catholic Church was now on the path of disaster, and it was breaking up. On account of the intense

---

[236] As late as AD 1572 on St. Bartholomew Night, Catherine de Medici persuaded her son, the king of France, to kill thousands of Protestants. This incident is known as the Bartholomew Massacre.

confrontations, it then also became too late to stop the splitting up of the Catholic Church.

The Depiction and Contempt of Pope Leo X

In hot pursuit, many Protestant were put to death by burning at the stake. Because of these confrontations and uproars, the authorities of Pope Leo X and the church fell to the ground.

Although many other countries, such as Spain, tried to follow the Catholic Church's example by prosecuting the revolutionary Jews, Muslims, and Protestants, the powers of the church and the authorities of the pope within Europe were diminishing.

So prophecies prevailed. Pope Leo X surely "stumbled and fell and could not be found" when Catholicism began a division amongst itself.

I believed the words 'stumbled and fell' is used as a phrase, meaning he met upon a force too strong for him. In fact, Pope Leo X was lost out of ideas to hold the Catholic Church together.

Although many still see Pope Leo X in a good light, it was said that by way of the pope handling of the matter regarding the Protestants Period, the Pope was not looked upon highly anymore by some within the statues of the church. Not look upon or was not seen with respect give the paraphrase, 'not be found'.

Read the following *Scripture* passage: "But he shall stumble and fall, and not be found" (Daniel 11:19 KJV).

Pope Leo X extravagance offended not only Luther but also some cardinals led by Alfonso Petrucci of Siena, who plotted to assassinate the pope but failed.

Apart from Pope Leo X's invention of indulgences and his worldly interests, a vicious scandal erupted concerning his sexuality.

Many contemporaries alluded to issues concerning his death. Officially some stated that he died of malaria on the December 1, 1521. He died so suddenly that not even his last and important sacrament was administered.

I wonder if the death of the pope was a manifestation of the judgment mentioned by the prophet concerning "the reproach" that shall fall on him by reason of the indulgences. The *reproach* laid by the Augustian Monk was so effective that Pope Leo X died (December 1521) so suddenly before his *last sacrament*[237] was taken.

Other Splits in the Catholic Church

Apart from Luther, another revolutionary Protestant (and a preacher) called John Calvin (1509–1564) disagreed with the teachings and worldly living of the pope and the clergy of Rome. He also broke away from the Catholic Church. Though he claimed that he was not a follower of Luther, being much harsher in his movement, his principle of thoughts were the same.

John Knox, a follower of John Calvin, took it up on himself also to introduce a stern version of the Protestant Movement in Scotland, and soon after that, King Henry VIII accepted the faith.

King Henry was to be remarried to a young girl named Ann Bullen, but the ruling pope, Adrian VI (1521–1523) refused. King Henry sent a message to the pope by protesting against his command and then went off to become a Protestant.

When Pope Adrian VI heard that Henry had gone ahead with his decision, he was very furious, which resulted in both King Henry VIII and Thomas Granmer[238] being excommunicated.

The following year King Henry appointed Thomas Cromwell, an ambitious politician, to look after the affairs of the church. The king named his ministry the Church of England, also called the Anglican Church.

In later days Emperor Charles V of the Holy Roman Empire realized that the Catholic Church was not proceeding in the spiritual

---

[237] Anointing of the sick with oil was usually a last sacrament by the Church.

[238] Granmer was a Protestant who assisted the king in his endeavors and was later appointed archbishop of Canterbury.

way that it should. The emperor therefore decided to call the council of Trent to settle the quarrels concerning the Catholic and the Protestant churches and bring about the reformation of the Church in the best way.

The council was not successful because of the presence of more Italians, so the votes were always one-sided, which benefitted the Roman Catholic Church. At this time Germany was more a Protestant state than a Catholic one, leaving Austria as the chief Catholic state of Germany during the Reformation Period.

The split in the church lead to quarrels between the princes of Germany and the Holy Roman Empire, resulting to Charles breaking up his empire. Emperor Charles V of the Holy Roman Empire retired in 1558 at the age of fifty-six to a monastery in Spain. The Holy Roman Empire disintegrated, various states turning away from Catholicism, choosing their own religious destinies during the sixteenth and seventeenth centuries.

Chapter 21

The Papal Rehabilitation and Ridicule

The Papal Rehabilitation

> *Daniel 11:20 (KJV) says, "Then shall stand up in his estate a raiser of taxes in the glory of the kingdom."*

When Scripture speaks of *estate*, it is simply describing the same allocation of the existing domain. Saying that someone will "stand up in his estate" denotes the uprising or election of an individual out of the same household, domain, or kingdom to maintain power and ruler ship.

Based on this, another king of the north[239] was given the honor of the kingdom and the papacy. His rule will allude to the auditing of the taxes to address the economical constraint and irregularities that were perplexing and pressuring the financial sectors by the ill doings at the hands of the past popes and cardinals.

By doing this, he would protect the finances of the Holy Roman Empire and stop the luxurious, worldly, and dishonest spending by the papal throne and its cardinals.

The auditing, correcting, and raising of the taxes would lead to the balancing of expenditures between both prominent and common

---

[239] This is the Papacy (Vatican) or Holy Roman Empire, which the Pope of Rome is the head administrator.

people, which in the long run will benefit and honor "the glory of the kingdom" in its policies of right and justice.

Count Braschi Ascension to the Papal Throne

Count Giovanni Angelo Braschi was an auditor in profession. His highly performed skill at the court of Naples won him the admiration of Pope Benedict XIV (1740–1758), who then appointed him as one of his secretaries in 1753. After he was engaged to be in marriage, the interest of the papacy took hold on him, and so he broke off the engagement, as he was ordained as a priest in 1758. By 1766, he was then appointed treasurer by Pope Clement XIII (1758–1769).

Count Braschi was feared and known greatly by his conscientious economic skills. Many who cunningly convinced Pope Clement XIV (1769–1774) to make Count Braschi cardinal and priest of Sant Onofrio on April 25, 1773, thought that he being appointed such position would result in their favor, giving more opportunities to do their mysterious deeds.

After the death of Pope Clement XIV in 1774, the priest of Sant Onofrio was elected to the papal curia on February 15, 1775. The priest on becoming Pope took the papal name Pope Pious VI. During his reign he put forth promising reformation in the complete administration of the papal state.

Pope Pious VI (1775–1799) reprimanded Prince Potenziani, governor of Rome, for failing to deal with the corruptions in the city, and he appointed new cardinals to remedy the economic problems the papal state faced. He cunningly relieved the pressures of the taxes, duties, and tributes that were demanded of the local citizens and placed some of these burdens on the upper classes. The annual disbursement of funds was reduced, and the pensions of many prominent individuals were denied.

As the word of the prophet declares, he will be "a raiser of taxes to the honor and glory of the kingdom." Here one can understand that Pope Pious VI implanted equal taxation on all citizens, whether rich or poor. The auditing of taxations was properly done, and the benefits were served and spent "in the honor and glory of the kingdom," as it was subscribed.

The demise of Pope Pious VI

> *Daniel 11:20 (KVJ) says, "But within a few days he shall be destroyed, neither in anger nor in battle."*

Because of the stern and effective action of the pope toward the financial and economic constraint of the empire, many were not allowed the usual access to the papal state funds, so Pope Pious VI was not all that loved by many officials of the Roman Empire. Apart from a few oppositions in the papal curia, other members of the Roman kingdom, especially France, were against the sovereignty of Rome and the authorities of the papal throne.

In 1793, the murder of the republican agent Hugo Bassville in Rome, who was charged with complicity by the French convention, gave rise to a new ground of offense, forcing Pope Pious VI to throw in his weight behind the league against France in the first coalition.

In 1796, Napoleon Bonaparte and his French republican troops invaded Italy and defeated the papal troops. This resulted in the occupation of Ancoma and Loreto.

In December 1797, a new pretext was afforded by the death of a brigadier general who had gone to Rome with Joseph Bonaparte as part of the French ambassadorship. General Berthier claimed that he was not advised of the visit by Napoleon. He marched into Rome and entered unopposed on February 10, 1798, and proclaimed Rome a Roman republic.

Napoleon Bonaparte immediate demanded Pope Pious VI denounce his authority, and upon his refusal, he was taken prisoner and escorted on February 20 from the Vatican to Siena and later to Certosa near Florence.

The pope died six weeks later after his arrival in the chief town of Drome on August 29, 1799. The pope's body was embalmed but was not buried until January 30, 1800. Embarrassingly not even a funeral service was held.

His entourage insisted that Pope Pious VI's wish was to be buried in Rome behind the Austrian lines. The French allowed his body to be taken from Valence on December 24, 1801. It was brought to Rome, where the pope was given a fresh burial on February 15, 1802.

The manifestation of the pope "being destroyed neither in anger nor in battle" explained him being overthrown and the papal official being dismissed.

As the news of the pope being dethroned reached Paris, rejoicing in his defeat brought the *burning* of Pope Pious VI's effigy (a sculptured image) in the garden of Palais Royal. This even was accompanied by jokes and songs.

The *burning* of one effigy was like demonstrating one's rise of power being demised. The demonstration by the public in Paris indicates their views on Pope Pious VI statues and moral etiquette. After this destruction of the pope's image was done, Napoleon Bonaparte, the French revolutionist, called himself the emperor of the Roman Empire and took advantage of the throne of the Holy Roman Empire.

The so-called emperor was later crowned officially in the presence of Pope Pious VII (1800–1823), which stirred issues amongst the members of the Vatican. Napoleon then extended his sovereignty above the Papal authority, and it was considered to administrate under his watch.

Chapter 22

The Existence of the Vile Person

In his estate shall stand up a vile person, to whom they shall not give the honor of the kingdom but he shall come in peaceably, and obtained the kingdom by flatteries.

—*Daniel 11: 21 (KJV)*

The Birth of the Vile Person

Early in the seventeenth century when the Protestant church claimed its liberty to worship, prosecution became widespread in Europe. On account of this, many individuals fled to the newly inhabited country New England (now called North America) to settle and make residence.

Most of these settlers fled to North America for at least one of these reasons: (1) to escape military persecutions, (2) to escape religious persecutions, or (3) to escape financial frustrations

1. Military persecutions—During the 1600s, Europe was plunged into constant war. Struggles were external, internal, civil, and religious. Young men were caught hold of, drafted at any time, and forced to join the army.
2. Religious persecutions—Any individual who refused to support the established religion of the king of England and the Roman Catholic doctrine was persecuted or bankrupted.

3. Financial frustrations—The benefits the landlords enjoyed were huge because they exploited those who leased and tilled the land.

By 1718, British colonization in New England was firmly established. The year 1732 marked the establishment of thirteen British colonies along the east coast of New England.

The first set of Indian settlers were pushed farther and farther west by the new colonists from Europe. It was clear that the rich and beautiful country of New England would soon become the new abode for European settlers.

As this country continued to establish itself as North America, it became stronger within its government, yet liberty remained the talk of the day. The Toleration Act in 1649 was already passed, and Maryland officially recognized freedom of worship.

As individuals addressed the toleration of any religious faith, the end of nineteenth century showed new breeds of religious faith and beliefs that spread all over North America. Some of these churches were as follows:

- Quakers—seventeenth century
- Baptist—seventeenth century
- Methodist—eighteenth century
- First Adventist—nineteenth century
- Seventh-day Adventist—nineteenth century
- Pentecostal and others—nineteenth century

All these religious sects preached and evangelized, claiming that they served a god as in the one and true Elohim (God) of Abraham, Isaac, and Jacob. Their conversations always brought religious disputes and confusions. Concerns often arose, as it was not likely that they were serving the same Messiah who preached unification in His kingdom.

North America, with its religious differences, nevertheless strengthened in governance and economy, becoming wealthier than most of the countries of the north. This then allowed North America to exist in power and strength, claiming European governance and dominion.

North American settlers then spread to the south of the land (South America), and the adjoining North and South American states, which are now called the United States of America, conquered many more non-European and European countries, proving themselves as the uprising *vile person* of the north.

Although the United States was the new Christian state out of the religious proceeding of Europe, its desire is to strive and become not only an overspreading of religions but adjoining lands (States) as well with Europe.

This binding of the United State of America with the European countries encouraged the filtration of the Roman Catholic faith within its borders.

The Pouring Arms of the United States

> *"And with the arms of flood they shall be over flown from before him, and shall be broken." (Daniel 11:22 KJV)*

The Return of Papal Power

Although the systematical approach of the United States was a beneficiary facture, it was evident that many European countries were against its principalities and powers over the northern kingdoms.

To hold and maintain its governance over the northern kingdoms, many peace talks were initiated. This was done to stem the growth of the northern rivalries and the opposing forces against the existence of the United States, the *vile person*.

Out of these peace talks initiations produced the Allies (also called the European Powers).

Many countries that did not obey the declaration of peace at the UN conferences were overthrown and placed under subjection. France, which had plagued Rome and its popes for years, was invaded by the Allies in 1813, deposing Napoleon Bonaparte. Shortly after that on May 24, 1814, Allied forces freed Pope Pious VII during a pursuit of Napoleon's forces.

Another great achievement that the US armies took part in happened at the Congress of Vienna in 1814–1815 when the Papal States were largely restored. This put a smile on Pope Pious' face. At this time Austria was the leading power in the new German Confederacy.

The United States also scored over the Turks, whose three hundred years of expeditions were conquests against the European kingdoms.

Despite the victory of the United States, the Turks continued their attacks on the southern Mediterranean coast. Pope Pious VII, who the main man (I believed) Daniel described as the "prince of the covenant," implored the United States of America to help suppress the Muslim barbaric pirates along the southern Mediterranean coast. They had been kidnapping Christians and asking for ransom or holding them as slaves.

The pope, showing his gratitude for the intervention of the *vile person* (USA), stated that the United States had done more for the cause of Christianity than any of the nations of Christendom.

Daniel 11:22 says, "And shall be broken: yea, also the prince of the covenant."

But what does this passage mean?

This explains the strategic task set out by the *vile person* or *vile kingdom*. Even the "prince of the covenant" (Pope Pious VII) was subdued by him. The pope was so convinced that even in his words he honored the United States.

I am not sure why the prophecy uses the reference *prince* instead of *king*. The word *prince* always suggests that someone else is above the person in power. This word could probably indicate the inferiority within the *covenant*. On the other hand, maybe the word *covenant* spells it all, meaning the union with Europe and the "vile person" in reference to the next "king of the north".

The Vile Person in Charge

> *Daniel 11:23 (KJV) says, "And after the league made with him he shall worked deceitfully, for he shall come up and be strong with a small people."*

The word *league* represents a union, and of course, a union was formed between the pope and the United States.

As the United States developed and became the economic and trade strength of the northern world, he was later to be seen as the superior force in that region. The vile person's *flood of arms* inspired the country to become the master of the western and northern world.

During many types of council, agreements were made as the United States was one of the spokesperson giving his peace speeches. The United States opinion as a dictator was to place any European countries or states that disobeyed the rules of these councils into subjection. Such countries or states are allowed to be governed by other individuals or countries within the European council.

As time went by and the nineteenth century closed, many northern countries gained interest in the fertile land of the south (Africa).

After invaders conquered the natives of these lands and gained possession of some of these territories, they exercised their greed, possessing more lands deep in the Congo for development and personal gain.

The possession of these lands on the African continent then became so worthwhile that people fought for them. Large Europeans powers engaged in rival activities as they claimed possession of particular African territories. This produced the Berlin Conference in 1884 so that people could settle the claims of Great Britain, France, Portugal, Spain, Belgium, Italy, and Germany. The United States was involved in dividing the African continent into spheres, Great Britain and France receiving the larger shares.

By then the Triple Alliance of Austria-Hungary, Italy, and Germany was already formed in 1883, and for a balance Great Britain, France, and Russia formed the Triple Entity.

From 1911 to 1912, there was also another change in the political map of Africa when the central Northern European powers decided to attack the stronghold of the Turkish Muslim barbarian. There was no opposition by the superior political power of the US government, so the Italians with other central powers engaged themselves and went against the Turkish Muslim tribe. The Italians were victorious and took over the Turkish regions of Tripoli and Cyrenaica and formed them into Libya.

As one could have guessed, the other central powers did receive their shares, which were digested[240] by the superior state known as the United States.

The year 1914 brought World War I, a struggle between the Triple Alliance (Austria-Hungary and Germany, without Italy) and the Triple Entity (Great Britain, France and Russia). On account of the Triple Alliance disregarding the agreement for peace, the United States was on the side of the Triple Entity and their cause, honoring them with the victory.

The states and colonies of Germany were then mandated to France, Great Britain, Belgium, and Portugal. Such arrangement was also digested by the vile person (the United States). The Austria-Hungary Empire was broken up into successive states—Austria, Hungary, Poland, Romania, Czechoslovakia, and Yugoslavia.

---

[240] The word here signifies agreed upon.

Italy, which disregarded the agreement of the Locarno Pact and took sides against the Triple Alliance, was awarded a small portion of the Austrian-Hungary territories[241] by the leading Allies (the United States and the United Kingdom) after the war.

Victory in World War I gave Italy a permanent seat in the council of the League of Nations.

The United States and the Triple Entity then initiated close ties. Hence, the decree of an alliance resulted.

Europeans Helped a Brother against a Brother

World War I also led to the loosening of the Turkish Muslim stronghold on the Arabian lands. This was done in gratitude and appreciation to the Arabian Muslims, as they assisted the Allies against the Triple Alliance during World War I.

The United States might not have played the leading roll, but for sure they had assisted along with the British and the French in overthrowing the barbarian Turks during the Arab Revolt (1916–1918).

> As the scripture says, "And he shall stir up his power and his courage against the king of the south with a great army: and the king of the south shall … battle with a great and mighty army: but he shall not stand: for they shall forecast devices against him." (Daniel 11:25 KJV)

The Arab Revolt (1916–1918) was initiated by the viceroy, Hussein Ali, under an agreement with the United Kingdom and the French. This agreement was to secure an Arabian independence

---

[241] Italy received South Tyrol, Istria, Trentino, and Trieste at the Treaty of St. Germain on September 10, 1919. The treaty was also called the Treaty of Peace between Allied Powers and Austria.

from the ruling Ottoman Turks, creating a unified Arab state with him remaining in control of the Hedjaz region of Western Arabia.

The viceroy, who was also a Muslim and unable to withstand the terror that the Turks consistently placed on them, put in his lot with the northern powers and conspired to end the Turkish barbarians' hold on the Arabian lands of the south.

During the revolt attacks the British Allies were advancing in full stride, but the victory could not have been completed without the help of Hussein Bin Ali, viceroy of the kingdom of Hedjaz in Western Arabia.

Scripture simply states,

> *"Yea, they that feed at the portion of his meat shall destroy him, and his army shall overflow: and many shall fall down slain" (Daniel 11:26 KJV).*

The symbolical explanation, "they that feed at the portion of their meats,"[242] simply denotes that they were as close as family.

Though they were all Muslim, the Arabian Muslims were uncomfortable living amongst the Turks. So for the viceroy of Western Arabia, it was necessary to betray and deceitfully turn against the Turkish Muslims so that he could regain their Arabian independence once more.

At the end of the war on October 1, 1918, the viceroy was not fully victorious because the Allies forfeited the initial[243] agreement. Nevertheless, he was placed in full control of the Hedjaz region of Western Arabia until 1925.

---

[242] *Meat* represents a lifestyle (e.g. philosophy) that they all enjoyed in common.
[243] Initially they agreed to unify the Arab states.

The Unspoken Peace

After World War I, many leagues[244] were initiated to stem the continuous rivalries between the European States and the religious war of the northern (Catholicism) and southern (Muslim) region.

As these frequent attacks on both the north and south—each done for political and religious empowerment—continued, further consultations within peace conferences and councils were made. Many treaties were then signed to encourage a global rest in the hemisphere and it surrounding areas.

Nevertheless, these peace talks between the north and the south did not last for long because they both were continuously threatened by each other, which resulted in many other battles. Consequently the United States would take sides and even command at times.

Sometimes it even seemed as if the Muslims and the Christians would tolerate one another on religious terms. But as the prophet Daniel spoke of the peace and said, "But it shall not prosper: for yet the end shall be at the time appointed" (Daniel 11:27).

We made previous reference to the Scripture passage as follows:

> *"And both these kings' hearts shall be to do mischief, they shall speak lies at one table, but it shall not prosper, for yet the end shall be at the time appointed" (Daniel 11:27 KJV).*

The phrase "both these kings" was not confined to only the king of Syria (north) and king of Egypt (south), but any *state* or *king* of the north and south that would rise to power.

---

[244] These leagues were the Leagues of Nations Union (1918 in UK), League to Enforce Peace (1915), the Covenant of the League of Nations (28th June 1919) and finally the Leagues of Nations (1920). These leagues were formed to stem the growth of wars, and disarm to the lowest point consistent with domestic safety.

And so today the Muslims (south), and Christianity of Rome (north) were at war against one another for religious and political reasons.

One must clearly note that the political and religious war is not confined to the borders of the papacy and the Muslim lands but extends as far as the civilized land of the United States of America.

Chapter 23

The Prelude of the Italian Government before and after World War I

Before we relate to Daniel 11:28 let us review certain history of the nineteenth century.

As one recalls, verse 27 speaks about the continuing deception of the kings of the north and south, which referred to the present and the time ahead. Inconsistently, verse 28 begins by saying that the king of the north shall "return to his land with great riches"[245], which does not tie or give a detailed follow-up with verse 27's deceptive actions on the part of the kings. However, this verse begins with another event immediately. It is therefore natural that one indicates, which person or event this part of verse 28 is relating to.

We should recognize that after World War I, there were few individuals of the north who pretended to stand out as the main men of the north at that time. Therefore, it is necessary that one point out this individual king of the north returning with *riches* to his own land.

As history pointed out, before World War I in the late nineteenth century, the greed for lands was very strong. After the Holy Roman Empire was ended in 1805, Austria had the leading role in the new German Confederacy at the Congress of Vienna in 1814.

---

[245] The word *riches* referenced his thought of possession and high-mindedness.

Austria then elevated in power and influence over the northern tip of Italy. Italy and Austria fostered each other, where Italian nationalism and Austrian interest clashed. After a while issues of the adjoining lands developed, which encouraged the three independence wars between Italy nationalists and Austrian interests, a conflict that lasted from 1848 to 1866.

A unification[246] initiative was brought about by Austria but was opposed by Prussia. Austria was deposed of after the Italian alliance with Bismarck, Minister President of Prussia (1873—1990), encouraged the Austro-Prussian War 1866. Bismarck's[247] victory allotted Italy the region of Veneto and Friuli, while Prussia's victory allotted them a greater portion of the German states.

In 1882, the disagreement against colonial expansion in the African continent was an issue. So Bismarck encouraged the Italian government to form the Triple Alliance with Germany and Austria-Hungary.

The continuous contentions between the factions holding claim on the African continent produced the Berlin Conference in 1884. The African continent was then divided up into shares, Belgium receiving the area they claimed. Britain and France received the larger shares of the areas remaining, which Italy after received, though they were still unsatisfied.

Again in 1912, when the Allies with Italy dismantled the Turkish Muslims' stronghold on the African continent, the map of Africa went through another political change. The lands were distributed between the Allies and Italian, Italy receiving Tripoli and Cyrenaica combining them into one Libya estate.

---

[246] This unification was to bring the lands within that border as one, both eastern and western Germany.

[247] Otto von Bismarck (or the Iron Chancellor) was originally named Otto Edward Leopold. He was born on April 1, 1815, and died on July 30, 1893. He was Minister of Finance of Prussia from 1862 to1890.

Again, after World War I in 1914, the Allies with Italy also divided the lands of the defeated Triple Alliance, Italy receiving some portions of the territories of Austria.

These countries of the north did return home with riches and land at the end of these wars. But the Italian government (both before and after World War I) became upset with the northern powers, especially since the issuing of the lands of Austria after World War I. This greed for more land enticed Italy, disregarding the peace covenant of the Allies, especially where the United State is concern, who continued to be the main strength of the north where war is concern.

The governments of Italy and Germany decided to resurrect the spirit of the Triple Alliance once more, aiming to prove themselves as the presumed vile person of the north. Nevertheless the Triple Alliance did not returned, but the *Axis Powers*[248] revealed itself.

Before we go any further, let us see how the Italian governments seek to showcase themselves as the *vile*[249] *person* of the north.

The Presumed Vile Person

After the invasions of the south by the northern countries (Europe), the south (Africa) was up for grabs in the 1800s. The United States played an important part in distributing the lands amongst the Europeans, including Italy, for ownership.

The Italian had conquered and invaded many territories, and their victories and riches encouraged the thought that they were the main power of the north.

---

[248] These are Germany, Italy and Japan. These were the Axis powers that fought in World War II against the Allied forces. The Axis formerly took the name after the Tripartite Pact was signed by Germany, Italy, and Japan on 27 September 1940 in Berlin. Hungary, Romania Slovakia and Bulgaria subsequently joined the pact by March 1941.

[249] This means a contentious in governance.

At that time the United States had invaded the European Empire and stood as the *vile person* (person in authority). In this manner United States became the sovereign and legislative bystander in the northern hemisphere.

The United States had illustrated to be the reigning voice at the United League and European Alliance.

The Italians, on the other hand, became a strong voice of opposition against the position of the United States within the European kingdom. On many occasions the Italian government maintained rivalries against many European states, indicating to the United States the Italian dominance within the kingdom of the north.

All these flattering peace conferences called by the United States of America and the Leagues did not seem to capture the attention of the Italians. Instead, the Italian government continued to project itself as the ultimate European power.

The hike of wealth determined the possessive power and control an individual state would have within the empire. So the Italian government, because of his wealthy ambitions, presumed themselves as king of the northern kingdom.

Power then became an issue in the European Empire. The consisting rivalries to presume one's country as the *vile person* of the European body continued with the United States and the European Allies against the Italians.

So here we see that Daniel was pointing to Italy, the further vile person of the north who returned home with his promoted fame and riches to make his claim as king. As the prophet says, "Then shall he return into his land with great riches" (Daniel 11:28 KJV).

The Italian Repudiation

Apart from the power of the United States, the pope remained the sole heir of the Papal States and head of Christendom.

The monarchy of Rome and the Papal States then resulted in the distress when the force ruled of anti-papal bodies, especially Victor Emmanuel II, who later becomes king (1861–1878). Victor seized most of the Papal States at the foundation of the Modern Unification of the Italian States in 1860 and the rest, including Rome, in 1870. As a result of this, the papacy and the Italian government have been in conflict ever since.

The Italian Army invading Rome in 1870 at the end of the Italian Unification cut short the first Vatican Council, which had been called to Rome at that time.

This was a council set by Pope Pious IX in 1869 to recognize, mention, and solve internal and external problems imposed upon the Catholic Church and its clergy men and decree papal infallibility.

Manipulation of the Papal and Political States by the Italian Government

Pope Pious IX was a strong figure in the early nineteen century. He was the longest reigning pope whose reign lasted for thirty-two years. Pope John Paul II was only pope for twenty-seven years, and Pope Leo XIII reigned for twenty-five years.

After the death of Pope Gregory XVI (1837–1846), Pope Pious IX succeeded the papal throne. The conclave of 1846 elected him as pope, and after the coronation he was placed with the title as "pontiff" and "king." So Pope Pious IX was not just an elected pope but also a king in his own little world.

Pope Pious IX was a secular ruler as the monarch of the papacy, but he was liberal in his way of life. He was also the last Pope to rule as sovereign of the papal throne as a combined power of church and state.

During 1848, the papal kingdom was faced with a revolutionary movement from not just Italy but all over Europe as well. One of the causes for these revolutionary acts was the fact that many decisions taken by the pontiff disturbed the allegiance of several European countries.

The pope's position was threatened at that time by the continuous attacks by the Italian statesmen commanded by Victor Immanuel II. This resulted in many outbreaks, and Pope Pious IX had to flee from Rome in 1848 for a short time.

After Pope Pious IX returned in 1850, the continuous ambition of Victor Immanuel II led to further attacks on the Papal States.

The pope refused to tolerate the ambitious call of Victor by protesting in a fashionable way, making himself immure[250] in the Vatican walls, where all popes have lived securely ever since.

While a prisoner at the Vatican, he was obliged to rely on French and Austrian soldiers to maintain order and protect his territories and domain.

The demise met by the Papal States was due to disagreeable advised and rejection given by the pope in earlier years. In 1859, Napoleon III of France and Cavour (premier to Victor Emmanuel II) agreed to go at war with Austria. Many European nations had encouraged the pope to do so, but he had refused.

Following the Battle of Magenta on July 4, 1859, the Austrian forces withdrew from the Papal States, giving their losses to Sardinia-Piedmont, hometown of Victor Emmanuel II. This left the Papal States vulnerable to any incursion. An army of volunteers was then created in defense by Napoleon III when the Papal States were invaded in 1860 by Victor Emmanuel II. These individuals within the army came from different countries, including France, Italy, Belgium, Holland, Canada, England, and the United States.

The US effective diplomatic relationship, which revived the papacy (since 1848), lasted only until 1867 when domestic pressures forced a closure between both countries, resulting in the withdrawal of the United States. Three years after that, Napoleon Bonaparte III's

---

[250] This refers to the imprisonment of one self.

forces were recalled because of the Franco-Prussian War, leaving Victor Immanuel II, who determined to position his government as the *vile person*, to proceed with his ambitions against the papal kingdom.

In 1870, the Italian forces of Victor Emmanuel fully controlled Italy. After his victory, Victor Immanuel II was then pronounced king of Italy.

After the takeover of the Papal States by Victor, the pope's authorities were relinquished, leaving the papacy only in charge of the spiritual needs of the people, while the political side was maintained by Victor Emmanuel II, who now defined himself as the *vile person* of the north.

The independent Papal States were then made subject to the Italian Unification, demanding the political and Papal States stay under the command of the government and unopposed King Victor Emmanuel II, leaving the Vatican to rely on the country's collected expenditures.

Pope Pious IX lived long enough to see the death of his opponent, Victor Emmanuel II, king of Italy, who was laid to rest in January 1878.

Pious IX, suffering from epilepsy, died one month later of sudden heart attack while he was praying the rosary prayer on 7th February 1878.

After Pope Pious IX died, Pope Leo XIII ascended the papal throne and reigned until 1903.

Chapter 24

The Nineteenth-Century Consummation against the Holy Covenant

And his heart shall be against the Holy Covenant.
—Daniel 11:28 (KJV)

The Selection to the Will of the Covenant

History has taught us that the Jewish nation was promised and covenanted by Yahweh to make them into a mighty race and a ruler of the world to come.

By the nineteenth century, even the Ethiopians had found out that they were listed by the genealogical existence of the Davidic dynasty and that they, too, were a Jewish nation formerly known as the Black Jews.

In the nineteenth century, much disastrous and inhuman wickedness was done to certain natives, including the Africans and European Jews.

According to the prophecy of Daniel, the soul of the northern kingdom "shall be against the Holy Covenant." To explain this reference, let's exam two Scripture passages—Exodus 34:5–17 and Jeremiah 31:29–34

As suggested, a covenant is an agreement between two or more parties (individuals).

In Exodus 34:5–7, Yahweh command that He would not make the "iniquity of the fathers" stop Him in blessing His children. He would have mercy on whomsoever He would, forgiving them of their iniquities and drive out the heathen from before them and let Israel inherit (rule) the earth.

In Jeremiah 31:29–34, the prophet prophesied concerning the words of Yahweh, saying, "Behold he will make a new covenant with the house of Israel and Judah." The passage goes on to say that this covenant would not be like the covenant that He had made with the forefathers after He took them out of the land of Egypt, a covenant and blessing Israel rejected, but this covenant would be a spiritual one that He would placed in our hearts.[251] Whosoever accepted the gift was selected to inherit the will of this holy covenant and would be his people and be saved.

Acts against the Holy Covenant

During the early 1800s at the tail end of slavery, there are three acts against the Holy Covenant, namely the Catholic philosophical teachings, King Leopold II of Belgium, and the Italian government.

The Catholic Philosophical Teachings

The Catholic teaching in the nineteenth century seems questionable with respect to the Holy Covenant.

As issues against anti–Catholic beliefs surfaced again during the reign of Pope Pious IX, many persecutions and new religious legislations in several European countries like Italy, Mexico, Spain, Germany Netherlands, England, and Whales were organized.

There were laws against the Jews, including the black nobilities of the land, regarding their freedom of rights of religion. To add to

---

[251] Acts 2:26, 28, 30–31; Acts 3:17–23.

this, the Jews were forbidden to attend any form of religious services or have any form of religious practices in public places.

However, this was abolished during the reign of Pope Pious IX, and a new plan, which was against the holy covenant, was formed.

According to the Word, the holy covenant of Yahweh will only be effective by the redemption of His holy people (Israel)[252] through Christ. Instead, during the reign of Pope Pious IX, the Church introduced the Mariology within the Roman Catholic philosophy. This feature became prominent in the nineteenth century when the pope appointed theologians to analyze a Marian dogma.

In 1848, the protocol of this research was introduced, and in 1854, the Immaculate Conception was declared saying that Mary had conceived without a *mate*[253].

In 1869, the first Vatican Council was called. At this council, the Marian Pope (Pope Pious IX) emphasized Mary as the "matrix of salvation." Here Mary was pronounced the "core producer and Mother of all Grace" and redemption and that all Christians achieved all things through her, the Mother of Christ.

I see this as a very ridiculous and presumptuous statement. I would understand if it said that "by Mary we have salvation," seeing that her matrix was actually the incubator that holds the giver of salvation, but you cannot say that "salvation was given through her." It is not the birth that brought salvation but what the Messiah did when He gave up His life[254] at Golgotha. His death served as an example that bound the thought of the assurance of the promise.

One could argue about the purpose of Christ and His baptism on the cross, being the author of salvation and giver of all grace, but what did the pope claim about the position[255] concerning Mary?

---

[252] "Israel" as a holy people is not confine to *physical* Israel as of the land ISRAEL, but also to those who accepted Yahweh and His Son, the Messiah.

[253] A male partner

[254] Hebrew 2:13–18; 8:3–8; Hebrew 9:11–18.

[255] This was probably the same contending factor according to the Council of

In understanding the *covenant*, it is said that the Mediator and *core* giver of Salvation was promise through Judah via the seed of Jesse. For reference, you can review Isaiah 11:1–5 and 11:10–11 and Acts 2:30–31 of the King James Version.

Seeing that the promise was made to Judah, one must not disrespect the blessing of Joseph.

The learned Faustus (Bishop of Riez) proving his point by saying that Mary was not from the seed of David but from the lineage of Levi by her father, Joachim,[256] who was also a priest but once had an issue[257] and could not serve at the temple. Though opposed by many, he continued to say that Christ was not the Son of God until after his *baptism*.

Scripture, neither in Matthew 1 nor Luke 3 when referring to the genealogy of the Messiah, does not point to Mary but to Joseph. Therefore, if the promise of the redeemer was through David's *physical seed*[258], then Mary could never be the only important factor of the matrix of grace. Seeing that Joseph was of the tribe of Judah, the seed and lineage of David, as the scripture made reference (Luke 1:27), his fatherhood would be of a necessity.

How could one forget that even the angel distinctly commanded Joseph to comfort Mary in his arms and be a father to the child when Mary gave birth? This clearly states the importance of Joseph to the prophecy. Making Mary the Levite to be the *Mediatrix*[259] would

---

Ephesus in AD 431, regarding Mary as the bearer of God (Theotokos) but not the bearer of Christ (Christotokos).

[256] Read *Lost Book of the Bible, the Gospel of the Birth of Mary*, page 17. This chapter gives a cited version of the work of Jerome a father of the Catholic Church who flourished in the fourth century AD; its introduction also gives the suggestion of the Bishop of Riez, concerning the tribe of Mary.

[257] Joachim was without a seed. According to Scripture, any priest out of the tribe of Levi that could not bring forth a seed should not burn a sacrifice at the tabernacle (Leviticus 21:16–24; 22:1–4 KJV).

[258] Not spiritual by some divine orders as mentioned but out of his loins.

[259] The *Mediatrix* was described in the Roman Catholic Mariology where it states that the Virgin Mary is the Mediator for the salvation of redemption by her son

simply be promoting the promise of the prophecy concerning the Davidic monarchy to no effect.

This issue of the Mariology led to the request of many like the nuns to evoke the words, "Mary, Mother of Jesus."

This Mariology declared the *presumptuous* attitude against the *holy covenant*, neglecting the real purpose of the Messiah and His work of redemption. He clearly stated that "no man cometh unto the Father but through Him" (John 14:6, 13–18 KJV). Obviously the message He is giving us is that redemption comes not through Mary, His mother, or His father (Joseph), but Yeshua (Jesus).

So by this manner, the Mediatrix and author of salvation, who is also the mediator between Yahweh and man, was separated from the holy covenant and replaced with "Mary, Mother of Jesus" as the author and redeemer of the covenant.

This being confirmed in 1854 with the support of an overwhelming majority of Roman Catholic bishops proclaiming Mary's Immaculate Conception, I say, disrespects the original word used by the prophet Isaiah.[260] The prophet used the word *halma*,[261] which simply expresses his knowledge of the maiden at or after birth. As a matter of fact, if the prophet had used the word *bethulah*,[262] then we could relate the expression as such that she was a virgin, but we can't make the expression to suit our own desires and fantasies.

At the first Vatican Council, the majority of councilors requested to add "immaculate virgin" to the Hail Mary, and some also requested the dogma of the Immaculate Conception be included in the creed of the Catholic Church; however, it was opposed by Pope Pious IX.

Pious IX, although opposing the inclusion of this dogma in the Catholic creed, strongly enforced a close relation between the

---

Jesus Christ, and that He bestows grace through her.

[260] Isaiah 7:14.

[261] This Hebrew word means damsel or young maiden, which is not precisely a virgin.

[262] This Hebrew word means virgin.

Immaculate Conception of Mary and her being taken up into heaven. This then indicated to me that Pope Pious IX is saying Mary was taken up to Yahweh and His throne, making her His goddess by reason of her conception.

During the first Vatican Council, the papal kingdom administered under the leadership of Pope Pious IX was determined to make his word a declarative and unquestionable utterance. The decisions were made, and the pope's words were pronounced to be infallible.[263] This first council was cut short because of the invasion of the Papal States by Victor Emanuel II in 1870.

Pope Pious died in 1878 and left behind all these legacies of conspired traditional and signed philosophical agreement for the papacy to follow, which all popes accepted and continued.

Exploitation of the Congo

> *"And he shall do exploits, and return to his own land."*
> *Daniel 11:28 (KJV)*

Another phantom against the holy covenant was this giant of Belgium. His work was according to the exploitation within the Congo. Though he could not reach the safe land of the Ethiopians,[264] his forceful deeds were performed on the natives of the Congo.

This phantom was Leopold II, king of Belgium from 1865 until his death in 1909 at the age of seventy-four. His sister was Emperor Carlota of Mexico, and he was also cousin to Queen Victoria of England.

Leopold's marriage to Marrie Henrietta, archduchess of Austria in 1839, also meant he was part of the Hapsburg family.

---

[263] This means that they declared him incapable of error.
[264] Ethiopians are known now to be a mixed Semitic breed of people, which some are namely called the Black Jews.

In 1862, one of his daughters married Prince Napoleon Victor Bonaparte, head of the Bonaparte family at that time. This marriage influences additional hierarchy in both the Leopold family and the Bonaparte family. Napoleon Victor Bonaparte[265] later became Napoleon III of France.

The Leopold family became a strong force. Leopold was king of Belgium and cousin of the powerful Queen Victoria of the United Kingdom, and he was adopted into two of the most powerful families of Europe, namely the Hapsburg family of Austria and the Bonaparte family of France. I guess one could say that these were part of the factors that made Leopold the giant that he was.

Now colonization was the next order of the day even up to the end of the nineteenth century. Colonization was set to authorize a labor force, which was beneficial only to the colonial masters, and such life also disintegrated the families and family life of those held in labor. Sometimes the forceful laborers were persecuted until death.

Many parts of the African continent were being depressed by the colonial masters of Western and Northern Europe. Many European countries found it an interest to acquire colonial territories to benefit their homeland.

In 1876, King Leopold II of Belgium decided to organize a body called the International African Society disguised as an International Scientific Association.

With the support of a famous explorer name Henry Morton Stanley, through the channel of many disguised efforts, the king of Belgium set up an established colony in the Congo region.

During these times many European countries were at rival about ownership of lands on the African continent. The Congo region was one of these territories.

As a result of these rivalries, the Berlin Conference of 1884–85 was called. During the Berlin Conference, fourteen representatives of

---

[265] Emperor Napoleon III assisted Pope Pious IX during the harassment and pursuits by Victor Immanuel.

the European countries and the United States of America recognized Leopold II and Stanley as governor of most of the area they laid claim on. The others were divided between Great Britain, France, Portugal, Spain, Italy, and Germany.

In 1885, the region claimed and occupied by King Leopold II of Belgium was called the Congo-free state. It existed now as the Democratic Republic of the Congo.

Leopold II established a rubber industry in the Congo and forced the natives to labor for him.

During these times the enslaved workers who could not work and those who refused to work would have their hands and certain parts of their bodies mutilated, and then they were left bleeding to death. Pregnant mothers would work through pregnancy and give birth in the fields.

Estimates of the overall death toll ranged from two to fifteen million.

Encyclopedia Britannica estimates the population losses at about thirty million people. Some individuals claim that the accurate figures could not be determined, as recordings were not available.

By 1896, sleeping sickness had killed up to five thousand people in the village of Lukolela on the Congo River. Sleeping sickness and smallpox spread so quickly that it decimated the population.

Because of these outrageous exploitations and the widespread human rights abuses in the nineteenth century, an international investigative was declared.[266]

Auspices of the Congo Reform Association led by British diplomat Roger Casement and a former shipping clerk E. D. Morel made many reports on Leopold II's secret society of murderers.

Leopold II's excuse for his inhumane action was that bringing Roman Christianity to the Congo *outweighed a little starvation*. This excuse of Leopold could be interpreted as to say that the

---

[266] Roger Casement and E. D. Morel formed the first massive human rights movement supported by an American humorist named Mark Twain.

enforcement of Roman Christianity was more harmful than his principle in the Congo.

The slaughtering and torturing of Leopold II's rubber workers in the Congo continued until the turn of the century when the conscience of the Western world forced Brussel to call an end to Leopold II's doings. It was said that France, Germany, and Portugal adopted the principles of Leopold II on their rubber plantations as well.

Leopold II's statue was erected twice but was struck down by the people of the Democratic Republic of the Congo because many did not see him in a positive light. Leopold II, the king of Belgium, died in 1909.

The First Italian–Ethiopian Invasion

> *Daniel 11:29–30 (KJV) says, "And at the time appointed he shall return, and come toward the south: but it shall not be as the former or the latter. For the ships of CHITTIM shall be against him."*

Chittim[267] is noted as an island or as an isle below the south of Asia Minor. This isle was originally the coastal area of the Phoenicians. The Phoenicians, as already discussed in previous chapters, were from a Semitic Afro-Asiatic race, and sometimes they were referred to as the Canaanites. The Phoenicians' trading coastline was between Chittim and the cities of Tyre, Sidon, and others.

The prophet Daniel linked the period of his era to the future. He does this when he uses the phrase "ships of Chittim." Usually this coastline was protected by ships, and of course in those days wars were more prominent on seas because of the continuous battle for trade and port dominancy.

---

[267] Cyprus was the early name given to the place of which Chittim was a part. For some reason, the whole land is now called Chittim.

The prophet, citing the future, indicates that the attack along the coastline of Chittim would be an invasion against the Semites race of the Afro-Asiatic group, "but it will not be as the former[268] or latter"[269] attacks in earlier times, for the Semitic race will be organized, standing up against whoever should come through the coastline against them.

The conquest against Assyria and Babylon by the Macedonian king was referred to, by some theologians, as the declaration of the prophecy in Numbers 24:24 (KJV), where the Scripture speaks of a set of people who "shall come from the coastline of Chittim to destroy Asshur[270] and Eber."[271] Others thought this referred to the Romans from the Mediterranean coastline of Italy.

On the contrary, reading from Numbers 24:21–24, we see the prophetical pronunciation spoken by the prophet Balaam as concerning the dwelling[272] place of the Kenites[273] and how they would be conquered by the king of Asshur. At the end, although the translation says "ships shall come from the coastline of Chittim and conquered the land of Asshur and Eber," it does not necessarily mean that these "ships" would originate *from* this "coast line". The prophecy could be relating to a fleet of ships coming *from* the north coast, taking the route of "the coastline of Chittim".

However, the coastline was rooted in the region of Canaan (Joppa to even Sidon) and across to Cyprus. Whether one pronounces the place as Citium or Cittim, the prophet was referencing *this* (between Cyprus and the Phoenicians coastline) coastline.

---

[268] Macedonian conquest 333–331 BC

[269] The Romans (Scipio) conquest 149–146 BC

[270] Asshur is referred to as present-day Assyria.

[271] Eber is referred to as some areas of the Assyria and across the Euphrates River bordering the Medes and Iraq (or Babylon).

[272] Their dwellings were on the plains of Canaan.

[273] The Kenites were from the descendant of Ken, otherwise called Kain. Although some historians referred to them as descendant of Cain, their origin is not specifically known, but they also resided in the land of Canaan (Judah in northern Israel).

At the time of the revelation of the prophecy of Asshur (Assyria) and Eber (Babylon and Medo-Persia), when King Nebuchadnezzar and King Cyrus the Medes took over the Kenites lands, the Phoenicians were already in control of the domain of this coastline from as early as the eighth century, becoming dominant at sea by 500 BC. It could not have been the Phoenicians that the prophecy was referring to as coming "out of the coastline of Chittim," fulfilling the prophecy against the Kenites. It had to be someone coming from the north. However, Alexander, the Macedonian[274] king, came *along* (not from) the coastline of Chittim and conquered the Phoenicians, absorbed the Kenites as well, and then passed *through* Canaan, Assyria, and Babylon between 333 and 331 BC.

The Phoenician coastline was then destroyed by the Macedonian conquest, but it was later rebuilt by the Seleucids Empire.

As time went by, the Phoenicians who inhabited the land of Tunisia[275] advanced in commerce and trading. At this time for the Phoenicians, Carthage became the main trading port via the coastline of Chittim.

Dominance for commerce and other trading ports encouraged rivalries between Carthage and Italy, especially Rome. The ongoing war[276] between them both led to the devastation of the Phoenicians' trading port via the coastline of Chittim. By the end of the Third Punic War (149–146 BC), the Italians had destroyed the city of Carthage and their coastline completely.

So here we see that the first destruction of the coastline was done by the Macedonians in 333–331 BC and then by the Italians in 149–146 BC. On this account the prophet determined the third invasion as "not like the former or latter" (see Daniel 11:30 KJV),

---

[274] The apocryphal book of the Maccabaeus represents Chittim as the land of the Macedonians in Numbers 24:24. The Latin Vulgate uses Italy in Numbers 24:24 instead of Chittim.

[275] The city of Carthage was founded on Tunisia.

[276] See chapter 6.

but that this time these natives will be ready to defeat the northern people that "shall come along (through) the coastline of Chittim."

History detailed a particular ethnic Semitic[277] group of people who, according to their genealogical point of view, were defined as the Black Jewish race from the Solomonic dynasty. Their home was the land of Ethiopia, deep in the south of Africa. Ethiopia was situated parallel to the Red Sea coastline just below Eritrea.

While the Ethiopians were enjoying their lot of the continent of Africa, the ethnic groups in the Congo were under exploitation by the king of Belgium and other European powers that were traveling along the coastline of Chittim, until they reached the Ethiopian borders.

The eyes of the Europeans were then fixed on these lands of the Ethiopian ethnic groups. As for the Italians, who had an appetite for more lands within the African continent, they continued thinking of ways to catapult themselves diplomatically across the borders of the Ethiopians.

Unfortunately in 1889 after the death of Ethiopian Emperor Yohannes IV, the country was plunged into great disorder. On March 25 of the same year the Shewa ruler, Menelik II, having conquered Tigra and Amhara with the support of Italy, declared himself emperor of Ethiopia.

Barely a month later on the May 2, a treaty of amity was signed between the Ethiopians and the Italians, giving the Italians control over Eritrea along the Red Sea coast northeast of Ethiopia. In return, the Ethiopians receive the recognition of Menelik's ruler ship in Ethiopia.

However, Menelik II of Ethiopia found out that the Italian's version of the treaty expressed a different kind of acknowledgment than the one that had been written in Amharic.

The Italian's version declared Italy as sole protectorate and governance of Ethiopia, while the Amharic version barely stated

---

[277] This ethnic Semitic group of people, though not living at the coast of Chittim, were descendant of the *Jewish* race.

any business of trade consultation with Italy. The Italian diplomats claimed, however, that the version they had was verified, and Menelik signed a modified copy of the treaty.

As the Ethiopian emperor refused to abide by the Italian's claimed copy of the treaty, a military solution was planned for Ethiopia.

One must remember that Daniel 11:27 speaks concerning the so-called treaties of the north with the south in that these treaties hold only for the time appointed. In contrast, verse 29 said that "at the time appointed *he* [Italy] shall come toward the south, but it shall not be as the former or latter."

So at this time the treaty of peace was spoiled by Italy. His diplomatic gesture to gain control of the Ethiopians' lands to exploit more people and commit work against the holy covenant was wittingly in his grasp.

To achieve this, the Italian government's tactical response was to bring divisions amongst the Ethiopian borders. He thought that separating them would bring chaos and split up of individual tribes. This would then shrink the tribe of Menelik in number and allow the Italians to bring about an easier victory against the Ethiopian king. He thought that once he had defeated the Ethiopian king, the others at the borders would be in his grasp.

Things did not turn out as the Italian *vile* person planned. Instead, all of the ethnic Tigrayan or Amharic people flocked to the aid of Emperor Menelik, displaying both nationalistic and anti-Italian feeling, while the uncertain loyalty of the sultan of Aussa were watched by imperial *garrisons*[278].

Because of the earlier defeats of the other ethnic groups on the borders of Ethiopia, the Italians thought it would be easy to defeat the forces of King Menelik II.

As the Italian army occupied the Tigrian capital, Adwa, in December 1894 after they crushed the rebellious forces of Bahta

---

[278] Stationed troops

Hagos, who had fought in support of Mengesha, they then went against Mengesha in January 1895 and fought at the Battle of Coatit. In retreat, Mengesha ran for safety.

At this time Menelik II decided to seek help from France by offering a treaty of alliance. Menelik thought that if they made an alliance with France, then the deceitful, treacherous, and *land-greedy* Italians would reconsider attacking Ethiopia.

Sadly for the king of Ethiopia, the French were in no way abandoning the Treaty of Bardo. This treaty was signed approval to help the Italians gain control of that part of the African continent, and the French would gain control of Tunisia, which was in their best interest. On this note Emperor Menelik and his fellow ethnic groups were left alone to defend Ethiopia.

In December 1895, the emperor of Ethiopia then made a proclamation asking for help from the tribesmen of Shewa to join his army against the Italians.

In the same year the Italians and Menelik's army clashed at Amba Alagi. During the battle the Italians underestimated the strength of the Ethiopian forces, which led to the Italians retreating to Eritrea.

The following day the Italians were quickly surrounded by Ras Makonnen's Ethiopian troop in Maqele. To prevent the Ras from attacking his army, the Italian commander Oreste Baratieri surrendered and used his negotiating skills with the intention to outsmart Ras Makonnen. However, his effort failed.

Emperor Menelik's, accompanied by his queen, Taytu Betul, and led large with his forces early January 1896 against the Italians who then surrendered. Menelik generously provided them with mules and escorted them out of Maqele with their weapons.

Francesco Crispi was not willing to accept an Italian defeat by a non-European country, so he ordered Commander Baratieri to prepare for another campaign, which resulted in the Battle of Adowa in March 1896.

Commanding General Baratieri thought of surprising the Ethiopians, so he planned an early morning attack, thinking his enemy would still be asleep after a celebrative feast.

Evidently the Ethiopians were religiously cultured and had devoted themselves to early morning worship.

As they made their way to the early morning service, the Ethiopians learned of the Italian advance and made ready their instruments of war and set off to meet the Italian soldiers.

The Italian army was crushed and 9,500 to twelve thousand died in addition to the two thousand *Eritrean Askaris*[279] who were captured and killed.

In the end the imprisoned Italian were treated fairly, while eight thousand captured Eritreans Askaris who were regarded as traitors against Ethiopia had their right hands and left feet amputated.

The Battle of Adowa in 1896 was listed as having the greatest number of European causalities during the nineteenth century. Even Napoleon's confrontation could not compare with this figure.

After the Italian–Ethiopian war at Adowa, riots broke out in many Italian-conquered cities, and within a few weeks the Crispi government collapsed because of the interventions of foreign powers.

The Treaty of Addis Ababa was secured in October, which marked the borders of Eritrea, forcing the Italians to recognize Ethiopian independence.

Delegations from the United Kingdom, France, and other European powers whose colonial claim lay next to Ethiopia visited the Ethiopian capital to negotiate newly formed treaties with the newly proven Ethiopian sovereignty.

During his era Menelik developed and expanded the Solomonic estate as no ruler had before.

---

[279] *Askaris* (Arabic word meaning soldiers) are local soldiers serving in the armies of the European colonial powers in Africa. These Eritrean Askaris were from the land Eretrea.

Chapter 25

The Twentieth-Century Consummation against the Holy Covenant

Therefore he shall be grieved, and return, and have indignation against the Holy Covenant: so shall he do; he shall even return, and have intelligence with them that forsake the Holy Covenant.

—Daniel 11:30

After the defeat of the north (Italy) by the south (Ethiopia) in 1896, many constitutional reforms were made by the papacy and other European countries. Conferences were called to gain the support of the European United Nations against the dominant rule of the southern[280] nations.

The main idea was to put an end to the ruling sovereignty of the south and make classifications of their cultures by modernizing their aspects of religions to the northern and western world.

An appeal was also made on November 30, 1919, by Pope Benedict XV, inviting all Catholics worldwide to make sacrifices for the Catholic mission, and he also said that these missions should foster local cultures and not import European culture. However, in the end many European cultures and ways were imposed upon the Africans and Asians because during the time of Pope Pius XI (1922–1939),

---

[280] Two of these southern nations were part of the African continents, and another was the Muslims provinces.

those who had accepted the ways of the Catholic faith and became missionaries had to abandon their cultural ways or face deportation.

Rules of governance and politics also became an issue, in that Communist, capitalist, and Socialist were constantly under pressure by the papacy, especially Pope Pius XI.

Opposing his predecessors from the nineteenth century who favored monarchy and dismissed democracy, Pope Pius took a pragmatic approached toward a different form of government.

In 1933, the pope addressed the Roman Catholic Church in the republic of Spain. At this gathering he advised that the Church was not bound to any one form of government, unless that government instilled the right of the citizens by giving them the privilege to exercise the principles of the Christian oracles according to the Roman Catholic faith. On this ground he implied that he would be against monarchies and their rule. He argued that one man should not acquire the power to govern a country throughout his life unless politically and freely chosen[281] by the people.

Many countries in Africa, Asia, Arabia, and the Middle East whose people accepted this culture began to fall apart. The citizens of these countries ignorantly denounce their cultural aspects because of the imposed politics and human rights offered by the Catholic Church. This decision actually helped to foster Catholic doctrine in some of these countries.

Democracy for the Catholic Church became the leading course for the nineteenth and twentieth century. In doing so, the pope and his entourage set out to stem one-man governance, which Communists encouraged.

Although the pope's reason of opposition against capitalism and socialism produced some humanitarian gains, such as employment, salaries, working legislations, impact against slavery and colonization and its kind, there were stipulations to adhere to as well.

---

[281] This is a political election where one has the right of choice. This right is part of a democracy.

With the intent of victory, the pope supported the northern kingdom by blessing the European countries, sending them out to battle with whatsoever force was necessary. And force was used against any nation that opposed them on the issues.

Of course "arms did stand" on the pope's side. Many attacks were organized against those who opposed the Catholic faith, many with the usage of arms. When we read about the Crusade, books tell us that the pope "preached a holy war," and of course the use of arms was ratified. On the other hand, the usage of arms was inevitable, for the Saracens and other opponent took up the same practice. As the word of the prophet says "And arms shall stand on his part" (Daniel 11:31 KJV), so we see it fulfill.

The Catholic Church set precedents in various countries, and these precedents proved themselves fruitful because some of these countries that were not of Catholic faith at that time, have then adopted Western culture and governance.

As time went by, some of those who ascended to the Vatican throne continued to *diverge* from the *holy covenant*, while some individuals in the political office within the European empire were then strengthened with prejudicial tendencies against the holy covenant.

They were three characters from the nineteenth and the twentieth centuries who acted upon issues that were seemingly contrary to the holy covenant—some popes, including Pope Pius IX (1846–1878) and Pope Benedict XVI (2005–2014); Benito Mussolini (1922–1943), who was prime minister during the reign of Victor Immanuel III, king of Italy (1900–1946); and Adolf Hitler, chancellor and then later president of Germany (1933–1945).

The Pope's Acts Differed from the Holy Covenant

I don't think these popes acted on a willful platform but surely their actions caused concern.

For instance, Pope Pius IX called the first Vatican Council in 1869, and Pope John XXIII called the second Vatican Council in 1962, where both acted in their best concern regarding the beautification of the mother of Yeshua the Christ, but the procedures needed validity. Pope Benedict XVI also does his part and endorses the Mariology and her Mediatrix of grace.

Although Pope Paul VI, Pope John Paul I, Pope John Paul II, and Pope Benedict XVI did not speak much on the issues of the Mariology, they were present during the second Vatican Council, which completely inaugurated its purpose and blessing. The commission of the second Vatican Council was then closed by Pope Paul VI in 1969 AD.

> *"And they shall pollute the sanctuary of strength, and shall take away the daily sacrifice, and they shall place the abomination that makes desolate" (Daniel 11:31 KJV).*

At this final council, many aspects of religion were discussed, but the main concern was the dogma of grace concerning Mary.

After many discussions, Mary was then made the ultimate issue concerning our *daily sacrifice* and throne of grace, which had previously been the Messiah.

Mary as the major step to salvation or Mediatrix of Grace highlighted by Pope Pius IX saying that "all Christians achieved all things through Mary."

Pope Pius X (1903–1914), who ascended to the Vatican throne after Pope Leo XII (1878-1903), also encouraged frequent reception of Holy Communion of the Eucharist, saying that the "Holy Communion is the safest and shortest way to heaven." These words do not keep with the original teaching of the ancient gospel, giving the impression that there is an easier or shorter way to get to heaven.

Pope Benedict XV (1914–1922) placed statues of Mary in many public places and declared a day of feast to celebrate Mary as the center of all grace, which undermined the Messiah. In this instance the commandment[282] of Moses stating that "one should not make unto them any craven image" was made void.

Many sanctuaries had statues of Mary dressed[283] in priestly robes, and believers bowed down in reverence at the statues' feet, beseeching Mary for the forgiveness of their sins. Many prayed to Mary in various ways, disrupting the daily focus on Christ and His death on the cross.

Scripture speaks concerning the Messiah, saying two thousand years ago that "one should ask anything in my name, and that no man can ask anything of Yahweh but by Him, Christ" (John 14:6; 15:16).

Although there was confusion over this doctrine, some Christians did not adhere to it but held on to the fullness of their Elohim and Christ (Yashua). Such people held on to the fullness and were evangelistic, teaching many to be strong and giving the one true Elohim praise by calling upon His name.[284]

As Daniel said, "And such as do wickedly against the covenant shall he corrupt by flatteries: but the people that do know Yahweh shall be strong, and do exploits" (Daniel 11:32 KJV).

Mussolini against the Holy Covenant

Fascism Inauguration by Mussolini and Hitler

During Pope Pius XI's reign (1922–1939), there emerged two main tyrants of the north, namely Benito Mussolini of Italy and Adolf Hitler of Germany.

---

[282] Exodus 20:3–5.

[283] Statues were clothed to show royalty, and the people presented themselves at their feet, giving reverence. Although Pope Benedict XV spoke out publicly against the misuse of these statues, they initially convinced the Christians of Mary's sacredness.

[284] Compare Daniel 9:26–27 with Daniel 11:31–32.

Mussolini's (1922–1943) militancy reign made him His Excellency Benito Mussolini, head of the government, the *Il duce*[285] of Fascism, and founder of the empire. Mussolini was one of the key individuals in the creation of Fascism.

In 1917, Mussolini at age 34, with the help of a British intelligence, started out as an editor of a right-wing newspaper and with the help of this newspaper profession he was abled to spread daily propaganda. Mussolini decided that socialism as a doctrine had largely been a failure, so in 1918, he made a declaration[286] asking for a man "ruthless and energetic enough to make a *clean sweep*"[287] to revive the Italian nation.

By 1919, he proclaimed socialism as a doctrine dead and that "it continued as a *grudge*[288] against other entities". On March 23, he reformed the Milan Fascio as the Fascist Italian Combat Squad, consisting of two hundred members and resulting in the formation of the fascist group on March 31, 1919. The Nationalist Fascist Party became fully active in 1921.

Mussolini and his Fascist Party marched into Rome and declared himself prime minister of Italy on October 31, 1922. This was encouraged by the ruling monarch, King Victor Emmanuel III of Italy (900–1946), who was not in favor of the present Prime Minister, Luigi Facta. Victor Emmanuel III gave Mussolini full support and his assistance with the Italian military.

In its earlier stages, Fascism opposed discrimination against class and supported nationalistic sentiment with the goal of strong unity. These were some of the ideas meant to raise Italy up to the level of its great Roman past.

---

[285] *Il Duce* is an Italian term "the leader."

[286] Probably also wrote it in his daily newspaper, *Il Popolo d'Italia.*

[287] *Clean sweep* would mean to do what is necessary or removed all obstacles.

[288] Probably what Mussolini is saying is that *Socialism* is like a stumbling block, not letting go, blocking the way for the future.

Later, Fascism encouraged war and aggression as well as the oppression of communism. It also promoted an alternative to democracy.

Mussolini and his Fascist members became a revolutionary and traditionalist sect and vastly different from anything else in the political climate at the time. It was sometimes described as the Third Way.[289]

During the Italian tyrant's first year in office, he developed the attitude of a totalitarian leader and thus began to perform as a dictator, calling himself the Supreme Leader (*the II Duce*).

By 1925, on Christmas Eve, a law was passed, changing Mussolini's formal title from president of the council of ministers to head of the government. Now he was no longer accountable to parliament and could only be removed by the king. Thus, he was only person who could determine the agenda of the state.

Fascism then became the order of the day. Benito and his Fascist members proclaimed that Fascism was the doctrine of the twenty-first century, replacing liberalism, communism, and democracy.

Democracy and its rules became impractical as Benito turned from his earlier principles, which he had maintained at the beginning of his Fascist government. He had claimed that his party would instill justice and equality for the people.

In 1927, Mussolini was baptized by a Roman Catholic priest in order to appease the fearful Catholics in opposition. These Catholics were skeptical of him because of the continuous ill treatment the Italian government had been inflicting on the church, including the removal of the papal properties and the blackmail of the papal power.

Italy, however, existed under the reign of Mussolini as a one-party state, and the people who opposed his Fascist government were outcast and destroyed by 1928.

---

[289] The Third Way is a political way of governance other than democracy and communism.

After the year 1929, Benito thought that getting the papal chorea on his side would convince many Catholics to support him in his cause against communism.

Catholic gave early support to Mussolini, yet there were still many differences of opinions between Pope Pius XI and the Italian's dictator.

The Italian tyrant bombarded the ethics and morals of the Catholic teachings. Teachers in schools and universities had to swear with an oath to defend and uphold the sentiment of the Fascist regime. Speech and news editing by the press were also controlled by this regime, which made the laws of *democracy* ineffective.

Benito Mussolini and his tirades against the laws of humanitarian consciousness highlight his plan "against the holy covenant."

This blessing and overspreading of the children of Israel, as it is said, was a promise made by the Eloi (God) of Israel, and this promise was treated as a covenant between Yahweh and His people.

In earlier days of the Nationalist Fascist Party, Mussolini had a relationship with the Jewish author named Margherita, the "Jewish Mother of Fascism," as she has been called. On account of the relationship, Mussolini hypocritically respected the existence of certain Jewish communities at the time.

During that time, although Fascism had been constantly changing its main position on racialism between 1920s and 1930s, Italian Fascism never discriminated against the Italian Jewish community because Mussolini recognized that a small contingent of Jews had lived there "since the days of the kings of Rome, and so they should not be disturbed."

The relations between Margherita and Mussolini in collaboration with the undisturbed Jewish community resulted in some Jews taking sides with Mussolini and his fascist group. Some of these unscrupulous Jews joined the National Fascist Party. One such person was Ettore Ovazza, who in 1935 founded the *Jewish Fascist Paper.*

According to Scripture:

> *And they that understand among the people shall instruct many: yet they shall fall by the sword, by flame, by captivity and by spoil many days. Now when they shall fall, they shall be help with a little help: but many shall cleave to them by flatteries. And some of them of understanding shall fall, to try them, purge them and make them white, even to the time of the end: because it is yet for a time appointed. (Daniel 11:33–35 KJV)*

One gives thanks and praises that although many Jews adopted the ways of deceit showed to them, a few stood fast and instructed many in the right path, having faith in the promise according to the seed of Israel and the Messiah according to the seed of David.

Against Jewish Blessing and Overspreading

By 1928, Mussolini had already realized the growth of the *Black Jewish* people (Ethiopian) and other colored nations that were striving to exceed the population of the Italian nation, and he was furious and suspicious of the danger that this growth represented.

He then acted deceitfully and contrary to his former concept concerning races and the free will of the Jewish people and emphasized the importance of the future of his Italian race.

His speech at that time was as follows:

> When the city dies, the nation is deprived of young lives and the blood of new generations, in which the city is now made up of people who are old and degenerated and cannot defend itself against younger people which launches an attack on the now unguarded frontier ... This will happened, and

not just to cities and nations, but on an infinitely greater scale: the whole White race, the western race can be submerged by other colored races which are multiplying at a rate unknown to our race.

Mussolini and Hitler's Laws of Anti-Semitism

By then the relationship between Mussolini and Adolf Hitler of Germany had become a contentious one. Although Hitler regarded Mussolini as a benefit to the future, Mussolini had little regard for Hitler, especially after the Nazis of Germany assassinated his friend and ally Engelbert Dollfuss.[290]

After the assassination of Dollfuss, Mussolini attempted to distance himself from Hitler by rejecting Hitler's form of racialism and anti-Semitism that German radicals had endorsed.

These two were in a war of words against each other for some time. The Germans called the Italians a mongrelized race, while Mussolini retaliated by laughing at the Germans' claim of racial purity on several occasions.

Mussolini suggested the Nazi decree, which stated that all Germans must carry a passport with either their Aryan or Jewish racial affiliation marked on it. He then laughed at such notion and proclaimed in his 1934 speech, "Does there exist a German race?" And he answered himself, "A Germanic race does not exist."

In 1935, the destiny of the two was determined, and they both reunited in friendship and formed the Axis Powers.

Two of their main policies were anticommunism and racialism, which included anti-Semitism. By 1938, the influence of Hitler had overshadowed Mussolini once again, and the Rome-Berlin relation with the introduction of the *Manifesto of Race*[291] was seemingly clear.

---

[290] Engelbert Dollfuss was an Austrofascist dictator of Austria in 1933.

[291] The *Manifesto of Race* (Racial Manifesto) was a manifesto published on the 14th July 1938. This was a set of laws in Fascist Italy, which were regarded as antiemetic

This manifesto was modeled by the Nazi Nuremberg Law, which enforced the stripping of the Italian Jewish citizenship of any profession or position in the government. The German influence on the Italian policy upset the established balance in Fascist Italy and proved highly unpopular among most Italians. In this case, even Pope Pius XI and his successor, Pope Pius XII (1939–1958) protested against these new Fascist laws.

Then Mussolini adopted the *Manifesto of Race* in 1938 in order to strengthen Italy's relations with Germany. His diplomatic pattern with Hitler and the manifesto was just a way of building that bridge between him and the German *Tyrant,* in getting the go-ahead when confronted by the League of Nation, all but confirming an attack on the Black Semitic race of Ethiopia.

Renouncing and Denouncing the Gods

Mussolini's onward actions manifested the declaration of the prophecy and its revelation as pointed out by the Scripture, that such "vile person" as "king of the north shall do according to his will." Notwithstanding, "he shall worship the god of forces," excelling in luxuries and power.

> *Daniel 11:36 (KJV) says, "And the king shall do according to his will: and he shall exalt himself, and magnify himself above every god, and shall speak marvelous things against the Elohim of gods."*

---

in nature, disallowing the Jews to hold any government position and stripped them of their Italian citizenship.

Then Daniel 11:38–39 (KJV) says,

> *"But in his estate he shall honor the god of forces: and a god whom his father knew not shall he honor with gold, and silver, and with precious stones and pleasant things."*

> *"Thus shall he do in the most strong holds with a strange god, whom he shall acknowledge and increased with glory: and he shall cause them to rule over many, and shall divide the land for gain."*

Benito Mussolini then declared himself an atheist, which prior to his conversion[292] was not widely accepted or appreciated. His earliest political pamphlet was titled "God Does Not Exist." During public speeches he even dared Yahweh to strike him dead.

He continued to say that "religion is a germ of mental disease that encouraged a pathological[293] reaction on mankind, and that the god of the theologians is the creation of their empty heads."

Two of his main proclamations were that the "history of the saints is mainly the history of insane people" and also that "science is now in process of destroying religious dogma." He essentially thought that the dogma of the divine creation was absurd.

Denouncing the ways of Catholicism and Christendom and the God of his fathers, Benito forcibly spoke out against those who thought that being religious was a matter of one's conscience, encouraging conversion to a better way of life. He announced that "science had proved that Yahweh did not exist" and that "the Jesus of history was an ignorant Jew whose family thought up a mad religion."

---

[292] Mussolini was baptized by a Roman Catholic priest in 1927.
[293] Symptoms caused by mental disorder.

Hitler against the Holy Covenant

Pope Pius XI realized that there was a greater evil than that of Communists, capitalists, liberals, and Fascists. The racism perpetrated by Hitler (1933-1945) was the most devastating of them all.

On October 15, 1918, Hitler went to the hospital, suffering from temporary blindness because he had been hit during a mustard gas attack. During this temporary blindness, English psychologist David Lewis and Bernard Horstmann suggested that Hitler's conversion[294] to anti-Semitism could have been influenced by this temporary blindness, which could have affected his nervous system. Hitler himself explained that he became convinced that the purpose of his life being spared was to "save Germany."

Hitler became involved in politics in 1919 and commenced his attack on the Jews during many public speeches in Germany.

On November 8, 1923, Hitler's Nazi Party copied Italy's Fascist ideas and imposed some of Benito's policies. The German *tyrant* also decided to emulate Benito's "March on Rome" by staging his own campaign in Berlin.

According to the plan, Hitler and his fellows decided to form a coup with the idea to overthrow the Bavarian government of Germany. They were not successful, as Hitler's coup was dismantled, and some of his members killed by the police force.

Hitler then contemplated suicide but was soon captured and charged with treason. His unsuccessful march on Germany resulted in the sentence of five years imprisonment in Landsberg prison on April 1, 1924. Hitler was so popular in prison that even the guards treated him with favor. On December 20 of the same year he was imprisoned, he was pardoned and released from jail by the Bavarian Supreme Court. The order was dated December 19, 1924, opposing the state prosecutor's objection of Hitler's early release.

---

[294] At that time this conversion was a disorder known as hysteria.

Adolf Hitler spent little more than a year in prison, and after he returned, he tried many more times to gain power legally but still failed.

The Nazi Party in Power

Adolf Hitler was still not a legal citizen of Germany, so he became a citizen in 1932. After he became a citizen, he then formed a party that won more than 35 percent of the vote during an election in April 1932. Although he lost the election, his party was seen as the realistic alternative in Germany.

During the reign of the victorious party, trouble developed in Germany, giving rise to a vote of no confidence.

The Nazi Party governed by Hitler gained power the morning after Hitler was sworn in as chancellor of Germany at the office of President Paul von Hindenburg on January 30, 1933.

With his new executive and legislative power after the Enabling Act, which was passed in March 1934, Hitler's government was encouraged to further suppress the remaining political oppositions. The Communist Party of Germany and the Social Democratic Party were banned. Eventually all other political parties were forced to dissolve. The Nazi Party then became a legal dictatorship and the only legal political party in Germany on July 14, 1934.

The aging President Paul von Hindenburg died on the August 2, 1934. Instead of holding a new presidential election, Hitler's cabinet passed a law proclaiming the presidency dormant and transferred the roll and powers of the head of state to Hitler as leader and chancellor (*führer* and *reichskanzler*). As head of state, Hitler now became the supreme commander of the armed forces. Now all soldiers and sailors joining the army swore their loyalties to Hitler.

During his reign more massive colonization of certain parts of Africa took place. Hitler having *craved* also for lands and power, at the conference of Leagues of Nations in 1935, he demanded for the return of the former German colonies in the African continent. These were lands confiscated by the Allies after World War I.

Hitler's Anti-Semitism and Nuremburg Law

Hitler's early manifestation of anti-Semitism was apparent in Vienna. Vienna had a large Jewish community, including Orthodox Jews who had fled the programs in Russia. Vienna was a bed of hotheaded traditional religious prejudice and nineteenth-century racism.

Influential ideologists and anti-Semitic individuals like Lanz von Liebenfels and Karl Lueger[295] led to Hitler and his quest against the Jews.

Hitler's earlier conviction and anti-Semitism was based on religious grounds, but later he developed a more gruesome attitude toward the holy covenant by introducing racism.

Strong words proceeded from the mouth of Hitler, another *tyrant* who proclaimed that his purpose of life was to exterminate the Jews of Europe.

Because of the promise Hitler gave in 1933 about the enactment of the Nuremberg Law,[296] the Germans became furious when they saw that it was not yet put in action. On the other hand, in the spring of 1935, the Gestapo's report stated that the rank and file of the Nazi Party was declaring that they had a solution in place to solve the Jewish problem. Nazi Party activists began a wave of assaults, vandalizing and boycotting the German Jews. To satisfy the Germans, Hitler then passed the Nuremberg laws on the eve of September 5, 1935.

---

[295] He was the founder of the Christian Social Party and Mayor of Vienna.

[296] This declares a ban on sexual intercourse and marriage between Aryans and Jewish Germans.

By this time the Italian–Ethiopian aggression was on the way. This was an attack that Hitler endorsed, thinking of it as a beneficiary factor to the European African colonization.

Hitler's quest against the holy covenant was to destroy the holy people of Yahweh and lay waste the Jewish nation. In so doing, this giant of the north slaughtered and persecuted many thousands of Jews.

Yahweh, knowing beforehand that Jerusalem would be targeted for ruin, had already scattered His holy people to the four corners of the earth so that when the appointed time arrives, "He shall *hiss* for them and have them returned in the last days."

More on Hitler and his atrocities against the Jews can be found in Robert G. L. Waite's book *The Psychopathic God: Adolph Hitler.*

Chapter 26

Characteristics of Adolf Hitler

There are three main characteristics that induced the personality of Adolf Hitler—Hitler's religious beliefs, his issues on sexuality, and his thirst for war

Hitler's Religious Beliefs

> *Daniel 11:36–37 (KJV) says, "And he shall exalt himself, and magnify himself above every god, and speak marvelous things against the Elohim of gods ... Neither shall he regard the God of his fathers ... nor regard any god: for he shall magnify himself above all."*

Adolf Hitler was raised by a Roman Catholic priest; however, after he left home, he abandoned mass attendance by not receiving any sacrament, although it was said that he continued to pay tribute and taxation to the church in Germany.

On many occasions in order to get the attention or admiration of the members of the hierarchy in the Christian Catholic Society, Hitler diplomatically spoke as if he was embedded in the heritage of the German Christian culture.

Hitler adored himself as a god and manifested his service as the revengeful messiah.

On the other hand, Hitler professed a belief in an Aryan faith, a messiah whom he claimed fought against Jews. For this cause he established a continuous fight against the said Jews whom he thought had rejected and crucified "his Jesus" (not the Jesus of Christianity).

Opposition by the papacy then gave him more reasons to attack the Catholic Church, for they had allied themselves with these Jews. Therefore, the German vile person's views were then strengthened, so he could abandon and destroy Christianity within the Reich (the army).

His public relationship with the Catholic Church in Germany worked as a strategy to meet his immediate political ambitions. His affiliation with the church only worked as a face card to get aid in creating the league of anti-Semitism.

Hitler's Issues on Sexuality

It is rumored that during his reign Hitler acted upon irregular sex relations, which this propagation fits according to the prophecy as follows: "Neither shall he regard the god of his fathers, nor the desire of woman" (Daniel 11:37 KJV).

Many have said that Hitler took women for granted. By using his charm convincingly, he solemnly turned around and broke their hearts.

Three of his close relationships with females went sour. Two of his lovers even committed suicide.

It is said that his ways with women allowed him to acquire sexual fetishes, including urolagnia.

Hitler disregarded the issues concerning a woman's freedom and privacies. He would forcefully imprison a woman and restrict her movement in public places unless she was chaperoned by him.

On account of his wide disrespect for women, Hitler's demonstration of love was repudiating and negatively determined by even him. This led to his private life being scrutinized by the eyes of the public. Many even thought he was a homosexual.

Lothar Machtan argued on the issue, and he wrote in a book titled *The Hidden Hitler*. This book gives details on Hitler's love affairs.

Many writers have confirmed Hitler's love life and sexual relationship with British Fascist Unity Mitford (a female). She had sexual encounters with a few of the Fascist soldiers, probably to get back at Hitler, who took advantage of her feelings for him.

Hitler's Thirst for War

> *Daniel 11:38–39 (KJV) says, "But in his estate shall he honor the god of forces … Thus shall he do in the most strong holds with a strange god, whom he shall acknowledge and increase with glory: and he shall cause them to rule over many, and shall divide the land for gain."*

Hitler used the estates of the country and his power to determine the destiny of Germany. In his hype "he honored the god of forces" and made the claim and acted as a warlord. The great warlord had his basic achievements and goals set out as planned. He thought that by using the intimidation of large forces, his plan could not be stopped.

Back in March 1933, Hitler presented a memo with a declaration advocating the following with Austria:

1. The restoration of the frontiers of 1914
2. The rejection of part five of the Treaty of Versailles
3. The return of the former German colonies in Africa
4. A German zone of influence in Eastern Europe as a goal for the future

However, at the World Disarmament Conference (WDC) in Geneva (Switzerland) in March 1933, British Prime Minister Ramsay MacDonald presented the compromised MacDonald Plan.

Hitler diplomatically endorsed the plan; guessing correctly that nothing would come of it and that he would win over London by making his government seem moderate and the French government seem obstinate.

This WDC in Geneva was held to resolve the deadlock between the French demand for *security* and the German demand for *equality of armament.*

The German *tyrant,* who decided to prove Germany as the *vile person,* was so caught up in his desires for arms and war that at every decisive moment his attitude involved bloodshed.

In June 1933, Hitler was forced to terminate the services of Alfred Hugenberg of the German National People's Party, who suggested a program of colonial expansion in both Africa and Eastern Europe while he was attending the London World Economic Conference.

This created a storm in Europe because the thought of this colonial expansion would involve war.

Hitler was furious with Alfred Hugenberg for these reasons. In 1933, Hitler had commented that Germany required several years of peace until it had sufficiently rearmed enough to risk war. Until then he introduced and encouraged a policy of caution. He stressed his supposed pacific goals and willingness to work within the international system in his *peace speeches* on May 17, 1993. However, after the first meeting of his cabinet in 1933, he privately made arrangements to accumulate funds to pay for rearmament. As the vile person and warlord, he never had been speedily interested in a colonial expansion of Africa but rather in control of Eastern Europe.

"Honoring the god of forces," Hitler then attempted to collaborate with Britain, thinking that with the help of England the goal of the national Socialist foreign policy would spell the destruction of Russia.

To start this initiative in May 1933, Alfred Rosenberg, head of the Nazi Party's Foreign Political Office, visited London as part of a disastrous effort to win an alliance with Britain.

Hitler was displeased that the *unified forces*[297] did not glorify him with his wishes, so he pulled Germany out of the League of Nations and World Disarmament Conference in October 1933. Hitler's reason for this was that the "French demand for security was a principal stumbling block for war."

Although behaving irrationally, Hitler was still advocating the necessity of an Anglo-German Alliance.

On this note, during a meeting with British Ambassador Sir Eric Phipps in November 1933, Hitler made a scheming offer. He said that Britain was to support a strong German Army of three hundred thousand men in exchange of Germany's support of a guaranteed British Empire. The British replied by saying that there should be a ten-year waiting period before any *support*[298] of Britain regarding that nature. Therefore, Hitler assumed that Britain strong ties with the Soviet Union encouraged this presumptuous reply.

Becoming creative and believing in the "god of force", Hitler developed relations with Poland. Secret talks in the fall[299] of 1933 with Poland led to the German-Polish Non-Aggression Pact in January 1934.

In March 1935, Hitler rejected part V of the Versailles Treaty. He did so by announcing publicly that the German Army would be expanding up to six hundred thousand men, which was six times the number stipulated by the Versailles Treaty.

---

[297] Some of these nations of this *unified force* were Britain, Italy, and France.

[298] Britain could not support such arms development because that would on the other hand encourage war, and also because of the Treaty of Versailles that was signed June 28th, 1919. This treaty was called and agreed by these countries including Britain and Germany to *impose* peace.

[299] Autumn

Hitler's rejection of the Treaty of Versailles was condemned by Britain, France, Italy, and the League of Nations. He convinced his opposition that his goals were aimed only at peace. On those grounds no actions were taken by the opposition, and German rearmament continued.

Later in Berlin in March 1935, Hitler held a series of meetings with British Foreign Secretary Sir John Simon. During these meetings the tyrant successfully evaded the British request for Germany's participation in the regional security pact by demanding the return of the former German colonies in Africa. This security pact was to serve as an Eastern European equivalent of the Locarno Pact.[300]

After all was said and done, Hitler, the German tyrant finally got his wish. On June 18, 1935, the Anglo-German Naval Agreement (AGNA) was signed in London. The agreement authorized the increase of the German Army by up to 35 percent so that it equaled the British Navy.

This marked one of the happiest days of Hitler's life because he thought that this agreement would give rise to an Anglo-German Alliance. However, the AGNA was made without consulting either France or Italy, directly undermining the League of Nations and the Treaty of Versailles.

In June 1935, Hitler then created the Anglo-German Alliance in collaboration with all other societies, coordinating them into a new Reich Colonial League, demanding again the restoration of the former German African colonies.

For the next few years this new Colonial League waged aggressive propaganda campaigns for colonial restoration.

---

[300] The Locarno Pact was formed after World War I at Locarno, Switzerland, in October 1925. It was signed on December 3 of that same year. It was a negotiated agreement in which Western European Allies and new states of central and Eastern Europe sought to secure the territorial peace and bring normality with defeated Germany.

In spite of all this so-call interest of Hitler toward these former German colonies in Africa, his intention was only to use this colonial demand as a negotiation tactic to force Britain to make an alliance with the Reich on German terms.

By then the two tyrants of the north (Benito of Italy and Hitler of Germany) had concluded the invasion of Abyssinia in 1936.

In October 1936, Hitler continued his thirst for war after he appointed freelance Nazi diplomat Joachim von Ribbentrop as German ambassador to the Court of St. James, sending him to get Britain to join the Anti-Comintern Pact.

An alliance was then declared between Germany and Italy by Count Ciano, foreign minister of Fascist dictator Benito Mussolini on November 25, 1936.

On the same day Germany concluded the Anti-Comintern Pact with Japan. Immediately invitations were sent out to Britain, China, Italy, and Poland to adhere to the joining of the pact. In reply, only the Italians agreed on signing the request, which they did in November 1937. During the latter half of 1937, Hitler abandoned his dream of an Anglo-German alliance, for the British leadership had turned down the offer to join the pact.

In September 1937, during a talk with the League of Nations' High Commission Carl Jacob Burckhardt for the free city of Danzig, Hitler made it clear that the British people were interfering in the German sphere of Europe. He then reconsidered not to have Britain as an ally within this *unit* (Anti-Comintern Pact), seeing that it would enable British authority to act as a stumbling block to German plans.

On November 5, 1937, Hitler then conveyed a war meeting with his war and foreign ministers. At this meeting he stated his intention to acquire "more living space" (Lebensraum) for the people of Germany. Therefore, he ordered they make plans for war against the east no later than 1943.

With his decisive tone, he told them that this war was meant to seize Austria and Czechoslovakia in the near future and that the time for action was now. His actual plan was to act before Britain and France would attain the lead in the European arms race.

This aggression against Austria and Czechoslovakia was intended to be the first localized war of its kind in Eastern Europe. This war was meant to agitate a final showdown with France and Britain against the Anti-Comintern Pact. Nevertheless, If the war between Germany and Austria proceeded, France would likely intervene because of the French affiliation with Eastern Europe, and if France intervened, then Britain would more likely to join as well?

On March 3, 1938, British Ambassador Sir Neville Henderson, who was still evasive in regard to joining the pact, met with Hitler with a proposal for an international *consortium* concerning Africa. This proposal stated that Germany would accept the leading role for much of the African colonies in exchange of a signed promise never to resort to war to change the monopoly already acquired by others. Hitler, who was now more interesting in acquiring more land in Eastern Europe for the benefit of the Germans, refused the British offer.

During his refusal he demanded all of the former[301] German African colonies, and that his interest is not in some international consortiums of running Africa.

In March 1938, Hitler pressured Austria into unification with Germany and made a triumphant entry into Vienna on March 14. By this time the glory of the "god of forces" was seemingly inevitable by the hand of the vile person.

Hitler then planned to strike at Czechoslovakia. He set his invasion for late September or early October 1938. After a suggestion[302] from Mussolini, he rejected his plan after many meetings with France,

---

[301] Some of these *former* German African colonies were German East Africa and German South West Africa. They were taken and scrambled among the Allies after World War II (WW II), which Britain received the larger share.

[302] Mussolini suggested that it will be a defeat on their part, seeing that Czechoslovakia will be strongly assisted by the Western Allies.

who claimed that they would honor their commitment demanded by the Franco-Czechoslovak Alliance of 1924, and the English Alliance and agreement that pledged to give France assistance.

Unsatisfied with the outcome and what he had been denied, Hitler invaded Western Poland on September 1, 1939. This aggravated the British and French, who declared war on Germany on September 3, 1939, although they did not act immediately.

Hitler built up a force on the German western frontier, and in April 1940, the Germans put their "god of forces" to the test again by invading Denmark and Norway.

In May 1940, Hitler's force attacked France and conquered Luxembourg, the Netherlands, and Belgium in the process. The attacks against France in May 1940 persuaded Benito Mussolini to side with Hitler in the war on June 10, 1940, forcing France to surrender on June 22, 1940. As a result of the overwhelming invasion, the British forces evacuated France by sea but continued to fight alongside other British dominions.

The vile person (Hitler) continued his quest for world power and ordered bombing raids on the United Kingdom. These were not as successful as he thought they would be. This failure propelled him to form the Tripartite Pact in Berlin on the 27 September 1940, with Saburo Kurusu of Imperial Japan and Galeazzo Ciano of Italy. The real aim of the Pact was to prevent the United States of America from interfering, giving aid to any European Allies, if war should break out between them (Allies of Euroupe) and any member of the Pact.

Hitler probably thought of the United States of America as a country that had fitted itself within the European sphere by using northern flatteries, and now placed itself as a stumbling block against the victory of an invasion on Britain.

The Tripartite Pact was then expanded to include Hungary, Romania, and Bulgaria. These nations collectively were known as the Axis Powers. By the end of October 1940, Hitler found himself equal in arms against the Europeans Allies and decided to attack Britain.

The German *vile person* ordered nightly bombings of British cities, including London, Plymouth, and Coventry.

Some historians claimed that the British refusal to surrender aggravated Hitler in such a way that he and his forces went and attacked the Soviet Union, which the Germans thought would be another[303] aid for the British.

As a result of this attack, Hitler seized large territories, including the Baltic States, Belarus, and Ukraine. Many Soviet forces were destroyed during the invasion.

Unfortunately for Hitler, his hope for a quick triumph failed because the German forces were stopped just outside of Moscow because of the Russian winter and fierce Soviet resistance in December 1941.

Hitler then decided to declare himself the final and supreme power of Europe by declaring war against the United States, but his thirst for war ultimately drove him to his end.

Hitler as well as Mussolini, who never accepted the United States as the *super state* of the north, now decided to seek their revenge against the United States with the help of the Axis Powers.

On December 11, 1941, four days after Pearl Harbor and the attack by the Empire of Japan, six days after the Nazi's German forces reached their closest point to Moscow, Hitler launched his attack against the United States. This attack then triggered World War II.

The force against the German *vile person* made up the largest coalition of its kind. It was comprised of the world's largest empire (the British Empire), the world's greatest industrial and financial power (the United States), and the world's largest army (the Soviet Union).

---

[303] The United States was considered as one of the sources to aid the British.

In late 1942, the German forces were defeated in the Second Battle of El Alamein.

In February 1943 at the Battle of Stalingrad, the German Sixth Army was destroyed.

After Operation Husky at the invasion of Sicily in 1943, Mussolini was dethroned and then surrendered to the Allies.

Throughout 1943–44, the Soviet Union and the Allies steadily forced Hitler and his armies into retreat along the Eastern Front.

In addition, on June 6, 1944, the Western Allies landed in Northern France, where Operation Overlord took effect, starting one of the largest operations in history. During this time certain realistic individuals in Germany thought that defeat was inevitable and plotted to remove Hitler from office. Hitler responded by ordering a savage reprisal resulting in the execution of more than 4,900 Germans.

By late 1944, the Red Army had driven the Germans back into Central Europe while the Western Allies continued to advance into Germany. At this point Hitler realized that he had lost the war, but he refused to acknowledge this fact to his fellow men. During that time he thought of making peace with Britain and America, but it was not sustainable. In April 1945, the Soviet forces attacked the outskirts of Berlin, but in defiance the tyrant was determined to die in the capital rather than surrender and admit defeat.

Throughout April 1945, Hitler continued to resist defeat and kept fighting even when he heard of the violent death of his companion Benito Mussolini on April 28, 1945.

On April 30, 1945, Hitler continued his fierce street-to-street combat, but as he realized that the Soviets could reach him, he decided to take his own life by shooting himself in the head.

On May 2 of the same year, Berlin was freed from Hitler's prevailing paws.

The Holocaust

During the reign of Hitler, many collaborative governments and recruits from countries committed to the Nazis had systematically killed somewhere between eleven and fourteen million people, including about six million Jews. This devastating act was called the Holocaust.

Daniel 11:33–35 (KJV) give the impression that the matter against the holy covenant shall be very destructive, that "some shall fall by the sword, and by flame, by captivity and by spoil many days." On account of the Holocaust, Hitler plainly declared this destruction in his "Prophecy Speech" on January 20, 1939.

> One thing I should like to say on this day, which may be memorable for others as well as us Germans: In the course of my life I have very often been a prophet, and I usually have been ridiculed for it. During the time of my struggle for power it was the first instance, the Jewish race, which only received my prophecies with laughter when I said that one day I would take over the leadership of the State, then of the whole nation, and there in after amongst many things settle the Jewish problem. The Jews laughter was uproarious, but I think that for some time now they have been laughing on the other side of their face. Today I will once more be that prophet. If the international Jewish financiers outside Europe should succeed in plunging the nations once more into a world war, the result will not be the bolshevization of the earth, and thus the victory of Jewry, but the annihilation of the Jewish race in Europe.

The proclamation of this *prophecy speech* by Hitler was pointing to the prophecy of Daniel 11:30 (KJV), which referred to the northern country returning "and have intelligence with them that forsake the holy covenant."

Since this speech, many debates concerning it have taken place. Historians such as Eberhard Jackel argued that shortly after Hitler had given his speech, he then committed himself to the genocide of the Jews as his central goal. I see this action of genocide an indication of how truthful and sincere Hitler is to his task and his prophecy speech.

Lucy Dawidowicz and Gerald Flemming argued that the speech was simply Hitler's way of saying that once he had started a world war, he would use this war as a show to perform his preexisting plan against the Jews (holy covenant).

Other historians say that in Hitler's speech there was no intention to reveal his plan of genocide but that he was mere bragging and coming out against the Jews and his opposition. I disagree with this assessment, seeing that after the speech and even during the war, Hitler had rightly committed these atrocities.

On May 15, 1940, Himmler, one of Hitler's right-hand men, showed him a list indicating treatments against any *alien* population in the east. This list explained the ways and means to *expel* the entire Jewish population in Africa, which Hitler endorsed.

During the invasion of the Soviet Union in 1941, the appointment book of Heinrich Himmler showed that he met with Hitler and asked him what to do with the Jews of Russia. Hitler response was, "Exterminate them as partisans." Some historians have commented that Hitler's answer to this question was surely one of his first steps for the Holocaust.

The Holocaust was pronounced as the "final solution for the Jewish question." This was planned and carried out by some leading Nazis, such as Himmler and Reinhard Heydrich, playing some of the most vital roles.

Evidence has also suggested that Himmler and Hitler decided upon mass extermination by gassing in autumn of 1941.

On February 22, 1942, Hitler suggested that the Holocaust was the final solution and the only way for the Europeans to regain their health, which meant the elimination of the Jews.

At the point of defeat in World War II, Hitler demanded the Holocaust to continue so that he could take a few more *souls* with him upon death.

Probably for the German *tyrant* it was necessary killing six million Jews to avoid the promise[304] not knowing that the promise given to Abraham, is in this time and age a spiritual set of people call by Yahweh's name, who reverend and hollow Him, and in time to come will inherit the earth.

One must clearly note, as I have said, Yahweh already shifted the physical promise noted by man to a spiritual blessing through His Son (the Messiah), which Abraham had already received through faith. The blessing was not listed through physical Jewry or Israel of the flesh anymore but through a nation that would accept His love and see Him (Yeshua) as the redeemer.

What should I say then? In fact, the Jews and the Israelites who did not see the Messiah (Yeshua) as the presented one could not follow the prophecy of His second advent as King presenting a new way of the messianic order that would lead to the throne of grace. So those who acknowledged Him as such were numbered amongst the spiritual elect, not by writs or rights but concepts of the hearts. On this note, the killing of the Jews at this time by the German government was not harmful to the inevitable growth of Yahweh's people (spiritual Israel). I should mention that a few Jews were still obedient to the cause of the Messiah, who led charge and delivered the truth. Yes, many diligent believers were also killed during the Holocaust, but it did not daunt the minds of those individuals who kept to the promise of the Father and the Second Advent.

---

[304] This is the *promise* of the *covenant* between Yahweh and His *holy people,* to let them be a mighty nation and inherit the earth.

Chapter 27

Second Italian-Ethiopian War

And at the time of the end shall the king of the south push at him: and the king of the north shall come against him like a whirlwind, with chariots, with horsemen and with many ships; and he shall enter into the countries, and shall overflow and pass over.

—*Daniel 11:40 (KJV)*

During the twentieth-century consummation against the holy covenant, this king of the south realized the intention of these *tidings* against the *elect*. These tidings were planned as a European colonialist expansion that Italy, Germany, France, and the United Kingdom endorsed.

During this time, the Italian tyrant, Benito Mussolini, who also shows aspiration to place Italy as the *vile person* of the north, planned an attack against Ethiopia a country of Africa. This was the Second[305] Italian-Ethiopian invasion against an Ethiopian king. Emperor Haile Selassie I, now king of Ethiopia (1930-1936, 1941-74)[306] was certain of this invasion and decides to push at the force determined.

---

[305] The first Italian-Ethiopian invasion took place at the Battle of Adowa in1896.
[306] Emperor of Ethiopia Haile Selassie I was crowned king in 1930. He went in exile after the Italians invasion of 1936, but was reinstated 1941 where he remain emperor until his overthrow by the Marxist dictator Mengistu Haile Mariam I 1974.

Italian dictator Benito Mussolini had strong desires to build a new Italian Empire. Like the old Imperial Roman Empire, Mussolini's new empire would rule over the Mediterranean and North Africa.

This new empire had to also avenge past Italian defeats. One of the outstanding amongst these defeats was the Battle of Adowa, which took place in Abyssinia on March 1, 1896.

The dictator's aspiration for this victory was his promise to the people of Italy about "a place in the sun." This place would make Italy equivalent to that of the extensive empires of France and Britain.

All the major European powers, including Italy, had already colonized many parts of Africa and committed many atrocities.

Many countries were caught up in greed, bidding for possession of land for colonization. The Christian mind-set, however, was geared toward the conversion of the African continent, changing the native culture into Western culture.

After the European imperialists scrambling for Africa after World War I, Ethiopia, which was governed by Emperor Haile Selassie I, was one of the few remaining independent African nations left. Acquiring Ethiopia would be the ultimate for Benito. Since he desired to successfully develop Italy into a promising empire, Ethiopia would serve to unify Italian lands held in Eritrea[307] and Italian Somaliland.[308]

Hitler, who agreed with Benito Mussolini, felt that Italian aggression against Abyssinia would open great opportunity for Germany as part of the European body in this colonial effort for the African continent. Therefore, as someone who was also "against the holy covenant," Hitler saw this partnership as one way to strengthen a friendship with Benito by encouraging the invasion.

---

[307] This country bordered by the Sudan in the west and Ethiopia in the south. Its northern and eastern parts have an extensive coastline that runs along the Red Sea.

[308] Was a colony of Italy since the Victor Immanuel II, and its geographic position is present-day northeastern, central and southern Somalia.

In 1928, Mussolini gave a concerned speech about a *colored* race that populated areas at a rate much faster than the White race did.

The Italian *vile person* was pointing to the black race of Africa. Assuredly this black race of Africa had proven that they were *connected* with the dynasty of King David[309], and was indeed *filled* with black descendants of the Semitic Jews. Mussolini and Hitler must have known of this fact, and capitalizing on their hatred for the Jews, they pointed to this side of the world and started eliminating the Ethiopians.

These two[310] were determined and had proven by their actions that they were resolute in the elimination of the Jews and the black Semitic race.

The Italian's Incursion on Ethiopia

In 1928, the Italio-Ethiopian Treaty stated that the border between the Italian Somaliland and Ethiopian lands was seventy-three miles parallel to the Benadir coast. In 1930, Italians forfeited this agreement by building a fort at the Welwel oasis in Ogaden, which was beyond the seventy-three miles stipulated by the treaty.

The Italians then converted the fort into a garrison with frontier troops commanded by Italian officers.

In November 1934, the Ethiopians, realizing that Italians were encroaching on Ethiopian borders, protested against the Italian's deceitful manner. On this note, the British were involved in this commission and withdrew to avoid any international contention, but the Italians stayed and continued to encroach on the Ethiopian lands.

---

[309] As recorded by many, His Imperial Majesty King Selassie I of Ethiopia came from the loin of Jesse and said to be a grandchild of King Solomon and the queen of Sheba.

[310] Benito and Hitler

The Ethiopians, having the right to defend their possessions and property, decided to push the terrors at their borders. This action of the southern king manifested the prophecy of Daniel that says:

"And at the time of the end shall the king of the south push at him" (Daniel 11:40 KJV).

In early December 1934, the encroachment led to the Welwel Incident. The result of this clash left approximately 150 Ethiopians and fifty Italians dead, and this event also brought on the Abyssinia Crisis at the League of Nations.

Conceited Action of the League of Nations

During the discussion at the League of Nations, both the Italians and the Ethiopians were exonerated for the eruption. You could also imagine that there was never an indication from the league saying to the Italian, he should desist from his encroachment on the Ethiopian borders.

This point was never strongly discussed. France, one of the main perpetrators, was more diplomatically willing to protect its friendship with Italy so that they could remain strong in combat against Germany if in the future a war would break out between them.

Before the kickoff of the First Italio–Ethiopian War 1896, the French commented at the League of Nations that the Italian aspiration was only for peace. Therefore, the French used this same diplomatic excuse in protecting the will of the Italians at the League of Nations in 1935, protecting their portion of Africa stipulated in the treaty signed January 7, 1935.

Because the League of Nations gave no rejection against the Italians' encroachment, the incursions on the Ethiopian borders continued.

The Italians soon began to build their forces along Eritrea in conjunction with the Italian Somaliland. The intention was to create a force large enough to plan an attack from that fort when they battled against the Ethiopian at the time appointed.

Before the Welwel War, the United Kingdom, Italy, and France had being acting in conceit for two reason.

Firstly in April 1935, Italy was invited to the Stresa Front, a body organized to curb Germany's war and arms expansion. I believe that the tyrant of Italy disregarded the interest, for he saw the tyrant of Germany as a comrade in similar fashion. Nevertheless, France did not interfere with Italy's refusal of the Stressa Front invitation, which showed the intention to keep Italy as ally.

Secondly, in June 1935, the British and the Germans signed the Anglo-Germany Naval Agreement (AGNA) without consulting the League of Nations. Italy and France agreed that the act by and large undermined the Treaty of Versailles.

So the French found themselves a diplomatic companion with Italy, while Italy, on the other hand, was Germany's companion. So France and Germany's defensive attitude at the League of Nations concerning the Italian's incursion on the Ethiopian boundaries was only in their best interest.

The emperor of Ethiopia, King Haile Selassie I, seeing that he would derive no aid or benefit out of meeting with the League of Nations, then turned to Japan as his only and last hope for assistance in turning away the evil that beset the Ethiopian people. He thought that Japan would provide aid because the Japanese citizens often expressed a love of the African Empire at that time.

Japan, serving as a model for many Ethiopians intellectuals, unfortunately had already assured Mussolini on July 16 that they had no interest in the political and colonial will of Africa. They had given their commitment to the Italian tyrant to stay neutral in the events of the Italian-Ethiopian conflict.

On August 2, 1935, the Ethiopian government approached the Japanese government about the decision to assist the Ethiopian people in regard this invasion. The request was denied despite the strong protest given by the Japanese popularity.

Immediately this king of the south, His Imperial Majesty (HIM), emperor of Ethiopia, realized the inevitability of this attack by this *vile person*, Mussolini of Italy.

Ethiopian Army Outlook

The mobilization of the army of Ethiopia had begun. Emperor Haile Selassie's army was weak compared to the forces of the Italians. His weapons were outdated, and some of the men within the army had little or no training.

The Ethiopian king, determined to push at the northern invader, did not focus on the possibility of defeat but continued to mobilize his army with great consistency to withstand the pressure that the Italians were about to apply.

The most up-to-date units were the emperor's imperial guard. The imperial guards were better trained and equipped than the other Ethiopian units. The uniforms of these guards were greenish khaki like that of the Belgium Army, which color provided a less target for the Italians weaponries.

Italian Army Outlook

In collaboration with the Royal Army and Royal Air Force, the Italian Army took residence in East Africa. To support the Italian Army, there were eight regular mountain and *black shirt*[311] infantry divisions that arrived in Eritrea, and four regular infantry divisions landed in Italian Somaliland. This huge army in East Africa also included many support units, including two hundreds journalists.

The Italian forces were well organized with highly sophisticated weapons. These weaponries included machine guns, artilleries, tankers, and aircrafts.

---

[311] This is a paramilitary movement of the Fascist Party in Italy during World War II. These soldiers are used as a "Voluntary Militia for National Security" (MVSN).

The Italians also had tons of ammunitions, food, and other necessary supplies.

During this campaign the Italians acquired some of his soldiers from its colonial possessions of Eritrea, Somalia, Libya, the Middle East, and Egypt. An independent troop, the Azebul Galla, was also present.

Independent Troop

There were also some independent troops that fought for the Italians, such as the Azebu Galla, who fought from the north.

Amongst others, the Azebu Galla was a set of tribesmen from the Oromo ethnic group found in Ethiopia, Northern Kenya, and part of Somalia. They spoke the native language of Oromo, which is part of the Cushitic branch of Afro-Asiatic language family.

As Oromo, the communities in the east were of Islamic faith, while the north practiced Orthodox Christianity.

Somehow, different from their religion, they seemed to neglect tolerating one another, and the tribal warfare between both Oromo's communities developed, contributing to a continuous power struggle for land.

The king of Ethiopia was of Oromo descent by both parents. He was an Oromo Ethiopian king. To strengthen his army, the Ethiopian king went and made a bid with the Muslims of east Oromo. The meeting was seemingly a satisfactory, which an agreement was made to help against the Italian Army.

During the Italio-Ethiopian War, the tribesmen of the Azebu Galla *turned* their hands against His Majesty, and for many reasons they enjoyed seeing the Ethiopians Christians flee.

Like the Azebu Galla, the Yemens who were composed of some Muslim tribesmen from the south of the Arabian lands alongside the Gulf of Aden, also threw in their lot against the emperor of Ethiopia.

Sultan of Olol Diinle

The sultan of Olol Diinle, who commanded a personal army, fought for the Italians and advanced into northern Ogaden. This sultan was angry with the Ethiopians for taking his people's lands, and with this helpful attack, it became seemingly possible to regain these lands.

De Bono in Command of the Italian Army

Mussolini and his armies did not spare time. He was so hungry for victory that he set out immediately with an evasive attack on Ethiopia.

He thought of humiliating the emperor firsthand before enjoying his victory. The Royal Italian Air Force dropped fliers asking the Ethiopians to rebel against their king, Emperor Haile Selassie, and support the true emperor, Lyasu V, who was forty years old at the time. He had been deposed of many years earlier and placed in custody.

On March 28, 1935, General Emilio De Bono was named the commanding chief of all Italian armed forces in East Africa. He was in command of the forces attacking from Eritrea, the northern front.

General Rodolfo Graziani was De Bono's subordinate and commanding chief of the forces invading from Italian Somaliland, the southern front.

At precisely 5:00 a.m. on October 3, 1935, De Bono crossed the Mareb River into Ethiopia from Eritrea without a declaration of war. Seeing this, the Ethiopians then declared war against their invaders, the Italians. Unfortunately after they crossed the Mareb, the dirt track roads created a problem to the Italian armies commanded by General Emilio De Bono.

De Bono, threatened by Mussolini because of his slow pace toward victory, marched through Adwa to the holy capital of Axum in October after it had been captured. He even showed off his victory by entering the city and riding up on a white horse.

De Bono continued to demonstrate to Mussolini how far he would go to ensure the victory of Italy by his persistent approach, capturing Makale on November 8, 1935.

Eventually he was promoted to the rank of marshal of the Italian army on November 16, 1935, but was then replaced in late December by Pierto Badoglio as the new marshal of Italy on the grounds that he was still progressing slowly. It was quite clear that Benito Mussolini desires a *speedy*[312] victory, which the marshal of the Italian armies must produce.

The Christmas Offensive

After he was informed of his command, Emperor Haile Selassie decided to test this new Italian commander with an offensive of his own. This retaliation was known as the Ethiopian Christmas Offensive.

To defeat the new marshal of Italy, Pietro Badoglio, and his forces, the king of the Ethiopians realized that he would have to create a force larger than that of the Italian force commanded by Major Critini, which was advancing toward the Dembeguina Pass, Amba Aradam, and the Warieu Pass.

The Ethiopian Army was a fraction compared to the Italian forces. Nevertheless, the king of Ethiopia didn't hesitate to push at this new marshal of the Italian forces, and as he did, he made his mark. Though their troop was small in numbers, they were committed to fight for the cause.

Critini's force was encircled by the Ethiopian forces, which fired upon them from all angles. During this attack Major Critini was

---

[312] At this point Benito desires a speedy victory. The desires of the Italian tyrant to go against the Ethiopian *speedily* referred to the prophecy that says, "And the king of the north shall come against him like a world wind" (Daniel 11:40 KJV).

wounded, and two of his officers were killed. The Eritrean infantry was slaughtered. The tanks occupied by the Italians were swarmed by Ethiopian soldiers, in that they could not mobilize the tanks properly to exit the pass. Relief Columns that were to relief Major Critini were also ambushed on the way.

Ethiopians attacked from the high ground at the pass, rolling boulders in and behind the tanks, which immobilized the Italians. This immobilization allowed them to easily pick off the Italian soldiers by arrows and rifles.

The Ethiopians set the captured Italian tanks ablaze, which was very stupid because the tanks could have been of use in counterattacks against the Italians.

Although half of Major Critini's force had been killed, he and a few others of his squadron managed to escape the Ethiopians at the pass.

It is said that the Ethiopians managed to kill three thousand Italian troops during this Christmas offensive. This period was then known as the Black Period of the war.

Sadly progress began to decline for the Ethiopians and their Christmas offensive because the Italians used of a chemical agent known as mustard gas, otherwise called poison gas.

Poison Gas—The Ultimate Weapon

The Ethiopian king's strategy made nice progress. They were showing the Italians that although their forces have modernized weapons and heavy artilleries, the Ethiopians could still defeat them.

Unfortunately this soon changed. Although the Ethiopian king had the will of victory and believed that good would triumph over evil, the Italians had hatred combined with science and technology, which gave rise to many modern weapons.

After the Ethiopian Christmas Offensive on December 26, 1935, the new marshal of Italy, Badoglio, asked and was given permission to use poison gas.

Of course Emperor Haile Selassie did made some progress in fighting the war against these modern technological weapons of the Italians, but during the usage of this "war chemical agent" his people did not understood the "burning rain" that came pouring down on them from the skies, killing everything in its path and stole the victory from them.

As Badoglio received additional forces to strengthen his impending victory, he launched a northern offensive at the First Battle of Tembien between the Warieu Pass and Makale on January 20, 1936. The Italians made their attacks from many positions, and they were effective with the use of the gas, especially at the northern front. The bombers of the Royal Air Force sprayed the gas from special artillery canisters. Four days after that, this battle ended with the Italians suffering 1,083 casualties and the Ethiopians counting eight thousand casualties.

In late February at the Second Battle of Tembien, the armies of Ras Kassa and Ras Seyoum were destroyed. As usual, the usage of poison gas was the major turning point.

In early March 1936 at the Battle of Shire, the army of Ras Imru was attacked and bombed. Nevertheless, the Italians continued to face fierce resistance. The resistance of Ras Imru and his army angered the Italian commander Badoglio, and so he sprayed the Ethiopian army of Ras Imru with poison gas as well. Here the Italians suffered one thousand casualties, but upward of four thousand Ethiopians were killed.

On March 31, 1936, at the Battle of Maychew, the counteroffensive of the main Ethiopian Army commanded by the Emperor Haile Selassie was defeated. At this battle the Ethiopian Army was outnumbered, and the troops were also tired because of continuous attacks. The Ethiopians could not break the Italian defenses, although they performed nonstop attacks on the Italian and Eritrean defenders.

As the exhausted Ethiopians began to retreat, they were run down by Marshal Badoglio's army, and while they were pinned down at Lake Ashangi, the Italian Army dispersed, leaving the Italian Royal Air Force to finish off what was left of the emperor's army, spraying them with mustard gas. The Italians suffered four hundred casualties, while the Eritreans had 873 dead. However, the Ethiopians counted eleven thousand casualties.

It is assured that the Ethiopian's moments of defeat were decisively done by the method of *spraying* the chemical war agent called "poison gas."

Chapter 28

Mussolini's Borders of Generosities

But these shall escape out of his hand, even Edom, and Moab and the chief of the children of Ammon.

—*Daniel 11:41 (KJV)*

The Edomites were Semites from the Esau tribe while the Moabites and Ammonites were also Semites but from the loins of Lot, Abraham's brother's son. The conclusion is that all descended from Terah, the father of Abraham, and from the loins of Shem, Noah's son.

Now all of these tribes live today as Muslims with the faith of Islam, where the Mid East and its surrounding borders are claimed to be their main habitat.

According to Daniel 11:41 (KJV) that says "these shall escape out of his hand," which to my understanding the verse was pointing to those tribesmen that assisted during Mussolini's invasions, especially the Ethiopian-Italian War 1936. Some of these tribesmen were the Yemens from south Arabia, the Sultan of Olol Diinle and the Oroho tribe from the east, who were all of Muslim faith.

The word *escape* in this verse[313] does not mean escaped from captivity or death but a conceded action done by the Italian. These Muslims were allowed to keep their cities, seeing that they gave assistance to the Italian tyrant during his invasions.

---

[313] Daniel 11:41 (KJV)

These countries[314] were known to practice the Islamic faith, and history has indicated that many other Muslims tribes helped the Italian invaders and were treated gloriously during the reigned of the East Africa Italian colony. Mussolini actually reached out to the Muslims in his empire and in the new Muslim states in the Middle East. This outreach was a signal of his gratitude for the aid that was granted against the Ethiopians, even though some were coerced by force. Nonetheless, it was well appreciated.

---

[314] One should take keen observation of the Scripture, where in it did not make reference only of the ancestral land of these Muslims, but also refers to the habitat of their seeds as in their children (children of Ammon). So the inhabitants of these Muslims countries were children of the Canaanites, Moabites, Edomites and the Ammonites etc.

Chapter 29

Italian Invasion of Egypt

And he shall stretch forth his hand also upon the countries: and the land of Egypt shall not escape. But he shall have power over the treasures of gold and silver, and over all the precious things of Egypt.

—Daniel 11:42–43 (KJV)

Here in verse 42 we see the Italian dictator making his path according to Scripture.

Now before the Italians made their plan to conquer Egypt, they went on some other journeys to besiege lands. Many other countries were taken, such as Libya from as early as of 1912. This conquest continued until 1934 when most of Libya's land was in the hands of the Italians.

There were other countries that were of interest to Mussolini as well. Aside from Ethiopia, Egypt was of the most importance by reason of the Suez Canal[315].

---

[315] The Suez Canal is an artificial sea level waterway in Egypt, connecting the Mediterranean Sea and the Red Sea. The Canal went under ten years of construction and was finally opened in 1869 to be owned by the Suez Canal Authority (SCA) of Egypt. Several emperors including Cleopatra and Napoleon devoted a lot of effort to this project, and more than a few wars have been fought for it. For Europe, this Canal is a vital waterway for oil and trade with Asia. So where the Suez Canal is concern, it is of great importance to the European and placed Egypt on a high platform within the economy.

Now the British had already planted its platoon in the land of the Egyptians to defend the Suez Canal. Nevertheless, since 1935, the Italians desired its wealth.

The prophecy said that "he shall have power over the treasures of gold and silver, and over the precious things of Egypt." I believe this was in reference to the Suez Canal, and the British already had power there. Nevertheless, the Italian dictator saw it as his moment to seize that "power over the treasures."

Mussolini's commander Graziani ordered General Berti to prepare attack on August 27, 1940. However, on September 9, 1940, the air forces of both sides launched an attack.

The prophecy declares that "the land of Egypt shall not escape," but for me the Egyptians could not have seen any form of victory without the help of the British.

Chapter 30

Italy-Libya

And the Libyans and the Ethiopians shall be at his steps.
—Daniel 11:43 (KJV)

The history of Libya as an Italian colony started in 1911. That lasted until 1931. At this point in time the Italian government only controlled the coastal areas of the colony.

Mussolini waged a series of wars under the command of Pietro Badoglio and Rodolpho Graziani. This war was like a purification campaign that included brutal and bloody acts of repression. Resistance leaders were executed or flew into exile. By 1934, Cyrenaica, Tripolitania, along with Fezzan all merged into one Italia Libya.

Libya as a colonized country under the new Italio Bablo was also integrated amongst the Italians, and of course, they also filtered into the army of Mussolini.

By 1940, laws were passed that enabled, either by force or willingly, them to join the Fascist Party.

Note that the capture, possession, and filtration of the Libyans into the army of the Italians show how Libya was taken and placed under Italian rule. In 1937, the Muslims of Libya pronounced the Italian vile person as the "protector of Islam."

Chapter 31

Benito's Final Task against the Covenant

And the Ethiopians shall be at his steps."
—*Daniel 11:43 (KJV)*

As one can imagine, Mussolini was often between battles with different countries, and that must have been encouraged by his greed for power or his aspiration to prove that he was the *vile person.*

The annexation of Ethiopia was on the way where the continued act after the second Italian-Ethiopian Invasion was shown to be inhumane.

In early June, the government of Rome combined Ethiopia with Eritrea and Italian Somaliland into a single administrative unit divided up into six provinces called Italian East Africa or AOI. Marshal Pietro Badoglio was proclaimed the first viceroy and governor general of this new Italian colony. Unfortunately for Badoglio, he only held this position for a short time before he was replaced by Marshal Rodolfol Graziani.

During the new general's takeover, Mussolini's orders after the war were very clear. On June 5, 1936, Mussolini wrote from Rome to the new general, stating that all rebels who had been taken prisoners must be killed. Furthermore, on July 8, 1936, a letter was sent from Rome stating the following:

To his Excellency Graziani,

I have ordered once again your Excellency to begin and systematically conduct a politics of terror and extermination of the rebels and the complicit population.

Graziani made it his duty to have these atrocities carried out by Italians who found it entertaining. Besides using bombs laced with mustard gas, they also enforced labor, installed public gallows, killed hostages, and mutilated the corpses of their enemies. Captured guerilla fighters were thrown from moving aircraft while the Italians took pictures with men hanging from the gallows and crates full of the detached heads of the Ethiopian soldiers or civilians.

In July 1936, loyal supporters of the Ethiopian forces attacked the Italians who held Addis Ababa. The attack was a failure, and many Ethiopians fled; however, those who were caught were taken prisoners and executed shortly after.

By late December 1936, Graziani declared the whole of Ethiopia under Italian control. Nevertheless, the whole country was marked for regular guerrilla attacks against the Italians. The Italians retaliated by using the mustard gas over and over again on the Ethiopian rebels, and those who were caught were executed.

The attempt made on the life of the new colonial governor general and viceroy, Graziani, at Addis Ababa on February 18, 1937, resulted into the Italian security force firing discriminately into the crowd of civilian onlookers followed by the execution of thirty thousand persons, including half of the younger educated population.

The Responses of Emperor Haile Selassie I

As a result of the many attacks with the usage of poison gas on the Ethiopian people, the heart of the king of Ethiopia was pierced, and it was as if he was *bleeding* through his eyes.

The Emperor's Speech Reproving the Falling Rain

By late January after the attack at Makale, the emperor gave a speech informing the world about the weakness of the Italians to fight a fair battle without the use of the illegal weapon called the poison gas.

> It was at that time when the operations for the encircling of Makale were taking place that the Italian command, fearing a rout, followed a procedure, which is now my duty to denounce to the world. Special sprayers were installed on board aircraft so that they could vaporize over vast areas of territories a fine death-dealing rain. Groups of nine, fifteen and eighteen aircraft followed one another so that the fog issuing from them formed a continuous sheet. It was thus, that as from the end of January 1936, soldiers, women, children, cattle, rivers, lake and pastures were drenched continuously with this deadly rain. To systematically kill all living creatures, and more surely poison waters and pastures, the Italian command made its aircraft pass over and over again. That was his chief method of warfare."

In saying this, the emperor expressed his thought that the Italians wouldn't fight fair battles. As cowards who faced defeat and found no other route to escape, their only method of retaliation was the use of poison gas.

The atrocities set out by the Italians was so devastating; many Italian aircrafts with special machines installed on board were placed in groups, so that they could easily managed to exterminate anything in its path over a vast area of land.

The deadly rain was so disruptive that women, children, soldiers, lakes, rivers, cattle, and pastures were destroyed. The idea was to totally eliminate all living things and to make sure that all pastures and waters were poisoned.

After the Battle of Maychew on March 31, 1936, with the Italian Army commanded by Badoglio against the Ethiopian Army commanded by Emperor Haile Selassie, the defeat of the exhausted Ethiopians was approaching. On April 4, 1936, as the emperor stared at the wasted bodies of his soldiers floating along the riverbeds, his heart "cried" out with pain. The emperor looked with horror and sadness, and it was as if tears as blood ran down from his eyes when he saw the bodies of his people lying in the poisoned lake.

His Majesty Exodus Ethiopia Warning the League of Nations

Early on the morning of May 2, 1936, Haile Selassie I hastily boarded a train from Addis Ababa to Djibouti on the Imperial Railway. His Majesty Haile Selassie I sailed in the British cruiser. His first destination was Palestine on his way to England via Gibraltar. His Majesty's final destination would be England, where he would stay in exile.

On His Majesty Haile Selassie I's journey to England, he passed through Jerusalem. Two days after his arrival in Jerusalem, he sent a telegram to the League of Nations. In it he wrote,

> We have decided to bring an end to the most unequal, most unjust, most barbarous war of our age, and have chosen the road to exile in order that our people will not be exterminated and in order to consecrate ourselves wholly and in peace to the preservation of our empire's independence ... We now demand that

> the League of Nations should continue its efforts to
> secure respect for the covenant, and that it should
> decide not to recognize territorial extensions, or the
> exercise of an assumed sovereignty, resulting from the
> illegal recourse to armed force and to numerous other
> violations of international agreements.

The Ethiopian emperor's telegram caused a stir internationally, and many nations temporarily deferred their recognition of the Italian conquest and victory.

In his telegram, the soon-to-be-exiled king speaks concerning the *covenant* with the League of Nations to make effort and secure the covenant. The king's telegram about the *covenant* can be interpreted in two ways. In one way it could reference the covenant made between the king of Ethiopia and the League of Nations, while in another, his message could also be an attempt to strongly announce the prophecy spoken of by Daniel concerning the holy *covenant* between Yahweh and His people, which stresses the everlasting existence of Israel with extension to the Jews.

On June 30, 1936, Haile Selassie I spoke at the League of Nations and was addressed by the president of the assembly as "His Imperial Majesty, emperor of Ethiopia." At this address the Italian people, including some Italian journalists, were furiously shouting and saying that it was an insult to the Italian people and the people of Rome for the Ethiopian emperor to be addressed in that manner.

The Romanian chairman, Nicolae Titulescu, reacted to this objection by jumping to his feet and shouting, "To the door with these savages!"

At this point Haile Selassie could give his speech in denouncing Italy's actions and criticizing the world community for standing by and allowing the atrocities ordered by the Italians to take place. At the end of his speech, which appeared on news forecasts and in the papers, the emperor of Ethiopia warned the League of Nations that "they should not sit at ease because it is Ethiopia today but it will be you tomorrow."

The Italian Cheerful Moments

While Haile Selassie I was crossing the Red Sea in the British cruiser of Her Majesty Ship (HMS)[316], the Italians were rejoicing in Rome. King Victor Emmanuel III waited for the crowd to be silent in Quirinal Palace on Quirinal Hill, and then he began by saying, "A few months earlier I told a friend that if the Italians won I would be king of Abyssinia, but if we lost, I will still be king of Italy."

Well, the people of Rome *praise* Victor by shouting, "emperor, emperor, salute the emperor." Victor Emmanuel was pronounced the first emperor in Rome in the last 1,460 years.

Emperor Victor Emmanuel being silent gives way for the Italian Fascist dictator Benito Mussolini letting his voice heard by applauding his victory. As one could imagine, the crowd in the Piazza Venezia in Rome was not informed of the use of poison gas in aiding the victory they cheered so much for now, and of course, the question of the cause of victory was of no concern.

In Mussolini's hour of triumphant, he bellowed that "the victory over Ethiopia has given the people of Italy the empire that was destined, and now peace is restored."

The International Response

The response to the Italio-Ethiopian invasion was a mixed one. Although the emperor gave a stirring speech against the League of Nations and their recognition of the Italio-Ethiopian invasion, there still remained a few within the league who turned their backs, leaving his speech unrecognized.

---

[316] This is always an abbreviated term used for British naval ships named after the Queen to recognize her authority.

On July 4, 1936, the League of Nations voted to lift the sanction that had been called against Italy in November 1935. On July 15, 1936, the sanction was lifted.

Only five nations within the League of Nations refused to recognize the Italian sovereignty over Ethiopia, and by and large they respected the Ethiopian request for independence. These five nations include the United States[317], Mexico, the Soviet Union, New Zealand, and the Republic of China.

Japan, one of the countries that agreed to lift the sanction against Italy, recognized with diplomacy the Italian empire on November 18, 1936. By December 11, 1937, the League of Nations voted again to condemn Italy, which resulted in Mussolini's withdrawal from the League of Nations.

Unfortunately the invasion of Ethiopia by the Italians meant that the Stresa Front was at an end, which encouraged the German dictator Adolf Hitler, who supported the Italian invasion long before it even started among his prolonged endeavors.

In 1938, France and Britain on behalf of their own greed decided to recognize[318] Italian control over the Ethiopians. Winston Churchill called it a complete triumph for Mussolini.

The Western Democrats' condemnation of the Italio-Ethiopian invasion increased daily, resulting in their isolation from Fascist Italy and Mussolini.

The increasing condemnation and isolation was driven by concerns given by the league, which was saying that the reconstruction and development of the infrastructure of the colony was much more than they anticipated and that the Italian's revenues were well below the standard to help support reconstruction. So the League of Nations

---

[317] Surely the United States would be amongst the few. The Italian government was always at odds with the United States, which was the proven vile person of the north.

[318] Here again France and Britain sided with Italy in a diplomatic (and hypocritical) attempt to keep allies against Germany.

saw it necessary to disagree, which resulted in Mussolini and Hitler joining forces with Japan to form the Tripartite Pact.

The Catholic Church's Statements and Responses

The church's responses were mixed. As for the Vatican fearing an attack from the National Fascist Party, they, too, made some of their responses with biasness.

Viewing the statements of these "prisoners of Christ," I asked this question: Could the words of these bishops show the benevolence of good against of evil? I have listed their statements here so that you may make your own conclusion. These quotations come from Anthony Rhodes's book *The Vatican in the Age of the Dictators.*

Bishop of Udine

In the pastoral letter sent on October 19, 1935, the bishop of Udine wrote, "It is neither timely nor fitting for us to pronounce on the right or wrong of the case. Our duty as Italians and still more as Christians is to contribute to the success of our arms."

Here the bishop of Udine was being diplomatic in his speech by praising the *benefits* of weaponry given and claiming it as a Christian success. The was so, seeing that they as Catholic Christians could step in and play their parts in Christianizing the Ethiopian nation, having the Ethiopians to be more in line with the culture of the Roman and Western world.

Bishop of Padua

In the letter sent on October 21, 1935, the bishop of Padua wrote, "In the difficult hours through which we are passing, we asked you to have faith in our statesmen and our armed forces."

It is obvious that this bishop directly asked the world to pray and hold firm so that victory would be secured in the hands of our[319] statesmen, including Mussolini and his outrageous and barbaric forces. Christianity is simply saying that *faith[320]* in their armed force surely will bring victory against the king of Ethiopia.

Bishop of Cremona

On October 24, 1935, the bishop of Cremona consecrated a number of regimental flag[321] and said, "The blessing of God be upon these soldiers, who, on African soil will conquer new and fertile lands for the Italian genius, thereby bringing to them Roman and Christian culture, may Italy stand once again as the Christian mentor to the whole world."

Christianity's actions and contributions to the invasion of the Ethiopian people are very illogical and tragic.

I for one will speak no harm against the Christian church, but as history unfolded, there pattern of behavior was not logical according to the commandments.

Without excuse, people surely knew the aspirations of the Italian dictator. He was not benevolent to the spiritual logistics of the Church, but the spiritual authorities had agreed to the atrocities by laying hands and blessing the Italians to pursue their goals of victory.

For thought, I will say it is obvious that in some aspects of life we all are under the influence of the flesh as humans, where by the weaknesses of the spirit to amend had not recognized our failure as servants of the living Elohim (God).

---

[319] Italians statesmen

[320] Should faith be in arms or the Almighty

[321] These flags bear the sign of the cross, which was given by Constantine and consecrated by the bishop of Rome. The emperor of Rome and the Catholic pope declared to use the sign of the cross to represent the Church.

Should anyone who is good pray for an active force, which desires to conquer a nation by killing thousands of innocent people, in order to spread the Christian faith?

Pope Pius XI

Pope Pius XI, who condemned totalitarianism, never stopped criticizing the works of racism, and it created a storm surrounding the papacy and Mussolini's Fascist government. Mussolini and his regime called the papacy a "malignant tumor in the body of the Italians that must be rooted out once and for all." He believed that there was no room in Rome for both the pope and him.

In spite of all this, the pope like the local bishops of Rome projected a field of defense around the warriors of Mussolini and his confederates by praying and blessing them.

When all is said and done, one must agree that the Catholic Church, though not in battle physically, did battle through faith with the attempt to tear the king of Ethiopia from his kingdom.

The King of Ethiopia Reinstated

After the Ethiopian invasion, Mussolini and Hitler joined forces between 1936 and 1939 during the Spanish Civil War. In May 1939, both signed the Pact of Steel and continued to crave the possession of land.

The exiled king, seeking to regain possession of Ethiopia, did not get the support of the Western Democrats until his prophecy[322] of truth revealed itself when World War II broke out.

On January 21, 1941, Emperor Selassie I crossed over into Ethiopia with the Gideon Force. In May of the same year the king

---

[322] His Majesty did warn the League of Nations that if they did not act now, their time would come soon, and it did.

entered into Addis Ababa, and by the end of 1941 during this East African campaign, the Ethiopian was freed of the grips of the Italians.

It was not until the last part of 1943 when the Italians formally surrendered. When they signed the peace treaty on February 10, 1947, in Paris, the Italians vowed to the victors of World War II to recognize Ethiopian independence and agreed also to pay $25,000,000 in repatriations.

The lion of Judah, as he was called by some, being replaced as the crown king of Ethiopia, stand out by presenting his bill of compensation of a total of 184,746,023 pound for the damages done during the course of Mussolini's colonial adventure.

After World War II, the League of Nations continued to stem the horror within the walls of the north. Thus, they provided peace for a time, but another factor began to germinate beyond the boundaries of the north, namely the *tidings of the east*. This terror created some storms for the United States (the outstanding vile person of the north), which he determined to quench somehow.

Chapter 32

Troubling Tidings of the East

But tidings out of the east and out of the north shall trouble him: therefore he shall go forth with great fury to destroy: and make away many.

—*Daniel 11:44 (KJV)*

The contending factor of the south becomes no more an obstacle to the main man of the northern kingdom. After World War II, the policies of politics and the commitment[323] to the League of Nations gave result to minimal war fare and greed for possession lands.

After World War II, the United States and the League of Nations took full control of the estates of Germany and Italy. The United States undoubtedly then became a strong voice once more in the northern hemisphere. Therefore, its presence as the *vile person*[324] of the north took effect, and it became the top country of the League of Nations.

From time to time there developed internal differences amongst the nations within the league, but on account of the *vile person* and its attitude, things were laid to rest.

---

[323] This commitment was an agreement to stem the enrichment of nuclear weapons and arms.

[324] *Vile person* always represent the way of governance, not necessarily a male person. An example could be drawn from the Scripture and its references of Ram or male sheep, which represents a country and its approach against opponents.

The league surely had some problems, but what started to disturb and affect the vile person most of all were the tidings out of the east.

The Bible has commented on the "tidings of the north," but for me that was not so much of an issue to the vile person as yet, although in times to come, the driving force to stir up the tidings of the north would come from the east.

Tidings from the east became such a strong force against the vile person that eventually *these tidings* pursued making residence[325] within the borders of its land (the United States).

The Middle East became the cradle of terror against the European Economic Community (EEC) and the Group of Eight (G8). Speaking of all these, the cradle of terror places most of its emphasis on destroying the United States of America.

The terror of the Middle East was *natural* in his stead. This I say on account of the *trumpets*[326] that was sound by the prophet Daniel and even other prophets as well. So what is to be must be by the powers of Yahweh Almighty as it was declared by His prophets.

One should remember that the Moabites, Ammonites, and the Edomites had lands that were left alone by Mussolini, these were the lands inhabited by tribesmen who had adopted the faith of Islam.

The Middle East and all surrounding borders are havens of the sons of Shem and Ham, who were the sons of Noah, and their faith is called Islam.

The *main* man of the north, having a personal desire to gain power and to remain in control, got involved in the Middle East concerning their borders respective to their claimed birthright.

After the flood the inhabitant of the earth were made up of the three sons of Noah. These three sons are Shem, Ham, and Japheth.

---

[325] The *terror* of the *East* against the United States reaches as far as the US soil.

[326] The *trumpet sound* indicates a prophetical declaration, which is set to be fulfilled under the command of the Almighty.

My two main concerns pertaining to the Middle East and its borders involve the *Ham man*[327] and *Shem man.*[328]

The Ham Man (Hamitic) and His Borders

The Ham man's main habitats came from Cush, Shinar (Babylon as in the tower of Babel), the land of the Philistines, Amorite and Canaan land, whose families dwelled in Sidon, as well as Gaza, Sodom, and Gomorrah. So we should agree that the Ham man's families lived anywhere from Egypt to the borders of Iraq.

One must not forget that according to Scripture, it was the Ham man's sons, the Amorites, that the children of Israel were held as slave in Egypt (Genesis 15:13–21 KJV). The Ham man's sons also made families and spread their residence within the Middle East and its surrounding borders. They, too, exercised the faith of Islam in this time.

The Shem Man (Semitic) and His Borders

Abraham

Scripture mentioned that the Shem man also "found himself a place in the mountain of the east." Abraham's birthplace and the nativity of his father was in Ur of the Chaldean (Ur of the Chaldees), a place in the east known as Mesopotamia that we now called Iraq. Nevertheless, Abraham,[329] whom the blessing was bestowed upon, never had a resting place of his own but only that which was promised

---

[327] The word *"Ham man"* (my word) derived from Ham, a son of Noah, while the word *"man"* means kin or person of the seed of Ham. Regular word used for this term is Hamitic.

[328] The word *"Shem man"* (my word) derived from Shem, a son of Noah, while the word *"man"* means kin or person of the seed of Shem. Regular word used for this term is Semitic.

[329] Abraham was from the bowel of Shem.

to him by his Elohim, and that was the place of the Ham man. Read Genesis 15:18–21.

Abraham had a brother name Haran, who had a son named Lot. He, too, was a Semite of the bowel of Shem. During Abraham's journey after he had passed through Egypt and returned to the mountain on the east of Beth-el, where he had already pitched tent and prayed to the Adoni (Lord), his herdsmen and Lot's herdsmen were at odds because the land they occupied was too small for both of them and the cattle they reared.

Abraham and Lot decided then to separate their dwelling from each other. Lot journeyed to the east and chose all the plains of Jordan at Sodom while Abraham dwelled in Canaan amongst the Ham men.

After Sodom and Gomorrah were destroyed, Lot went in the mountain of Zoar, and his two daughters lay with him. This action produced two offspring, Ben-ammi and Moab, and their families dwelled in the lands of the Ammonites and Moabites in the Middle East at the surrounding borders of Jordan.

Abraham, being a traveler and having no abiding place, was also a sojourner in Egypt with his wife, Sarai, who was also his sister[330] as the daughter of his father but not the daughter of his mother.

After they were in Canaan for ten years, his wife, Sarai, whose name changed to Sarah and who bore no children unto him at the time, told him to go into her handmaid, Hagar the Egyptian, the daughter of the Amorites, to bear seed unto him. As a result, a son named Ishmael was born unto him.

Shortly thereafter, Sarah bore Abraham a son named Isaac. Abraham also had other sons of the concubines[331] he had, and to these concubines he gave gifts before his death and sent them in the east countries away from before Isaac his beloved son. Thus, many half Semites also took resident in the Far East and Middle East long before Israel had been formed.

---

[330] Read Genesis 20.

[331] Hagar was one of these concubines.

Ishmael

Ishmael's mother came from the loins of Ham and the tribe of the Amorites and the Egyptians. Ishmael's mother, Hagar the Egyptian, took her son from the presence of Abraham and his other son, Isaac, and went and dwelled with her brethren, the Amorites of Egypt.

There she gave Ishmael the daughters of the Egyptians to be his wives. Ishmael has twelve sons, and their dwelling stretched from Havilah to Shur eastward toward Assyria. So here we find that Ishmael, although a son of Abraham, went and made residence amongst his fellow brethren of the *Ham man*.

So those who inhabited these lands situated before Egypt and stretches eastward was children from the loins of Ishmael. However, they were partly Amorites and Semites but of a more *clear blood*[332] of the Ham man.

Isaac

Isaac, who was Abraham second son and born of Sarah, made him of a stronger blood line of Shem and of the Semite tribe.

Abraham, honoring his lineage and the covenant of the Elohim, demanded his oldest servant to swear "that thou shall not take a wife unto my son of the daughters of the Canaanites among whom I dwell" (Genesis 24:3 KJV).

After Abraham's command, the servant went to the kindred's' household at Ur of the Chaldees in Mesopotamia and to the city of Nahor, Abraham's brother, and brought a wife[333] to Isaac.

---

[332] *Clear blood* indicates a royal bloodline of the (Ham man) Hamitic tribes. This means that the families of Ham were in marriage with each other. Where an Amorites were betrothing to Moabites or Canaanites the bloodline of the Ham man remains intact (pure blood line of Ham) and the offspring would then be predominantly of Ham's blood lineage.

[333] Isaac's wife name was Rebecca.

Isaac's wife's father, Bethuel, was a half Syrian of a Syrian[334] mother.[335] Read Genesis 25:20. Bethuel was son to Nahor, a brother to Abraham of the sons of Shem. So Isaac's seed was mixed with the Syrian and Shem lineage. Because Isaac was Semite and his wife was Syrian and Semite, it allotted their children to be more of a Semite blood, only partly showing the visage[336] of Syrian kin.

Isaac's wife, Rebekah, who was also his cousin, conceived and bore twin. Scripture said that they both were at war with each other in the womb. Read Genesis 25:22, 23.

The first born was red and hairy and was named Esau. The second born was named Jacob, and he came out holding the heel of his brother, Esau, with the intention to pull him back into his mother's womb.

These twins separated from each other, forming two separate nations.

Esau

The firstborn, Esau, was a red man who hunted and ate flesh for his meals, but because of hunger, he sold his birthright to his brother, Jacob, for portage made up of lentils and beans. Therefore, he was called Edom, the father of the Edomites.

The Edomites lived between Kadesh, Gaza, and the mountain between the Suez Canal. Esau's seed was also a mixed[337] one. His

---

[334] The Syrians, as was told by many historians, were never precisely referred to by Moses until the time of Rebecca. But undoubtedly after the flood, as mentioned by the books of Moses, the ark came to rest on Mount Ararat in Armenia. It seems that the sons of Japheth rested in the north with one of its boundaries at Armenia. The sons of Ham and Shem rested with them, producing a semi-Caucasian breed, the Syrians.

[335] Bethuel's mother's name was Milcah. She was daughter to Haran, the father of Isaac and Lot.

[336] This is the actual complexion. Read Genesis 11:29, 24:15, and 25:20.

[337] Esau was mixed in the sense that he, too, was a half Syrian and half Semitic.

generation was made up of the Hittites of Canaan and Ishmaelites of Egypt born unto Ishmael, which were composed of the souls of the Ham man. All these tribes turned in their lots against the children of Jacob. Read Genesis 26:34–35 and also Genesis 28:8–9.

Jacob

The second born unto Isaac was Jacob,[338] who never ate of his father venison[339] but rather used herbs and beans as his food. On account of the Scripture, it seems like Isaac ate[340] the same type of venison as Esau's more than Jacob's.

At the point of death Isaac chose to bless his firstborn, Esau, but because of Rebekah's love for Jacob, Isaac was tricked into giving the blessing to the second born, which was not the custom in the family of Shem. Therefore, the blessing from Yahweh concerning Abraham and his seed was handed[341] down to Jacob and his seed.

With the intention to keep the blessing in the generation of Shem, Isaac commanded Jacob "not to take any daughter of the Canaanites for a wife, but go to Padan-aram to the house of Bethuel his mother's father and take a wife of the house of Laban[342] his mother's brother" (Genesis 28:1–5 KJV).

On his quest for a wife Jacob came to Padan-aram the land of the people of the east. In the east he found the household of the children of Haran and Nahor. At the well in Padan-aram he was shown Rachel,[343] the daughter of Laban, who was the son of Bethuel. Bethuel was the son of Nahor and Milcah. Nahor was Abraham's brother, and Milcah was Abraham's sister-in-law.

---

[338] Jacob was also of the Syrian blood (Deuteronomy 26:5).

[339] Nutritious meal

[340] "Isaac loves Esau, because he did eat of his venison" (Genesis 25:28).

[341] Isaac may have intention to honor the traditional ways; however, the Elohim's *covenant (blessing)* was inevitable, and that was determined through Jacob.

[342] Laban was also a half Syrian. He was a son of Nahor and a son of Shem.

[343] Rachel was Jacob's cousin.

Jacob served his uncle Laban, his mother's brother, for fourteen years and received Laban's two daughters, Rachel and Leah, as wives.

Jacob stayed in Padan-aram, where twelve sons and one daughter were born to him from both wives and their handmaids, Bilhah and Zilpah.

The Intertwined

Years after Israel profaned the command of their fathers[344] and begun to intermix and have children with other nations. Moses was also accused of taking as a wife a daughter of the Ham man's seed, the Ethiopian woman. Scripture declared that the exodus of Egypt was comprised of some Egyptians who had been accepted into the families of Israel in some sort of ways.

During the journey to the Promised Land, Israel was involved in many relationships with the countries they conquered. Moses warned Israel "that after reaching the promise land they will turn their back on the laws of Yahweh," and mingled[345] with the people of that land and told tales and fables.

As a result of their hard-hearted desires, they were scattered amongst the nations of the earth. This mingling allowed Israel to *dilute*[346] the *purity* of the bloodline with a mingled seed by fusing with the conquered nations.

On account of this intertwining, Yahweh decided to cleanse[347] Israel for Himself once more. By so doing, He sent the Messiah to redeem Israel unto Himself, therefore procuring Israel in the spiritual sense. Israel was no longer Israel of flesh but one in Christ, whether

---

[344] Abraham.

[345] Deuteronomy 7:1–9.

[346] This is a weakening of the clear blood line of Shem.

[347] This word is used instead of prove or select.

Jew, Greek, or Gentile, they all worshiped together as long Christ is recognized as the testator[348] of the New Covenant.

Does the physical Israel have any hold on the ownership of Yahweh or His promise? I say no. Israel in the Middle East cannot claim any land in regard to Yahweh's promise to father Abraham. To speak on the other side of things, whether Semites, Israelites, Amorites, Moabites, or any other race, they all are one mingled seed of Shem and Ham.

While these mingled seeds were fighting for the ownership of land and the promise of Abraham, others within the Middle East who held the faith of Islam decided not to sustain the unity negotiated by the vile person of the north, the United States of America.

The United States was looked upon as a busybody, getting involved in the matters of the Middle East. His strategic way of rising to power and his method of instilling Western culture in the east gave some in Islam reasons to view the United States a threat to the glory of Allah. Many saw the United States as the stumbling block that must be stopped from rising to power.

Many took it up on themselves to devote their lives to this cause, committing suicidal attack in the name of Allah. This pattern of behavior troubled the United States, allowing him to pay special attention to the Middle East and the tidings that unfolded.

Some of the tidings that unfolded include the Iraq-Iran War, the Iraq-Kuwait War, the Iraq Invasion, and Afghanistan and Osama bin Laden

Iraq-Iran War

Iran, also an Eastern country, was involved in a bed stream of tidings that created a *storm* after being provoked by the attempt

---

[348] This Testator will reveal Himself in three forms—first as the Lamb, second as King of Kings, and thirdly as the High Priest.

invasion of Iraq under Saddam Hussein's[349] regime (1979-2003). As a usual, the United Nations as well as the United States had to step in putting an end to any conflict known, so with preferential assistance the conflict between Iraq and Iran was stopped.

It is said that this Iraq-Iran War was stimulated by some drawn-out disputes over land. Under Hussein's regime, Iraq claimed ownership of some particular lands at the border of both countries. One of these lands was Mohammareh, which the Ottoman gave to Iran. The Iraqis persistently claimed that Mohammareh was part of the property of Iraq.

In 1969, the deputy prime minister of Iraq announced that part of these disputes over lands was the result of Arabistan (Khuzestan), which the foreign rulers had given to Iran.

Many conflicts, as regarding to ownership of land and its borders, were end result of interference of foreign powers that get themselves involved in the distribution of original eastern domains. So the United States, who claimed himself a pattern of a "god" in justice, conveniently placed himself to severe the tidings of the east they themselves willingly or unintentionally kindle.

This Iraq-Iran War was known as the Imposed War, Holy Defense in Iran, and Saddam's Qadisiyyah in Iraq. The Pos-Gulf War, as it is referred to at times, lasted from September 22, 1980, to August 1988. The Western world has called it the First Persian Gulf War before the Iraq-Kuwait War on August 2, 1990.

The Iraqi president, Saddam Hussein, with his right to defend the ownership for his claim concerning the Iraqi's lands and its borders, intended to confiscate the possession of the Iranian oil fields and replace Iraq as the dominant Persian Gulf state within that territory.

On September 22, 1980, Saddam Hussein made his attack on the Iranian soil with full assurance that his plan would be a success.

---

[349] Saddam Hussein was President of Iraq from July 16, 1969 until he was invaded by the U.S. – led coalition on April 9, 2003.

Surprisingly Hussein and his force made little progress. The Iraqi Army began to retreat in mid-March 1980 as the Iranian Army accumulated strength in resistance.

As the Iranians were in controlled of the war, the UN Security Council along with the United States of America called for a cease-fire on September 28, 1980. Despite the call for a cease-fire, the Iraq-Iran War proceeded, and hostilities intensified.

By June 1982, all captured territories that were in the hands of the Iraqi President were restored. For the next six years Iran was on the progressive side, and Iraq was in trouble.

Although many lives were lost on both sides, the Iranians were still in control of the war, forcing Saddam to use chemical weapons like mustard gas, killing Iranian troops, Iraqi civilians, and Iraqi Kurds.

The UN Security Council, knowing that these atrocities had been committed by the Iraqi government, did not see it in their best interest to investigate at that time and instead allowed the United States to prevent the condemnation of the Iraqi methods of war.

The fact that these acts were illegal did not deter the continuous progress of the Iranian attacks but lead the Iraqis to a continuous retreat.

The Iraqis, who were under pressure from the Iranian forces, could not stand, so they expected aid in combat, weapons, and ammunitions from the United States, the United Kingdom, the Soviet Union, NATO, France, Brazil, Yugoslavia, Spain, Italy, Egypt, and Saudi Arabia. Iran, on the other hand, sought war aid from North Korea, China, Lydia, and Israel.

While the Soviet Union supported both nations with weapons, some information suggested that the United States had been supporting Iran with the importation of weapons.

In 1987, the Iranians developed another offensive method and attacked from southern and northern Iraq. The Iranians were stopped at the south but were more successful at the northern end with continuous attacks threatening to capture the oil rich Iraqi city of Kurkuk and other northern oil fields.

One must not forget the statement of President Ronald Reagan and his government proclaiming that the battle within the east between Iraq and Iran must be determined, where that the battle must benefit the United States of America by allowing Hussein's forces to claim victory.

The Reagan government went on to say that they could not afford to let Iran win the war, and in preventing this, he would do anything necessary to uphold that promise.

That promise was manifested again when the UN Security Council, seeing the near victory of the Iranian forces, tried to deter the Iranian success by passing the US–sponsored Resolution 598, which called for an end of fighting and return to prewar boundaries. This resolution was to proceed in the benefit of the Iraqis because they were on the brink of losing the war.

Saddam realized that he had lost many important pieces of lands during the war and diplomatically accepted the resolution. Iran, who decided not to give up possession of land taken from the Iraqis, especially when total victory was close, opposed the resolution of the UN Security Council and the United States of America, resulting in a continued conflict.

The interference of the United States and the United Nations stir some ill feelings from the Islamic revolution against Western bodies, which Iman Khomeini urged to be done in unity[350].

Saddam Hussein and his government, on the other hand, dishonored Iman Khomeini's Islamic union in the revolutionary act against Western world oppressions, inviting the United States with foreign bodies to strengthen his force against Iran, another Muslim state.

---

[350] Iman Khomeini's intention was to unify all Islam states and have them fighting together, not against each other.

Khomeini Ayatollah Ruhollah was engaged in developing an Islamic state that would inflict terror against the Western world, which has oppressed the Islamic world. Iran was seemingly an associate of these terrorist developments. Hussein, on the other hand, had refused to have Khomeini entrenched this plan of Sheik and Kurdish terrorist behavior in Iraq, and thus, his position became part of his reason for his invasion. On this note, Khomeini urged all Iranians to understand that the "motive of Saddam Hussein is to bring Islam to *blasphemy*[351] and polytheism." He went on to say that "if America becomes victorious granting victory to Saddam, Islam would receive a blow not able to raise its head again, and so the battle must be Islam against *blasphemy* and not Iran against Iraq."

The voice of the revolutionary leader Khomeini had no effect on Saddam Hussein's invasion, the attack continued none the less. During 1987, all forces along with the United State and the UN Security Council came to the aid of Saddam Hussein. By April 1988 and July 1988, progression in the war changed, and Iraq was now on the offensive side.

Iraqi President and his forces dropped chemical cyanide bombs on the Iranian Kurdish village of Zarda, killing hundreds of Iranians in one blast. Those who survived these blasts still suffer from variety of physical, nervous, and mental disorders.

At this time, Iran was no match for the chemical weapons and nerve gas, and consequently there were many losses and setback on the Iranian side.

With no other alternative, on August 20, 1988, Iran then agreed with the UN Security Council and the proposed resolution of the United States, and peace was restored.

---

[351] Saddam's action against Iran, and his union with the United States would be like disrespecting the *holy* cause of Islam, which would bring shame upon their belief.

Then came the aftermath, which the UN Security Council pumped millions of dollars in aid to both countries in an effort to restore their financial growth and quell their economic setbacks.

However, was this aid given on behalf of the Iraqi Presedent a matter of mere justice, or was there a political or economic benefit to be earned by the United States?

Iran Will Return

Now within this twenty-first century, Iran is still a country that exists at the peak of economic balance. It has returned to its former glory during an era of tidings within the east.

History always repeats itself, and so one must realize that Iran will stand again in the near future as a threat to the Western world, especially the United States of America. There is no way to avoid the inevitability of universal stress that remains and will appear. Iran will shine as one of the counterbalancing forces of the east, stimulating World War III. Up to this present moment, Iran has had *bad blood* with the Western world, and it had the ambition to excel and produce a stronger armed force.

On the contrary, one does not say that the alleged action of Iran to disturb world peace is good, but if world peace must stand tall, then all major countries that introduced disarmament must first throw down their weapons and wave a white flag of peace.

But then how can this peace be when the continuous wanton of world power exists, which does not rehabilitated for peace but encouraged the will of weaponries, and the act of weaponries produced instability to the adversary's economy, and then all suffered.

One cannot refute the words of the prophecy as according to the book of Daniel[352] and the book of Revelation.[353] World powers will

---

[352] Daniel 11:45.
[353] Revelation 14:8; 17:15–18.

continue to exist, and the greed for this power will drive the desire of all opponents until the vile person is cast down.

Iraq-Kuwait War

Iraq became a hall of terror against the United States, acting up a storm even from the first Bush administration.

Under the Saddam Hussein's government, Kuwait had been undergoing enormous pressure. Saddam convinced his government that they had to take Kuwait. Being in command of Kuwait would enrich Iraq under his command.

After the Iraq-Iran War, the friendly relationship between both countries (Iraq and Kuwait) deteriorated because of economic and diplomatic reasons.

In 1989, Iraq accused Kuwait of stealing Iraqi oil through slant drilling on the border of Iraqi's Rumaila field. This so-called accusation led to the invasion of Kuwait by Saddam Hussein and his regime.

News reporters and other individuals gave many reports in regard to the Iraqi attack of Kuwait in 1990. Some of these included the following information:

I. It is said that after the eight years during the Iraq-Iran War, Iraq was under much economic pressures. Most of their oil fields had been destroyed during the war, and the prices now for oil were very competitive in the market. Therefore, Hussein decided that the best hope of survival for Iraq was to attain control of Kuwait to manipulate the oil prices in the Persian Gulf.

II. Kuwait, which was an Allie during the Iraq-Iran War, demanded the repayment of more than eighty billion dollars that they had loaned to Saddam during the war, but unfortunately Iraq was under financial stress and could not repay the loan. Some thought the invasion by Saddam's regime was planned to be a distraction because of the government lacked the funds to repay the loan.

III. Though referred to as bias by some conspiracy theorist, many believed that the Iraqi government thought that there were some covert collaborative efforts between Saudi Arabia, Kuwait, the UAE, and the United States to reduce the price of oil. In effect, this reduction would then stem Hussein's bid on the price of the Iraqi oil exports, which would place further stress on the country's economic burdens, putting a hold on Iraq nuclear arms and also reducing the size of the Iraqi armed force.

Saddam Hussein strengthened his intentions and actions by saying that "Kuwait was a part of natural Iraq, which had been marked off by British Imperialism." He claimed that after the signing at the Anglo-Ottoman Convention in 1913, the United Kingdom disastrously split Kuwait from the Ottoman Empire into separate sheikdom.

The Iraqi government persistently argued that Kuwait had always been a part of the Ottoman province of Basra.

It was noted that although the ruling dynasty[354] during 1899 had made a protectorate agreement in regard to its foreign affairs with Britain, they did not attempt secession from the Ottoman Empire. These borders were never carved out, and they never distinctly separated Kuwait from the rest of Iraq.

The separation happened when the British high commissioners came and claimed superiority of the northern and Western world. They engaged themselves with the domestic issues of the east, having diplomatic intentions for the oil in Kuwait, and they drew lines to restrict the future Iraqi government so that they would not have

---

[354] The Al-Sabah family was ruling at the time.

the ability to threaten Britain dominance of the Persian Gulf. The Persian Gulf then became a major interest and especially one of the hopes of Hussein's future control.

In addition, the Rumaila oil field was the center of attractions between the Iraqis and Kuwaitis. The dispute over the Rumaila oil field did not begin during the reign of Hussein. It started in the 1960s when the Arab League declared the marked Iraq-Kuwait borders two miles north of the southern tip of the Rumaila field. Many quarrels then emerged on account of the Rumaila borders, which were addressed and put to rest during earlier ages.

After the Iraq-Iran War, Iraqi production was way behind, while the Kuwaiti oil fields were progressing well. Hussein and his regime quickly developed a grudge that accused the Kuwaitis for performing slant drills and stealing oil from Iraq.

The Kuwaitis refused to acknowledge the accusation by the Iraqis, and a quarrel developed. In this quarrel the Iraqi leaders, however, managed to cite the Rumaila borders as one of their reasons in invading Kuwait.

On July 25, 1990, the United States, realizing the conflict that was about to unfold between Iraq and Kuwait, made conversational links with the Iraqi ambassador April Glaspie.

Speaking in neutral terms, the US ambassador made concerned comments about the military preparation near the Iraq-Kuwait borders. Mrs. Gillespie went on to say that Washington sought to understand the disagreements between Iraq and Kuwait. However, the United States did not want to be seen as a busybody within the affairs of the Arab conflicts. The nation wanted to remain neutral between them both. The ambassador concluded that the United States did not intend to start an economic war against Iraq but that the war instigating should be provided.

However, when the Iraqi leader heard these comments, especially the last one from the ambassador, he thought the United States would not interfere, so he presumed he had gotten a green light to invade Kuwait.

August 2, 1990, at 2:00 p.m., Iraq launched an attack on Kuwait with four Iraqi republican guard divisions. The intense battle lasted for two days. Most of Kuwait's armed forces were overrun by the Iraqi guard, while others escaped to neighboring Saudi Arabia and Bahrain.

Kuwaiti civilians, members of the military, and the sovereign classes alike all fled. The emir of Kuwait, Jaber al Ahmed Al Jaber Al-Sabah, fled into the Saudi desert, while his younger half brother, Sheik Fahad Ahmed Al-Jaber Al-Sabah, was shot and killed by Iraqi soldiers as he tried to defend the Dasman Palace. As some have said, the younger brother's body was placed in front of a tank that rolled over him.

The state of Kuwait was also annexed and numbered as the nineteenth province of Iraq by Saddam and his regime.

Kuwait's vast wealth was looted. Human rights were ignored and violated, and hundreds of Kuwaiti people were taken to Iraq, many of which are still unaccounted for.

The victory of the Iraqi President, Saddam Hussein, did not ease the tension in the Middle East, but it encourages the pressure even more.

The United States and the UN Security Council, which had assisted the Hussein in his attempted invasion at the Iraq-Iran War in 1980, did not stand wholeheartedly against Hussein's early plan to invade Kuwait, but stand aside until Kuwait's defeat; they offered a helping hand to Kuwait. Nevertheless, the league and the UN Security Council decided to uphold the covenant of the league and help was given.

The annexation and the seven-month siege of Kuwait were unanimously and internationally condemned by all major powers. Countries that were close allies to Iraq, such as France and India, recommended the immediate withdrawal of the Iraqi forces from

Kuwait. Certain countries, such as the USSR and China, enforced armed embargos. NATO members were also critical of the invasion brought forward by Saddam and his regime.

In August 31, 1990, the United States led by the second Bush's administration and the UN Security Council, passed a resolution demanding the immediate evacuation of the Iraqi forces from Kuwait by January 15, 1991, but to no avail.

The stubbornness of Hussein and his forces agitated the vile person of the northern and western hemispheres, resulting in a US-led coalition by President Bush with the directive to attack Iraq on January 1991.

Many massive air strikes were made, but the Iraqi President and his forces managed to hold on to Kuwait until February 25, 1991, when Kuwait was finally liberated.

Further attacks on Iraq were placed on hold during the time of Kuwait's liberation, allowing Hussein to comply with world peace and limitation of nuclear development.

Insight of the United States—Iraq Invasion

The United States and the United Kingdom alongside other US Allies invaded and toppled the Saddam Hussein regime for twenty-one days of major combat. The invasion was considered a follow-up of the tidings attached to the Persian Gulf War (1991) and Saddam's invasion of Kuwait (1990).

At the time of the Kuwait invasion, Hussein's affiliation with the western and northern hemispheres was not good. Hussein was seeking a position of power in the Persian Gulf. Hussein had realized earlier that the possession of oil was necessary for power in the future, and he wanted to retain the high cost of oil so that he could maximize profits. The United States saw the idea as a challenge to the economy and did not see Saddam's aspiration as the best way forward.

Since the Gulf War, the United States and Britain had been keeping an eye on Hussein's government. They watched so that Hussein would put an end to certain type of weapons in his country, including his scud missiles and any weapons of mass destruction (WMDs).

The US president G. W. Bush and British Prime Minister Tony Blair encouraged each other by reason of an invasion meant to disarm Iraq's weapon of mass destruction, to end the Iraqi leader's support to Afghanistan terrorists, which were a threat to world peace, and to free the Iraqi people of the evil governance of Saddam and his regime. Although the Iraqi leader denied these accusations, the pressure continued to build across the Middle East between Iraq and the second Bush administration.

A BBC news forecast pointed out that George Bush consistently associated al-Qaeda and the Iraqi leader with the September 11 attack. President Bush's administration also added that Hussein was an enemy to the United Nations, which in turn made him also a threat to world peace.

One can understand the president of the United States being diplomatic in his approach by connecting Hussein and al-Qaeda as another threat to world peace. It is obvious that he thought that these words would bring the allies and other independent countries to his side, agreeing to the invasion.

Nevertheless, there was strong opposition concerning the invasion of Iraq by some US allies, including France, Germany, New Zealand, and Canada. These argued that even with all the scientific procedures and military searches done, there was no evidence found to conclude that there were any weapons of mass destruction in Iraq, which the report of February 12, 2003, clearly established.

The opposition against the attack continued up to the invasion, which the *Guinness Book of World Records* later listed as the world's widest protest as an antiwar rally. This protest included three million people in Rome, which made the total number of protestors thirty-six millions across the globe between January 3 and April 12, 2003.

Although the uproar drew attention, it did not daunt those who were for the invasion. There were key allies of the Unite States within NATO, such as the United Kingdom, who strongly agreed with the invasion. France and Germany, however, thought a different resolution might work better, such as doing more weaponry inspections.

After considerable discussions the UN Security Council agreed on a compromise plan. This plan was to allow for more weaponry inspections, and if the Iraqi government did not comply, there would be serious consequences. On the other hand, the Security Council's members, including France and Russia, distinctly argued that there must not be an intention to use force to overthrow the Iraqi leader, but the US administration had already thought to strike at the Iraqi government with or without the agreement of the United Nation if the Iraqi leader did not comply.

The second Bush administration had determined to make it their point of duty to terminate Saddam Hussein and his way of governing the Iraqis.

Nevertheless, more investigations to determine that Saddam and his regime were carrying out the productions of weapons of mass destruction were done. The results of these further investigations did not show a negative light, so the United States along with his confederates within the UN Security Council accommodate their intentions by accusing the Iraqi leader of the usage of mustard gas.

At the time of the Iraq-Iran invasion, which was endorsed by the United States, many attacks had proven victorious with the usage of poison gas. Many journalist and media personalities surely were aware of the gruesome acts involving the use of chemical weapons in the Iraq-Iran War, and during the council against Saddam Hussein and his usage of chemical weapons, this same vile person disallowed the council to condemn Saddam for his treacherous and gruesome act in 1980.

In fact, if they had placed Hussein, after the war, before the tribunal, he and his regime would have been punished for the usage of poison gas from that time, and he would not have thought about using it again on the Kuwaitis and even his own people.

On March 20, 2003, countries like the United States, United Kingdom, Spain, Australia, Poland, Denmark, and Italy began to bomb Iraq.

The invasion of Iraq was very brutal and disruptive. Many innocent citizens were killed, and may of Iraq's historical dwellings were destroyed.

On July 22, 2003, Saddam Hussein's sons, Uday and Qusay, along with one of his grandsons were killed in massive air strikes.

Saddam and many of his confederates were tracked for months. Saddam was captured on December 13, 2003, by the US Army during Operation Red Dawn. Saddam Hussein and his confederates were brought to trial by the United States at Camp Justice, which is now called Camp Bosnia in Bagdad. Saddam was hanged by his neck until he died on December 20, 2006.

Afghanistan and Osama bin Laden

Afghanistan, a country in the east, is also a "tiding of the east" to the United States of America. In Afghanistan, the US government sought to capture the leading advisor of the Taliban. It was alleged that this person had committed many atrocities, all in an attempt to destroy the government and people of America.

Bin Laden recruited many Muslims and trained them as warriors to give their lives in commitment to the assumed[355] purpose of Allah. Despite the presence of the US army and other countries of the north

---

[355] I said *assumed* because many Muslims separated themselves from this deed.

residing in Afghanistan, this committed leader was still accused of many ruthless attacks, some of which he had committed within the borders of the United States of America.

Osama bin Laden was founder of the Islamic extremist organization called al-Qaeda, and he is prominently known across the world for the September 11 attacks on the United States, which instigated many civilian deaths.

His brand of Islam and his dealing in the violent and extremist ways of jihad caused his wealthy Saudi Arabian family to disassociate themselves from him. When he was accused of these deadly deeds, he was immediately placed on the American Federal Bureau of Investigation list for the ten most wanted fugitives.

Bin Laden believed that the restoration of Sharia law would set things right in the Muslim world and that all other ideas—Pan-Arabism, socialism, communism, and democracy—must be opposed and stopped. He also believed that Afghanistan under the rule of Musiah Omais Taliban was the only Islamic country in the Muslim world.

The jihad extremist believed in bringing terror to the United States of America, and he preached that "Muslims must fight the injustice perpetuated by the USA and other non-Muslim states against Muslims." Osama's tidings of anger encouraged the elimination of the state of Israel and the withdrawal of a US presence from the Middle East.

His act of judgment is indiscriminative. He believed that the killing of women and children was acceptable and that they were legitimate targets of jihadist action. The al-Qaeda group sincerely acknowledged that a faithful bystander being killed would go to paradise (Jannah) while nonbelievers would go to hell. Although many Muslims looked upon his concepts of warfare as ruthless ones, it strengthened the terror and fear the Western world felt and made the tidings of the al-Qaeda group a great matter to deal with.

The al-Qaeda leader was looked upon as anti-Jewish too. He warned Jewish organizations, saying that they were grabbers of luxuries and would take all you have whether in this world or the next. Bin Laden's terror is not confined to the Western world alone, but it extends to anyone sharing the same platform with the United States of America. He speaks against "Shia Muslim being listed with heretics, taking brotherhood with the USA and Israel, and making all as the four[356] principal enemies of Islam."

Bin Laden's terror on the West became more extreme, which caused the FBI on November 8, 1990, to raid certain houses, including an al-Qaeda associate named Al-Mohamed. During the raid the plot to blow up the New York City skyscraper was discovered. The Saudi government heard of the plot and banished the leader of the al-Qaeda group from Saudi Arabia, as he was taking refuge there at the time. Osama bin Laden then went to live in the Sudan.

During the 1990s, bin Laden and al-Qaeda supported many organizations. They mainly supported Islamic struggles, urging wars rather than negotiations with any opposing forces and governments.

The atrocities committed by bin Laden affected the whole world. In 1992, he was involved in the bombing of the Gold Mihor Hotel in Aden. Al-Qaeda pronounced the death of innocent bystanders during the bombing of the Gold Mihor Hotel, saying that "those who will go to paradise will be welcome by Allah, and those opposing Allah will go to hell."

In May 1996, on account of the extremist and anti-Jewish action of bin Laden and his al-Qaeda group during his stay in the Sudan, the leaders of the Sudan, Saudi Arabia, Egypt, and the United States placed pressure on the extremist leader, forcing him to return to Jalalabad in Afghanistan. Bin Laden became proactive in reaching Afghanistan, raising money from resistance associates who were their allies from the days of the Soviet Jihad War, and Pakistan Inter-Service Intelligence.

---

[356] The four principal enemies referred here include Shia Muslims, heretics, the United States, and Israel.

The "tidings of the east" caused by Osama bin Laden continued to trouble the Northern Alliance. By May 1997, they came together, posing a threat to overrun bin Laden and his terrorist group in Jalalabad, forcing Osama to move his operations to Tarmak Farms in the south.

Although he was pressured by the Northern Alliance, his later effort was a success. He sent hundreds of his Afghanistan Arab fighters to help the Taliban kill between five to six thousands Hazarans, and he overran the city at the same time.

In 1998, four members of the Egyptian Islamic jihad along with bin Laden and al-Qaeda were arrested in Albania. In retaliation to that arrest, the US embassy in Africa was bombed.

The 2001 September 11 attack on the US World Trade Center in addition to the severe damage to the Pentagon in Arlington, Virginia, and the death of 2,974 people were initially denied by Osama bin Laden and the al-Qaeda operation, but later in 2004 a tape revealed bin Laden taking full responsibility for the bombings.

As a result of these notorious acts, the government of the United States and several other countries waged war against this tiding of terror to depose the Taliban operations in Afghanistan and capture al-Qaeda's regime. By this time the United Kingdom reached the conclusion that Osama bin Laden was the real culprit behind the destruction of the World Trade Center.

Bin Laden stated his reason for the September 11 bombing as a reaction to the unbearable injustice and tyranny of the American-Israeli Alliance against his people in Palestine and Lebanon. It was said that the American-Israel Alliance instigated the destruction of the Towers of Lebanon in 1982, killing women and children.

Bin Laden had made significant impact on all administrations of the United States.

Clinton's Administration (1993–2001)

Since the time of the presidency of Bill Clinton, it became the objective of the United States to capture bin Laden.

Shortly after September 11, Clinton urged that we make more of an effort to capture bin Laden dead or alive.

Before September 11, Paul Braemar admonished the Clinton administration to correctly focus on the bin Laden prospective, while Robert Oakley criticized the Clinton administration for being obsessed with the issues and "tidings of the east" concerning Osama bin Laden.

Bush's Administration (2001–2009)

During the second Bush[357] administration, the US government concluded that Osama bin Laden was present at the Battle of Tora Bora in Afghanistan in 2001. This conclusion of the US government gave rise to military officials and civilians criticizing the government, saying that had the U.S. gave a complete ground search at the Battle of Tora Bora, Osama would have been captured at the time.

After an exhausted search in 2005 by the CIA and also the dedication of paramilitary units to capture bin Laden, the operation was shut down because they had made no progress in locating bin Laden.

The United States and Afghanistan forces started the search again on August 14 in the mountain of Tora Bora. The search was triggered by intelligence about a pre-Ramadan meeting to be held by al-Qaeda members. During the search dozens of al-Qaeda and Taliban members were killed, but Osama bin Laden was not found.

Concerning the 9/11 attack, the Bush administration named Osama bin Laden and al-Qaeda as the prime suspects and offered

---

[357] There were two Bush administrations. The first was run by President G. H. W. Bush (1989–1993), and the second was run by his son, G. W. Bush.

people twenty-five millions dollars for information leading to bin Laden's capture. On July 13, 2007, this figure was doubled to fifty millions dollars. Still waiting on a strong lead on Osama bin Laden's whereabouts, George W. Bush said that one day he would capture Osama bin Laden dead or alive.

Obama's Administration (2009–present)

During the Obama presidency many military tactics were used to locate Osama bin Laden and al-Qaeda forces, but these often failed.

General Stanley McChrystal, the top US commander in Afghanistan, said in December 2005 that the Al-Qaeda operations could not be defeated unless the leader, bin Laden, was captured or killed.

The commander also thought that bin Laden had become an Islamic figure across the world, emboldening many Muslims against the United States. Many thought it was a good thing and signaled possible success when Obama sent the thirty thousand troops to Afghanistan.

On the contrary, it was not so much a success because earlier in 2010, after relentless searches to capture bin Laden, Obama showed signs of fatigue by withdrawing a fraction of the US troops from Afghanistan.

In the year 2010, the ruling government of the United States of America declared that the withdrawal of some troops from Afghanistan was one of his ideas to solve the financial crisis surrounding US welfare.

This excuse to pull US troops from Afghanistan didn't seem validly to many people. Some claimed that Obama's government saw the search as futile. Because they were making no progress, the army needed to change it strategies.

At this point, Obama's government was starting to point to different strategies to capture the terrorists in Afghanistan.

Although the US army exists at its limits, the implications faced by the United States to capture the terrorist Bin Laden and his followers, the United States was placed in a confusing position.

Comments were made saying that more Muslims were interested in fighting for bin Laden's cause, not only in the east but in the Western world as well.

During a special interview on an international broadcasting station in September 2010, an official indicated that killing an al-Qaeda leader would be assuredly a small hit to stop the terrorist movement brought by bin Laden.

So, whether the extremist leader of the al-Qaeda operation would be dead or alive, the question about the United States being secure from terrorist will for some time remain unanswered. One must understand that even the death of bin Laden will not stop the terrors of al-Qaeda and the Taliban.

This *tiding* will last for as long as the prophecy of Daniel determined, and the destiny of its fulfillment will pronounce the fall of the *vile person*, which manifested himself as the United States of America.

These tidings of the east became such a distraction to the United States that the governance and even the welfare of the country deteriorated. Many critics already believe that the collapse of American dominance is the result of the war against terror.

Although these tidings of the east continued to unfold, this does not seem to be the only problem for the vile person and his allies. The wailings and gnashing of teeth prophesied by the prophets will take its course, and the "tidings of the north" will determine World War III.

Chapter 33

Tidings of the North

But tidings ... out of the north shall trouble him.
—Daniel 11:44 (KJV)

The tidings out of the north are not issues that I wish to elaborate on too deeply at this time. Such might instigate violence at the outset. Nevertheless, I will briefly explain that which has been shown to me through the years.

The prophecies had already declared all fullness, but the eyes of man are so dim that the vision of the prophecy is blocked from their eyes, resulting in man's path of dissolution.

I may not be as clear as I should; however, if man within the heights of his want for power does not think to resolve the fury that surrounds him, then the existence of the tidings that followed will be devastating, and the end will be as determine, which is World War III.

Let us consider the prophecy in Revelation 9:13–19. Here the prophecy mentioned the "angels that were loosed at the Great River Euphrates, and that they are to go and slay the third part of men who have not the seal of Yahweh." To comment, this part was speaking of a physical surrounding, namely the River Euphrates, which represents, according to biblical history,[358] an area enclosed

---

[358] This history reveals the conquest of David against the kings of the east (2 Samuel 8:1–6 KJV).

with the atmosphere of war. The setting that's free the angels denotes the setting that's free the tidings[359] to make war, which would divert to other parts of the world. So the River Euphrates is like a pillar or the center of the tidings of the east. One can then say the boundaries of the River Euphrates are the surroundings that manifest the tidings prophesied.

In Revelation 16:12, we can also see that the River Euphrates is like a *passage way*[360] to exit the east. Scripture mentioned the "river being dried up for the way to be cleared for the kings of the east." This explains the boundaries being removed and allowing easy access. Therefore, the prophecy inevitability prohibits the vile person's triumph over these tidings of the east, allowing the prophecy of the book of Daniel and Revelation of great effect.

The Scripture passages speaking of the "kings of the east" did not necessarily mean kings as on thrones or rulers of government, but these could have meant people who stand as high authorities within organizations. On this note, the ruler of the Taliban and al-Qaeda could be deemed as a "king of the east" as well.

One must understand that the tiding of the east will kindle the tidings of the north, and the tidings out of the north will proceed to World War III.

But which country of the north will the tidings unfold from? I would point to the Russians.

During the unfolding tidings of the Middle East, the Soviets[361] played a vital role by organizing arms deals in the Iraq-Iran War and selling to both sides to strengthen their own economic standpoint.

---

[359] This tiding is the overspreading of spiritual warfare.

[360] Water in general does not allowed easy access or smooth travel, so this simply means that the water level was lowered, therefore making access across possible.

[361] At this time the USSR known as the Soviet Union was under the leadership of President Gorbachev (1985-1991).

There were other counties that had followed suit during the Middle East crisis but the Soviets[362] got my attention concerning the crisis to come, which is the "tiding out of the north."

Since December 25, 1991, the Soviet Union had declared extinct and its attributes have been under the leadership of the Russian President, Bores Yeltsin. The Russians, still under the will and culture of that side of the hemisphere, would also follow the pattern of the Cold War where the Western Blocs[363] were against Eastern Blocs[364].

I can assure you that at this point of time in the twenty-first century; Iran poses a threat because nuclear expansion. If Iran and the US coalition should NATO go to war, then the Russians would deal arms to the respective countries involved. With his war strategies, the *vile person,* the United States, would utter an arms embargo between the Russians and Iran.

Desperate for economic development, the Russians would not adhere to the vile person's cause, and then the tidings would follow. Although chaos would follow, Russia and his allies would also be the outcome of unity, and communism will underline once more with the task of its own pursuit.

As we speak and as the tidings are near, the United States has been considering all things. The USA has been watching and looking for any one suspiciously dealing in arms. An outstanding International Broadcasting Media, during the month of November 2010, reported that an arms dealer was arrested in Thailand and was accused of intending to sell arms to a foreign country not within the umbrella of the UN agreement for arms deal.

---

[362] Though it's not under the leadership of President Mikhail Gorbachev since 1991, the Russian President (Yeltsin) will follow the pattern.

[363] This Western Bloc consists of the United States, its allies and others.

[364] This Eastern Bloc consisted of the Soviet Union and its allies in the Warsaw Pact.

Arms will continue to be manufactured; therefore it will remain a business for some, which will in the long run continue to encourage the path for World War III and ultimately the destruction of mankind.

When the tidings of the north unfold, Korea might also play a significant role. This I say since there is no interesting World War III without the Koreans (North and South). The question is this: Whose *side* will the Koreans take?

After World War II, the defeat of Japan led to the occupation of Korea north by the Soviet Union and subsequently the occupation of Korea south by the U.S. forces. These two entities[365] set up government in both north and south of Korea, where both governments go at war for the legitimate ownership of the Korean borders. The Soviet with China took side with Korea north and invaded Korea south on June 25, 1950.

The United States and the United Nations Security Council recognized the invasion against Korea south as an act of aggression. The US on that ground sent a large army to their defense but this did not yield the aggression, because the Soviet continues their attack, which ended in a stalemate. The fighting ended on July 27, 1953 and an armistice was signed creating the Korean Demilitarized Zone, separating the north form the south.

This is a natural thing to look into because these two entities will pay tributes to the side attributes should be given.

History makes it easy for us to comprehend and analyze the forecast of the prophecy concerning the vile person and his reaction during the tidings of the north. We can understand this if we follow the prophecies of Daniel and Revelation.

The vile person will make it his business to contend with all those who affiliate with his opposition.

---

[365] The Soviet Union and the United States of America

"Therefore he shall go forth with great fury to destroy, and utterly to make away many" (Daniel 11:44 KJV).

It is unfortunate, but the end that is determine was already destined by the Almighty (Elshadi). What must happen cannot be avoided.

Prophecy is a plague upon mankind. It is inevitable and served as a token of Yahweh's command, reminding man to turn from his wickedness but man decided to play gods, not turning from their evil ways.

The tidings of the north will continue until they agitate confusion within the League of Nations. This confusion will spread like disease upon the UN Security Council, the League of Nations, and the EU. The darkness that exists will overflow, and the nations affiliated with these organizations will then turn on the United States, the nation that had dominion over most of the earth.

Chapter 34

The Vile Person's End

And he shall plant the tabernacles of his palace between the seas and the glorious holy mountain; yet he shall come to his end, and none shall help him.

—Daniel 11:45 (KJV)

Let me refer to the symbols of the prophecy in Revelation 17 (KJV). Verse 1 speaks of the individual who sets upon much water. Verse 2 speaks of the woman riding upon the scarlet beast, who gave the nations of the earth to drink of her cup of fornication. Verse 5 speaks of "mystery Babylon the great, and mother of harlot and abomination of the earth." Revelation 17:15 continued saying that the "water that she rides upon with the beast are people, nations and multitudes of different tongues."

We can understand then that the *water* represents the nations or kingdoms that the *whore* ruled, those being manipulated by her power and wealth. Verse 18 says that this "woman is known as that city which reigned over the kings of the earth." This *city* in this time and age represents the United States, the vile person with the Statue of Liberty as its symbol placed between the waters and its city.

But how can we determine that the United States is both the *vile person* and the *woman* that rides upon the waters? When the prophet says that "the waters which thou saw, where the whore sits are people, and multitudes, and nations and tongues," the word *whore*[366] relates to the whole city in relation to its cultures, religions, and customs, but when declared as a *vile person*, this references points to its government and policies.

Now let us return to Daniel 11:45, which mention the vile person "shall plant the tabernacles of his palace between the seas and the glorious holy mountain." We have established that the *water* and *seas* represent the nations, people and their tongues (languages), while as for the *palace*[367] have been placed between the seas and the *glorious holy mountain*[368], speaks of the vile person pitching his office[369] and main attentions towards the nations of terror and the borders of Jerusalem.

The quarrel for the holy land and its borders will allows the vile person of the north to take great interest in solving disputes between Israel, Lebanon, and Jerusalem.

I asked what the vile person would do to stop this quarrel. Will he chop up the land as the earlier British government and intellectuals did years ago, disastrously splitting the borders of the Rumaila oil field and chopping off Kuwait from Iraq? If this same method is used again to divide the land in order to settle this dispute, then the tidings will continue. Nations in the east will then take sides, and the arms dealers will continue to trade and eventually take sides.

The Russians and Koreans (North Korea) will be watched keenly, while the United States will then place an arms embargo on the nations doing imports and exports of weaponry, which will automatically cause much confusion within the UN Security Council, NATO, and the EU.

---

[366] The word *whore* could prophetically symbolize the city Sodom and Gomorrah, but in this new age and time this word would be referring to the United States, as she gets *involved* in all their countries social and economical affairs.

[367] *Palace* refers to an office or some fixed monument for an ideal purpose.

[368] *Glorious Holy Mountain* in most cases referred to Jerusalem.

[369] *Office* means a fort, port or main attraction

On November 20, 2010, the BBC news gave details about President Obama in a NATO-Moscow Summit Conference making an agreement with Moscow about a European missile defense shield and a reduction arms treaty. He wanted that they stand together, not as adversaries from the Cold War but as allies in providing a route via Russia to Afghanistan to fight against the terror that exists.

However, this agreement will not stand. Eventually the northern tidings will strengthen, kindling the fire of World War III, and the prophecy of John on the Isle of Patmos will unfold as Revelation 17 says. "So he carried me away in the spirit into the wilderness, and I saw a woman sitting upon a scarlet colored beast, full of names of blasphemy, having seven heads and ten horns" (Revelation 17:3 KJV).

One should also consider the following: "And the ten horns, which thou saw, are ten kings, which have received no kingdoms as yet, but receive power as king for one hour with the beast. These have one mind, and shall give their power and strength unto the beast" (Revelation 17:12–13 KJV).

Finally readers might also want to analyze the following:

> *And the ten horns which thou saw upon the beast, these shall hate the whore, and shall make her desolate and naked, and shall eat her flesh, and burn her with fire, for Yahweh (God) hath put it in their hearts to fulfill his will, and to agree and give their kingdom unto the beast until the words of Yahweh (God) shall be fulfilled. (Revelation 17:16–17 KJV).*

Now let us discuss the detailed description of the beast. The ten horns are ten nations developed in earlier centuries, and by 1948, they were in alignment, demonstrating their purposes as the European Economy Community (EEC).

These ten nations include the following:

- Germany
- Britain
- France
- Italy
- Spain
- Hungary
- Poland
- Portugal
- Belgium
- Yugoslavia

They gave their power and services of allegiance to the power of Rome (Roman Empire) for a time. Later three were plucked up out of the union because of the disrespectful behavior to the laws of the league—Hungary, Poland, and Yugoslavia.

The EEC was then replaced by the northern nations as the European Union (EU). Although Germany played the leading role, the union was monitored by the vile person. Nevertheless, the EU was not enough. By 1975, the vile person was engaged with France to form the G6, which would bring together the six wealthiest nations—Britain, the United States, Italy, Germany, France, and Japan.

In 1976, Canada joined the group, creating the G7, and by 1997, Russia was added to the group, forming the G8.

Although the EU is a combined body of the G8 and other nations, both the EU and the G8 will come together and ride with the United States *(the Whore)*, being held in her *paws* by flatteries until the time appointed.

During the tidings of the north, the UN Security Council will be called, and at that council, opposing factors will kindle World War III. During that council, it will be like King Arthur at the Knights of the Round Table, they all will be thinking that they all has the power, when at the end they had none.

Who will stand against the vile person? History had always repeated itself, and as the saying goes, *where there is always fire the grass is never green*. This proverb indicates that once there is an action whether it is good or bad, there is always a reaction.

After the North Korean nuclear text May 25, 2009, relations deteriorated between North Korea and both Russia and China, yet Russia played a significant part in the process of U.N.Security Council resolution to solve the North Korean nuclear issue. One of his main suggestions was no aggression towards North Korean.

Since 2011 close relations had been made between the Russians and North Korea, where they marked the 63rd anniversary of bilateral ties on 18th of October same year. Also bears in mind that Russia's relations have improved with Iran since the breaking up of the soviet bloc, even closer since the US tensions. .

I am saying that the resurrection of the spirit of the Cold War will directly give the end result of a new treaty similar to the pass, where as North Korea, Russia and China being Allies to resurrect the spirit of the Cold War.

The pattern of the pass has already emerge in recent time when South Korea and North Korea were at each other's throats, promoting individual power. As the news suggested in late November 2010, North Korea fired destructive weapon on South Korea, and as it remains, President Obama reacted by saying that they would do what was necessary to stand by South Korea's defense because South Korea has always been their ally. So the prophecy will follow, where the end would be World War III.

If one studied the pattern of the prophecy of Daniel 11, you would understand that during the last sequence of the latter days many persons had decided to take the place of the vile person. The Russian however will decide to take this position as the vile person, during the call of the U.N. Security Council, which in his remarks at the council he would demand a new resolution of world power and this will stir confusion on the "whore" (the USA).

The confusion within the UN Security Council will then determine the fall of the vile person, and those with him shall be against him, for the north that was once his sweet haven shall be a sword against him by virtue of this confusion. Some will stand at his side, but those who don't shall make friends with the vile person's enemies and cling together for the moment of defeat.

At that time, a shout of rejoicing shall be made, and the United States shall be a ground of dead bodies. The prophecy of the future must come to pass, and as it is written, the end shall come to the vile person.

Is the prophecy a vain thing? Consider the words of this book say the prophet; for it shall be at the time appointed, in a short time, the "great city Babylon" is fallen. The prophecy of Daniel 11 (KJV) declared the whole aspect of the vile person's defeat, and as it details, so shall the end be, Selah.

Author's Note

As the author of this book, I would like to speak about the name and manifestation of Yeshua, son of the Elohim (God).

First I must say that throughout my book I have maintained the pronouncement of Yeshua as the name I see as more correctly used. In my task of worship I believe that name should not be translated. It should be kept in its sacred and original form and letters. Nevertheless, if you see fit to utter its translated form, then it's up to you.

Now Yeshua (Jesus) is noted without a doubt as the Son of the living Elohim (God). I have clearly explained in the introduction that He, Yeshua (Jesus), is the Son of the living Elohim (God) whose name is Yahweh, according to the name ascribed to Him by Moses.

As for the Immaculate Conception, one must understand that I hold no grudge against one's belief because I, too, firmly acknowledge the blessings of Mary and what she brought into this world for mankind. Nevertheless, one must understand that as the Bible said, "Salvation comes only through Christ Yeshua (Jesus)."

Now let me speak as a Christian. If we as Christians hold firm in the truth and cannot accept where we as a Christian nation went wrong in the past, then we serve the Almighty without reasons. History has show that the church has done many things contrary to the Holy Father's custom, which many popes in the twentieth and twenty-first centuries have acknowledged. Why shouldn't we as lowly followers accept and acknowledge where the church has come short and move to spiritual growth?

It was for this same reason that Martin Luther admonished the church to reconcile where we had gone wrong, but the pope at that time saw this admonishment as contempt, and the result was separation instead of reformation.

I see no one who loves the Almighty more than I do. For that reason I planned to make two donations. One is my continued service to Him for the rest of my life, and the other is to build him a tabernacle of worship.

On the matter of world peace, it is clear that man must ascribe to the intervention of the living Supreme Being, who gave His Son to die for us. Countries must declare world peace, and for that to happen, all individuals must disarm, including the United States.

There are many things that seem outrageous, including the atrocities against the Jewish people, but let me freely speak concerning what beset the Ethiopians.

As I am about to *speak*, I cannot because I am *burned* with the anger, anger that *pumped* rage in my head, *disturbing* the thought of my minds.

I will yet *speak* being not confounded about the wickedness done unto the Ethiopian people because of the desires for glory, and greed of the Italian king and government.

Oh, my people have suffered. I say my people because that's where I come from. What then should I say? Should we suffer more as an African nation after all that has been done through slavery? Why give more pain to the Ethiopian?

These atrocities continued because the Vatican and the pope blessed the tyrant of the north, Mussolini, befitting him with enchanted faith to commit these atrocities against the *holy covenant*.

Mussolini and Hitler intended to wipe out the existence of the black Jewish race with the use of poison gas, but then who Yahweh blessed no man cursed.

Is it a natural thing that prophecy has its place in the existence of mankind, or is it just coincidence that the words of the ancient prophetic fathers fitted in with the thought of mankind? If so, then the words of prophesy are the eye of the future, and on that path, it remains a plague upon mankind.

If prophecies would remain as plagues to mankind, then it will continue to manifest until the path is fulfilled according its purpose.

On this account, all kingdoms according to the prophecy will come to its end, and as determined, the *vile person* will fall. When the *vile person succumbs* to his *injuries*, a *kingdom* will take its place, and that future *kingdom*, as recorded in the prophecy, is the *kingdom* of the Elshadi (Almighty), the one and true Eloi named Yahweh by the prophet Moses.